IT'S ALL ABOUT WORK

IT'S ALL ABOUT WORK

ORGANIZING YOUR COMPANY TO GET WORK DONE

Stephen D. Clement, Ph.D.
and
Christopher R. Clement

Copyright © 2013 by Stephen D. Clement, Ph.D. and Christopher R. Clement

Organizational Design Inc.
PO Box 9859
The Woodlands, Tx, 77387
www.organizational.com

ISBN: 978-0-9886396-0-7

All rights reserved. No part of this publication may be reproduced, stored in a retrieval system or transmitted, in any form, or by any means, electronic, mechanical, recorded, photocopied, or otherwise, without the prior written permission of both the copyright owner and the above publisher of this book, except by a reviewer who may quote brief passages in a review.

The scanning, uploading, and distribution of this book via the Internet or via any other means without the permission of the publisher is illegal and punishable by law. Please purchase only authorized electronic editions and do not participate in or encourage electronic piracy of copyrightable materials. Your support of the author's rights is appreciated.

Printed in the United States of America

Contents

Special Acknowledgment 7

1: Are You Doing it Wrong? 9

2: Why Is Structure So Important? 19

3: The Work of Dr. Elliott Jaques 27

4: Organizational Preparation and Situational Awareness 39

5: Principle #1: Organize around Levels of Work 44

6: Principle #2: Clearly Define Accountabilities
   and Authorities for All Roles 78

7: Principle #3: Clearly Define the Nature
   of Working Relationships 94

8: Principle #4: Assess the Working Capability of a Person 126

9: Principle #5: Provide Effective Managerial Leadership 163

10: Organizational Structure and Customer Impact 190

11: Implementation Introduction, Sponsorship,
    and Education 200

12: Preparing to Analyze the Existing Structure 213

13: Constructing the Extant Organization 233

14: Creating a Proposed Requisite Organization 252

15: Implementing Your New Structure 263

16: Other Lessons Learned 272

Chapter 17: Bringing It All Together 280

Acknowledgments 286

Bibliography 288

Glossary 290

Special Acknowledgment

Dr. Roger Harvey has made a special and particular contribution to this book. In the early stages of formulating the overall design of this effort, he proposed a straightforward logic and flow that made intuitive sense. Building upon his recent experience in the U.S. Army Transformation Project, Dr. Harvey went on to provide invaluable insights regarding the scope and content of the key design principles described in this effort. His strong academic background and his recent small and medium business experience made his advice all the more meaningful. One of his primary concerns was to strive to make this effort both understandable and practical to the layman reader. We have indeed benefited immensely from his comments and recommendations regarding this manuscript.

Chapter 1

Are You Doing it Wrong?

The academics have studied motivation for years ... yet we still can't get our work done ... we are bombarded with "leadership secrets" yet I see poor leadership all around ... what I need is a system, a system that shows me how to build the foundation of a good organization, a foundation that allows my team to "nail the fundamentals" of our business ... then I can worry about developing leaders and motivating people.

—*CTO of a small technology business*

Organizational Structure as the Foundation

Historically speaking, today's business organizations are still in their infancy. The advent of the industrial age required new methods for getting work done. Max Weber, a German sociologist and economist, was the first "scientist" to study organizations from a social (i.e., people) perspective.[1] He believed that "bureaucratic organizations" were "technically superior" to any other form of organization. He correctly predicted their advance in the early 1920s. Today these bureaucratic organizations, in one

---

1 Numerous references and biographical information for Max Weber may be found by following the link: http://en.wikipedia.org/wiki/Max_Weber.

form or another, power businesses and governments worldwide. Yet, organizations have existed for thousands of years, mobilizing groups of people to get something done. And getting things done has often been called "work." Hierarchy has always been an integral part of these early work systems and the human interaction that occurred within them.

Government institutions fostered in the era of bureaucratic organizations and have steadily adapted since their inception in the late 1700s and mid-1800s. But, as Weber points out, most commercial organizations have only been around for just over a hundred years. Nonetheless, there are some organizations that exist today that have been, more or less, relatively unchanged for literally hundreds of years. Today's business professionals and organizational experts continue to seek the discovery of the organization of tomorrow or the organization for the new normal. Perhaps before we ask, "What does my organization need to look like tomorrow?" it would serve us well to first to take a look back into history and ask, "What can I learn from organizations that have adapted and survived for hundreds of years?"

Dr. Elliot Jaques, a little-known psychiatrist and organizational expert, did just that. His original studies of the sociological impact of people working in bureaucratic organizations eventually led him to research organizations worldwide, both public and private. As an inquisitive scientist, he proceeded to perform experiments and laboratory-style testing of a series of hypotheses related to what made these organizations work. In this book, we build upon his seminal work with a new outlook on modern organizations. We will outline a new set of organizational design principles that build upon Dr. Jaques's early work and his pioneering research of organizations. This deep dive into previous research focuses on organizations that have been built around levels of management and accountability/authority for hundreds of years.

Organizational structure is the foundation of any business. And, as such, many of today's organizations are lacking a solid foundational structure and supporting set of organizational principles. Many companies have simply ignored this foundational base. To be perfectly honest, organizational structure, accountability systems, and working relationships are somewhat boring. It is much more exciting to focus on influencing the hearts and minds of people (leadership?). Can you imagine a frenzied audience jumping up and down with excitement, pumping their fists, and high-fiving each other at an organizational structure seminar? Probably not, but you just might be able to envision this happening at a leadership or coaching seminar. So today's executives and managers have gravitated toward the excitement and enthusiasm of leadership and away from the boring and staid topic of organizational structure.

So the quest for magical charisma goes on. As a result of this thinking, the efforts at improving performance in today's organizations are never going to be as successful as they could be. Why? Because much of the performance gains are placed on top of a poor foundation, a foundation that may or may not support good leadership and long-term success. Our intent is simply to get people to change this traditional approach.

Much of the business community is enamored with leadership (and other performance improvement concepts, e.g., Lean Six Sigma) rather than organization and structure because they don't fully appreciate or understand the impact of structure and organization on individual behavior. For example, suppose that a struggling business makes a tremendous turnaround under a new manager or owner. The majority of the credit is subsequently attributed to the new manager's leadership skills. However, upon closer examination, one might notice that the leader made changes to the organization during this turnaround effort. Once dysfunctional teams became functional, perhaps because the leader had clarified roles with proper accountability and authority and then followed up by holding people truly accountable. The new leader may have made some personnel changes, perhaps because he had intuitively matched the capability of the employee to the level of work in the role. The new leader also could have made changes to the organization and its structure simply by applying what he believed to be good leadership practices. Good leaders don't simply implement effective leadership practices; they also routinely tailor the organization to best meet the constantly changing marketplace and work requirements. Imagine if you will a great leader who has been assigned to a dysfunctional organization. Our prediction is that over time the leader will have a significant impact on the organization and its attendant structure.

Structure Comes before Performance Improvement Concepts (and Initiatives) and Leadership

It is incumbent on organizational leaders to build an effective and efficient organization (the foundation) before embarking on major performance or continuous improvement initiatives or leadership initiatives. In this book, we describe the principles of sound organizational structure in sufficient detail to permit other organizational leaders to foster performance gains and leadership success stories. The leadership and consulting business is notoriously ambiguous with thousands of books, courses and "experts" available to assist you and your organization. Yet, many organizations are unsuccessful in their pursuit of improved leadership and performance initiatives. Consequently, the search for the latest leadership fad or panacea is ongoing. Soon, yet another book will be published and written by a successful former executive (leader) trying to present new ideas to apply to aspiring leaders and organizations. We suggest a different strategy. Take the time to read this book and digest the concepts and principles it contains and apply them as a solid base upon which to build your own leadership capability. We strongly believe that most of your people currently possess the capacity to be better leaders; they simply lack an adequate foundation to build upon.

What Are the Underlying Concepts and Principles?

Leadership does not occur in a vacuum. It always involves a relationship between people in some sort of social structure. That structure is important because it sets a context that profoundly affects all aspects of existing personal interactions. Structure is more than a simple pattern of roles and organizational charts; it also contains a set of key work-related variables that are central to getting work done effectively with a clear sense of accountability, authority consistent with that accountability, clear working relationships across normal organizational boundaries, roles occupied by individuals with the capability to get the job done, and leadership.

Elliott Jaques's early research explored how many layers existed in a successful organization. He found similar-sized organizations with varying numbers of layers, some with less than ten layers and some with far more. He also came upon an interesting anomaly, the U.S. Army. At the time, the U.S. Army had fifteen different soldier ranks and twelve to fifteen separate organizational layers in the non-warfighting side of the institution. Yet, the combat side of the army only contained seven "echelons" (battalions, divisions, etc.).[2] The interesting question that this finding posed was, Why, when the U.S. Army goes to war, does it do so with only seven layers of command and what happens to the other six to eight layers that exist in the non-warfighting side of the institution? We devote an entire chapter to Dr. Elliott Jaques's work later in this book. However, as he continued to explore successful organizations, he was struck by the similarity of many of his hypotheses to those principles already embraced by military organizations worldwide.

The military has always benefited from the presence of organizational doctrine or, in layman's terms, "How we do things around here." Intuitively, the institution recognized early on the salience of these variables to the leadership process. Their absence nearly always led to mission failure accompanied by the loss of soldiers' lives. These were simply unacceptable costs. Hence, the military always paid attention to these key variables. With the passage of time, they became the foundational building blocks for the institution as a whole. A basic description of these building blocks is presented below.

First, military commanders operate daily within what today would be called a relatively flat hierarchical organization. The number of layers in this hierarchy has been tested time after time in the crucible of combat and contains precisely the proper number of organizational layers necessary to accomplish complex missions. The number of layers reflects a hierarchy of command roles with each successive layer adding unique value to the layer below. This hierarchy of layers has remained essentially unchanged since the days of the Roman legion. There is a simple explanation for this unique layered structure. First, commanders who were separated from actual battlefield actions by too many layers of command (management) tended to put into place battle plans (strategic plans) that failed. These failures altered the course of history, and countless lives were lost by a commander who was too far removed from the battlefield (marketplace). Additionally, Dr. Jaques discovered

---

2   Elliott Jaques, Requisite Organization. (Arlington, VA: Cason Hall Publishers, 1996), 136.

that this hierarchical structuring also reflected an intuitive finding, refined over thousands of years, of the natural distribution of human capability to work at various organizational layers.[3] This hierarchical layering corresponds perfectly to the varying nature of tasks that have to be performed for a military (or business) to accomplish its mission. The magical number is seven. There are seven levels of command from the soldier to the highest general. There have always been seven distinct layers even though there are more pay grades than seven. Extra layers do not creep into combat military organizations because they are seen as adding no real value, and the cost of focusing on non-value-adding work in combat is often death. *Principle #1—Establish The Correct Number of Organizational Levels!*

Second, military organizational structure (in combat) has always been built around a clear sense of accountability. Commanders know precisely what they are accountable for and the penalties that follow if they are unable to effectively discharge their accountabilities. Commanders are also provided the necessary authorities they may need to discharge all assigned accountabilities. For example, in time of war, commanders are bestowed with the authority to order subordinates into harm's way under threat of court martial, if required. (Good commanders, however, rarely rely on this extreme basis of authority. But the authority is there nonetheless.) *Principle #2—Clearly Define Accountability and Authority!*

Third, the military has always recognized a requirement to clearly define the nature of working relationships that cut across normal organizational boundaries, especially in combat situations. Terms such as direct support or direct-support reinforcing describe the role of artillery (marketing) units in support of infantry (sales) operations. These terms are not left ambiguous or subject to individual interpretation. They are precisely defined, and military leaders at all levels understand them completely. Today's civilian equivalent of shared service centers or matrix support activities are often left so ill-defined that it is no wonder that operating leaders view them so negatively. Similarly, government department heads and corporate support executives (human resources, information technology, finance) often rely on a poorly defined concept

---

3   Elliott Jaques and Stephen D. Clement, Executive Leadership. (Arlington, VA: Cason Hall Publishers, 1991), 116.

of oversight to justify giving orders to organizational entities, thereby causing these entities to spend considerable resources in responding to such orders. Many of these orders are considered by operators to be non-value-added government or corporate meddling. *Principle #3—Clearly Define Working Relationships!*

Fourth, the military spends an immense amount of time developing and assessing the capability of combat leaders. It trains commanders exhaustively on how to take full advantage of their individual capabilities in striving to accomplish routine missions. Its after-action reviews (AARs) of training exercises are world class postmortem analyses of what went right and what went wrong during a given exercise. These AARs leave no stones unturned. They explore, at every level of command, every decision, judgment, and movement made during an exercise. (Rarely do civilian corporations apply the same rigor to their existing operations.) Leader performance is subject to constant scrutiny. Individuals are periodically assessed and rank ordered with promotions subject to sophisticated selection boards and processes. Only the best are selected for higher levels of responsibility. *Principle #4—Continually Assess Individual Working Capability!*

Last, leadership is always from the front. That is why the motto of the infantry is to "follow me." The military culture, including the operating values contained therein, is always scrutinized to ensure that it is supportive of frontline soldiers. There is a long and cherished history that reinforces this support of the frontline soldier. An indelible part of that culture is ensuring that commanders at all levels possess the character and ethics deemed essential to make them worthy of leading soldiers in combat. The military institution recognizes that if the leader is not competent and of impeccable character, then how can he or she expect subordinates to follow them enthusiastically and operate to their full individual capability. *Principle # 5—Ensure That Managers Are Competent to Lead!*

This book is not focused solely on lessons learned from military structure, but it does describe and build upon a set of principles that have found a home in the combat military for many generations. These same principles, however, do not exist in most corporate settings. Without a foundation of sound organizational principles, we believe many organizations are doomed to mediocrity, surviving from one crisis to the next. This book will tell you how to institutionalize these foundational concepts in your own organization in order to set a fertile stage for any subsequent challenges or changes you may choose to implement. At the end of the day, companies all over the world have near-equal access to the same information and technology. The only true source for achieving a competitive edge is the quality of your people. Why not provide them a proper foundation to permit them to operate to their full individual potential!

Who Should Read This Book?

The audience for our book is primarily individuals who are a part of complex organizations. By our definition, complex organizations may be for-profit or not-for-profit, business corporations or government agencies, or national or multinational institutions. They may be very large or small. Many may be seeking organizational growth to become the organization they think they need to be to overcome today's challenges and prepare for uncertain futures. Implementing our blueprint for small and medium-sized businesses (SMB) requires modification of some of the underlying concepts to best meet their unique organizational requirements. For example, smaller organizations need not be as concerned about clearly differentiating the number of layers within the organization. All sizes and types of organizations will need to ensure that work-related accountabilities and authorities are clearly defined. Finally, personnel issues relating to individual capability are vitally important to organizations of every size, as getting the most out of your people often constitutes the difference between long-term success and failure.

What is a complex organization? We don't know where simple ends and complex begins: it may be in terms of revenues, profits, headcount, geographic reach, or other quantifiable measures. But these organizations tend to face complex challenges or are experiencing an increase in the complexity of their current problems. To us, complex is defined in terms of the magnitude and complexity of work required to produce whatever value the organization produces. With work and people come complex and numerous working relationships, and with these types of working relationships comes the need for clear structure and role clarity. The people who are involved in these types of organizations and these types of work and working relationships are our audience.

How do you know when you're in a complex organization? Consider the following quote:

> *If you've spent any time inside large organizations, you know that expecting them to be strategically nimble, restlessly innovative, or highly engaging places to work—or anything else than merely efficient—is like expecting a dog to tango. Dogs are quadrupeds. Dancing isn't in their DNA.*
> —Gary Hamel
> *The Future of Management*
> Harvard Business School Press, 2007

If your organization is pretty efficient but dances like a dog, we hope your organization will be able to dance better after reading our book.

Introduction

In the first section, we review the theory and principles first published by Elliot Jacques, Lord Wilfred Brown, and one of the authors (Dr. Stephen Clement) on how organizations should be structured. This is what they and we mean by a requisite organization—an organization structured around the basic requirements of the work. We put those theories and principles to practice throughout our book, so it is only fitting that you understand the genesis of our organizational design and governance prescriptions right out of the gate. If you don't like prescriptions or being told how to do things, we hope you will read our book anyway—just write off our normative tone to our work with the army.

Over the course of years of research and practice, we have developed a model where we tie vision, strategy, and mission to organizational design, processes, and governance. Preceding all of this is a customer. All organizations have customers, and serving one's customer base is the underlying concept that gives an organization value. Our model allows us to address such questions as, how should we organize to generate the most value for our customers, should we have a flat or multi-tiered hierarchical organizational structure, how many levels or tiers should our organization have, and how do we change our structure to adapt to new strategies, environments, or new customer needs?

The Principles

In the second section, we walk you through the organizational design principles we believe are requisite for all organizations to achieve sound organizational structure. We will discuss the origins of our theory and the principles, research, and studies that form the foundation of each principle. We will follow this discussion with thoughts and comments on how these principles impact today's organizations.

Analysis and Implementation

The value of any principle or theory is truly gauged in real-world settings. In the third section, we discuss how you can analyze your own organization and implement these principles and some of the lessons learned from our years of experience in applying these principles in many different types of organizations: the dos and do nots of implementation.

Chapter 2

Why Is Structure So Important?

The decisive reason for the advance of the bureaucratic organisation has always been its purely technical superiority over any other form of organisation.

—*Max Weber*[4]

The history of organizational design goes back to Max Weber and his principles for managing large bureaucracies. The U.S. economy was transitioning from family farms and family businesses after the Civil War to the twentieth-century industrial revolution with large corporations, trusts, and holding companies. The challenge during this period of American economic history was how to organize large, complex corporations—challenges faced by Vanderbilt, Morgan, Rockefeller, Carnegie, Ford, and many other captains of industry. Max Weber and Fredrick Taylor offered solutions to corporate organizational design and management structure at the time.[5] But as bureaucracy and bureaucratic organizations became more commonplace, they were also viewed more negatively, and the theory and principles underlying them eventually

---

[4] Liesbet Hooghe (2001). The European Commission and the Integration of Europe: Images of Governance. Cambridge University Press. p. 40.

[5] Numerous references and biographical information for Max Weber may be found by following the link: http://en.wikipedia.org/wiki/Max_Weber. The link for Fredrick Taylor is http://en.wikipedia.org/wiki/Frederick_Winslow_Taylor.

fell from favor. Today, modern organizational theory and principles are focused on matrix organizations, flat organizations, teams, and in some cases, to no formal organizational structure at all. Notwithstanding research and publications heavily weighted to these topics, organizations today are larger than ever, more complex than ever, and more global. Governments as well are as big as ever. Our economy today remains populated by complex organizations, yet the literature seems particularly lacking in modern theories and principles that apply directly to complex institutions and their organizational strcuture.

This book will partially fill this void. In this book, we present theories, principles, and examples of organizational analysis and design. Our theories and principles apply primarily to complex organizations—to bureaucracies, if you will. However, they also apply to small and medium-sized organizations seeking to grow and improve their overall operating effectiveness. We have tested these theories in both the military and large for-profit organizations as well as numerous small and medium-sized businesses. From that experience base, we suggest ways of implementing these principles in your organization. It is our intent that you not only understand these theories and principles but that you are sufficiently confident in them to actually implement all (or a portion) of them in your own complex organization.

Background

The majority of people in industrialized societies spend the bulk of their lifetime in some type of organization. Working professionals spend far more time with those they work with than they do with their own families, and statistically speaking, far more people work in some sort of an organization than those who are self-employed or functioning as individual contributors. Even those who do not work for pay spend a tremendous amount of time working as volunteers with organizations such as churches, schools, and social organizations (youth sports, rotary club, etc.) in an effort to add value to their lives. So if organizations are such a large part of our adult lives, why do so many of them end up being dysfunctional? We believe that many of today's organizations spend much of their problem-solving energy focused on the wrong problems.

Let us use an old house as an example. Would you paint the walls of an old house if you had an indication that there was mold or dry rot in the beams? How about the foundation: do you even know if your house (organization) is built on a pier and beam foundation or whether there is a cement foundation to support the framework? If the foundation is aged, have you inspected it for cracks or shifting? By analogy, it is our belief that sound organizational structure, what Elliott Jaques called a "requisite organization," is the type of foundation and framework that is needed for long-term survival.[6] Good leadership and great products or services can make an old house look pretty good, but is your house structurally sound? Can it withstand the proverbial storms that we know the marketplace will throw at your organization? Your question should be, "Is my organization ready for the next storm?"

> *I see the storm on the horizon and I know his hand is in it, and if he has a time and place and work for me, then I believe I am ready.*
> —Abraham Lincoln, just prior to the outbreak of the Civil War

So, by reading this book and implementing the accompanying methodology, our teaching goal and your learning goal may be defined along personal and organizational lines.

Personal:

- Understand the theories and principles of organizational analysis and design in complex organizations based on our research and the research of Dr. Jaques
- Appreciate the relationship between your customers, your structure, and your organization
- Lead yourself and others in implementing organizational analysis and (re)design in your organization
- Understand how our principles and underlying concepts can create a solid foundation upon which to build your leadership

---

[6] Jaques, Elliott. Requisite Organization. Arlington, VA: Cason Hall Publishers, 1989, page pair 3.

development programs and performance improvement initiatives

Organizational:

- Define the right number of levels (layers or strata) in your organization and establish value-adding work at each level, including the time frames in which these levels should operate
- Define accountabilities by defining value-adding outputs as well as effective measures of performance
- Carefully and clearly define authorities assigned to levels and positions in the organization—requisite authorities to get the work done
- Create a system where managers can assess the capability of personnel in their roles by using sound judgment and principles
- Chart the workflows in an organization—both the flows that go up to the strategic levels of the organization and those that go down and out the door to customers
- Utilize our principles in analyzing your organization and implementing a new structure that is organized around the work

The economic turmoil of the last few years has resulted in lower revenue, budget freezes, and spending reductions for most businesses and government agencies in the United States and around the world. At the same time that budgets are frozen or reduced, these same organizations are expected to produce more products and services. So the challenge for organizations is to not only produce the same level of services with fewer resources, but to actually increase the quantity and quality of their product and service levels. This is the challenge of increasing productivity—one of the issues we address in this book. The financial challenge and the companion issue we address is, how can business enterprises and government agencies generate internal funds when their external funding is frozen or reduced (or otherwise constrained)?

Generally, most organizations generate additional funds by either raising prices or cutting costs. The former strategy is hard to pursue in difficult economic times, while the latter strategy generally involves personnel layoffs, introducing stringent cost controls, or implementing a major restructuring program. The imposition of strict cost controls is a favorite strategy for many companies that are struggling financially. And while such controls can staunch the outflow of funds, they do so at a considerable human cost to innovation, discretion, and morale. Eliminating personnel through restructuring or outsourcing, while typically effective in the short-term, also brings with it its own set of problems. Employees in these situations become fearful for their job and, hence, tend to behave in a risk-averse manner. Their response mechanisms further erode productivity and morale levels. There must be a better way!

The alternative to these two strategies is to find ways to do more with less, that is, to be more efficient by dramatically improving an individual's and an organization's overall productivity level. Most initiatives aimed at improving productivity levels involve the introduction of new ways of doing business, such as applying new technologies; convincing the workforce to work smarter, not harder; eliminating non-value-adding tasks; process reengineering; and so on. Rarely, however, do such productivity improvement initiatives involve focusing on an organization's structure and its attendant work system. These latter two factors have never generated more than passing interest by most executive leaders or government administrators. Instead, structure has generally been taken for granted and, more often than not, pejoratively referred to as "bureaucratic" in nature. The general feeling in most organizations is that structure is simply not that important.

Recent efforts to flatten organizations by eliminating management layers do address the structure question, but most of these efforts are done haphazardly, without the benefit of a proven theory or field-tested design principles. It is easy to remove an organizational layer, but if the designer doesn't simultaneously take out the work historically performed by the individuals occupying that layer, the actual workload for layers above and below becomes larger and possibly unwieldy. The work done by individuals in the eliminated layer now must get done by pulling the boss down a level to do it or by relying on individuals at the next lower level to step up to do the work. The risk is that individuals in the higher level are overqualified for the work or that the individuals in lower levels are in over their heads. The organizational design principles we present in this book eliminate this risk by aligning the number of levels to the complexity of the work and the capabilities of the individuals doing the work.

It is our contention that many of the productivity initiatives in organizations, while interesting, will only improve productivity levels short-term at best. In their place, we suggest that companies and government agencies go back to some of the old traditional management basics. One of these basics focuses on establishing a proper organizational structure to perform the essential work of the organization. Structure is important because it sets the context for all human interaction. The wrong or inappropriate structure can easily lead to dysfunctional interactions between members of any organization. Further, we believe that most contemporary organizations (including both corporate and government agencies) currently contain the wrong structure. These organizations find themselves with too many management layers; roles inappropriately crowded too close together, driving out the creative spirit of employees; a lack of clearly defined roles in terms of underlying accountability and authority base—frequently leading to individuals throwing their weight around to get things done; or poorly defined working relationships, resulting in needless friction and excessive conflict. And these are only a few of the problems associated with having the wrong structure.

All of these problems suck the creative energy out of an organization's people, resulting in abnormally low productivity levels. It is a vicious circle because, to offset these problems, companies frequently turn to more and more management fads to improve productivity. Sometimes the latest fad attempts to motivate individuals to work harder; at other times, everyone is encouraged to share increased information with everyone else; and sometimes managerial roles are eliminated and a matrix organization introduced with individuals nebulously reporting to multiple managers. We contend that the first step in any productivity improvement effort is to get the organizational structure right. We call this getting back to organizational basics. In the following pages, we hope to demonstrate how to do this and to illustrate the success you will experience when you apply our principles and theory.

In this book, we share lessons learned from several multiyear transformation initiatives: corporate, government, and small business. For many of these initiatives, the goal was to reduce the headquarters' size and other overhead expenses so that additional funds would be available for operating units. Similarly, in business enterprises operating in an era of constrained resources, the challenge is how to take reductions in one or more areas of the company and then to apply the savings to other more critical areas of the company. These more critical areas may be directly involved in profit generation or in the design and testing of new product or service offerings. At any rate, the reallocation of scarce resources is likely to be perceived negatively by those individuals in the organization who are required to give up resources. The real challenge is for organizations to generate additional funds internally. In the business literature, this reliance on internally generated cash flow is known as the *sustainable growth model*.

As mentioned earlier, we will share our lessons learned from applying our basic organization principles in a variety of business organizations, ranging from Fortune 500 organizations to small family-owned businesses. These businesses have weathered the storm of economic decline only to be faced with the daunting challenge of market uncertainty to an extent that many have never experienced. The old saying "change is the only constant" just may itself be changing to "change and uncertainty are the only constants," and both are now the new normal.

This book will propose a multistep application program of organization design principles to increase efficiency and productivity in any business enterprise or governmental agency. And, as we discuss in the next chapter, our principles are grounded in organization theory—theory developed and tested by Dr. Elliott Jaques and one of the authors (Dr. Stephen Clement).

We've all been there. You want to get something done at work that seems so simple. And yet it ends up being so, so ... hard. Too many layers, too many rules, too many cooks, too many everything. What's even more frustrating is that those at the top often aren't even aware of the frustrations. After all, they don't have to deal with them. The irony: they often put those complexities there in the first place. So they remain blissfully ignorant of the problems they've created. Until, that is, it's too late. Until the [organization] is toppling under the weight of its own inefficiencies.

—Editor's Note to the *Wall Street Journal/ MIT Sloan Management Review Business Insight* article "Too Big to Manage," *Wall Street Journal*, October 26, 2009

Chapter 3

The Work of Dr. Elliott Jaques

As cited earlier, the genesis of our principles is the research and findings of Dr. Elliott Jaques. Over a fifty-year period of research and publishing, Dr. Jaques developed what is known as *Requisite Organization Theory—an all-encompassing systems theory focused on designing, staffing, and managing work in organizations.*[7] Dr. Jaques' empirical-based theory is normative in the sense that it prescribes organizational structure parameters (dimensions); human cognitive capabilities; compensation and rewards; accountabilities and authorities; and managerial attributes required to bring the most satisfaction to people in organizations and, at the same time, maximize the value produced by those organizations. His years of research lead him to identify basic requirements for organizational design in large organizations, that is, what is "requisite" to meet the aspirations and goals of individuals in organizations and of the organizations themselves. "Requisite" to Dr. Jaques was "required by nature"—in this case, required for an organized workplace; hence, the name Requisite Organization Theory.

Over the past decade, we have tailored many of the concepts of Requisite Organization to reflect findings from our own research and studies. It was this tailoring process, supplemented by two decades of real-life application experiences, that led to the development of the

---

[7] Elliott Jaques, Requisite Organization, (Arlington, VA: Cason Hall Publishers, 1989).

organizational design principles described in this book.

Why Requisite Organization Theory?

Why principles based on Requisite Organization Theory rather than one of the many other empirically based theories and models?

First, Jaques's work focused on both large and small, complex organizations. Large organizations are pejoratively referred to as *bureaucracies;* we prefer the words *hierarchal organizations.* Large organizations are characterized by thousands of employees, complex working relationships, global operations, seven to nine organization levels, and multiple functions, products, and services. These were the types of organizations that Dr. Jaques studied. Some were corporate (e.g., Glacier Metals, CRA-Rio Tinto, and Whirlpool); some were governmental (e.g., U.S. Army, British National Health Care System, and the Church of England). Other organizations were smaller in size but still complex (e.g., Novus International, Ontario Hydro, and Gilbert Associates). Dr. Jaques concluded that nearly all organizations suffered from basic organizational pathologies that prevented them from being efficient or effective. According to Dr. Jaques, when organizations are properly structured, they are capable of releasing the full potential of employees and of achieving world class performance standards.[8]

Second, Requisite Organization Theory is a total systems theory. Like all systems theory applications, if designed properly, the whole is greater than the sum of the parts. To achieve the synergies associated with total systems theory, the organizational conditions underlying effective workplace systems must be studied and analyzed as well as the psychological conditions that affect each individual within the workplace. Requisite Organization Theory integrates multiple dimensions of people and processes with organizational design (see Figure 3.1). The human dimension couples psychological, social, cognitive, and motivational variables (i.e., the soft variables) with compensation, rewards, teams, accountabilities, and authorities (i.e., the hard variables).

---

8   Ibid., 2.

The Work of Dr. Elliott Jaques

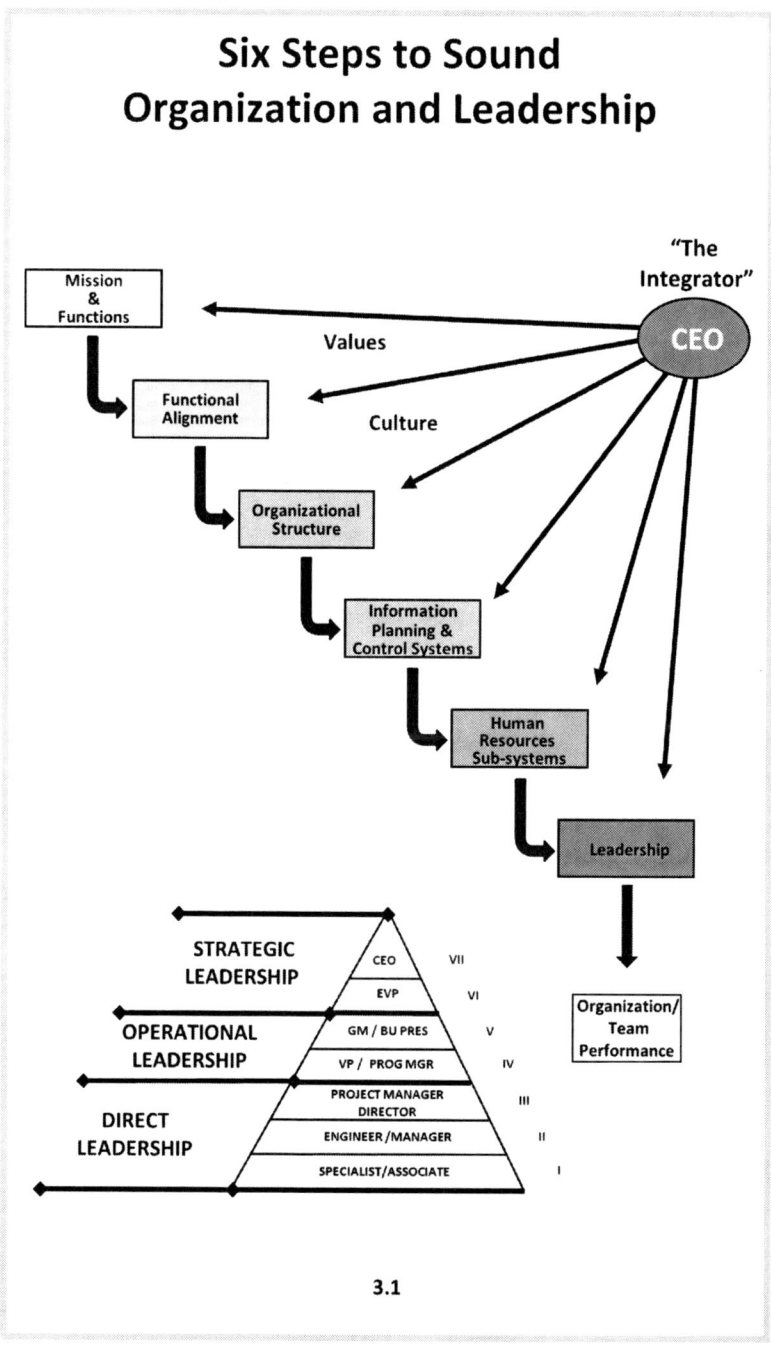

3.1

Increasing individual and organizational productivity requires that each step described in Figure 3.1 be properly addressed.[9] This means addressing structural issues early on, followed by ensuring that all existing systems and processes support desired behaviors. For example, the compensation system should actually pay people for producing desired outcomes, the planning system should be sufficient to encompass the proper time horizon necessary to deal with long-term issues (e.g., strategic uncertainty), and the human resource (HR) system should properly focus on reinforcing desired behaviors (e.g., ensuring that operating values are congruent with stated values) so that leadership challenges are met with tangible as well as practical solution sets and not limited to the latest leadership fad (e.g., follower leadership).

Like all systems theories, Figure 3.1 shows a complex set of variables, each of which is interdependent with all the others. Many corporate executives and agency heads shy away from trying to address the whole system because of the system's complexity. Instead, they look for a quick fix. In our opinion, no such fix exists. The real challenge facing senior executives in organizations is, how quickly can they address the full range of variables that are outlined in Figure 3.1? We shall endeavor to answer that question in the ensuing pages. Our principles do not employ all of Dr. Jaques's findings, but many of them are grounded in some part of Requisite Organization Theory.

Finally, and most importantly, our own experience has demonstrated that Requisite Organization Theory tenets work in practice. Additionally, we have found others who have employed Requisite Organization Theory with equal success.[10] Our personal success has been in tailoring the theory and principles to better meet contemporary organizational needs. For example, a key tenet of Requisite Organization Theory is use of the time-span instrument to measure the complexity of work. According to Dr. Jaques, the time-span measure reflects the level of work of a role.[11] The time-span measurement is the longest of the target-

---

9   Ibid, page pair 80.

10 Empirical research and publications may be found on the Global Organizational Design Society (GO) website: https://globalro.org/en/home.html. The GO website also contains a comprehensive bibliography on Dr. Jaques's work authored by Ken Craddock.

11 Jaques, Elliott. Requisite Organization. Arlington, VA: Cason Hall Publishers, 1989, page pair 16.

completion times of tasks in the role. Time spans have been found to become longer and longer as one analyzes higher and higher roles in an organization. In essence, Dr. Jaques found that time span reflected the planning horizon required of role incumbents at successively higher levels in an organization.[12]

As important as the time-span measure is in assessing the level of work in a role, we have found a sizeable shift in the time span of many executives in today's rapidly changing world. We call this concept *time compression*. This concept was first discovered in our work with military organizations in combat situations. In our research with the army, we found that leaders in combat situations were focused on progressively shorter time spans than what occurred in peacetime situations. We have seen similar shifts in many corporate settings as well, as senior executives in these companies focus on dealing with rapid change. We will discuss this shift in the time span of today's executives in more detail in the chapter devoted to levels of work and time-span measurement. We discuss the concept here only to demonstrate the tailoring process described previously.

Furthermore, we have also discovered individuals and organizations who have successfully applied Requisite Organization Theory and its tenets to organizations that one would think are far too small to utilize Dr Jaques's work. They have adapted components of the theory and principles to better meet contemporary business and economic conditions of today's small and medium-sized businesses.

Personally, we have successfully applied the aforementioned tailored principles in the Headquarters, Department of the Army, the U.S. Army Medical Command; Installation Management Command; many large business corporations (e.g., Rio Tinto, Whirlpool, Ashland Chemical, Lennox Industries, Pepsi, G&K Services, ConAgra Foods, Office Depot, and Textron) and more recently to many small businesses as well. The aforementioned principles have proven useful in our analysis and design efforts related to these organizations.

---

12 Ibid, page pair 37–40.

Dr. Elliott Jaques

"Who the Hell Is Elliott Jaques?" is actually the title of chapter 8 in Dr. Jerry Harvey's book (author of *The Abilene Paradox*) *How Come Every Time I Get Stabbed in the Back My Fingerprints Are on the Knife?*[13] Dr. Harvey introduces the reader to Elliott Jaques with a story of his checking out one of Elliott's books at his "beloved institution's" library to find that he was only the second person to ever check out the book, *A General Theory of Bureaucracy (1976)*:

> *Despite its absence from the New York Times best-seller list, I read it and found it to be one of the most creative, stimulating, exciting, rigorous, confrontational, intellectually demanding, and morally provocative pieces of work I had ever read in the field of management and organizational behavior. No, that's not accurate. I found it to be the most creative, stimulating, exciting, rigorous, confrontational, intellectually demanding, and morally provocative piece of work I had ever read in the field of management and organizational behavior.*
>
> In light of my reaction, I began to wonder how I, who pride myself as being a semi-bright, relatively well-read professional in the field of organizational behavior, had not heard of Jaques' work.

The first person to check out the book was the one who had referred him to Jaques's work in the first place, and that was three years prior.

Harvey then proceeds to network throughout the world of organizational behavior specialists, management thinkers, consultants, academics, executives, and students in an informal poll to find who would have reason to know Elliott Jaques and understand his work. Harvey writes that the majority of the responses he received were essentially, "Who the hell is Elliott Jaques?"

Elliott Jaques did not set out to be a management thinker; in fact, by education and profession, he began his career far away from organizations, specifically with a career in medicine. He received his M.D. from Johns

---

13 Harvey, Jerry. *How Come Every Time I Get Stabbed in the Back My Fingerprints Are on the Knife?* Josey Bass Publishers: San Francisco, 1999.

Hopkins followed by a Ph.D. in social relations from Harvard. Dr. Jaques moved to London and studied and worked alongside Melanie Klein in her work in psychoanalyzing children, some as young as two years old. During World War II, Dr. Jaques was tasked by the British Army to assist in identifying which young soldiers might one day be officers and generals. It was while working in the British Army that he first began to ponder the role and impact of the organization on the individual.

Consistent with this concern, Dr. Jaques became one of the first serious management theorists to address the social role of the corporation way back in the 1960s. His whole study of organizations was centered on pondering some of the most fundamental questions of human society: *What is a good social institution? Can individuals be free in an organization? Can there be fairness, justice, and liberty in a hierarchy of authorities? At the heart of these issues, according to Jaques, is the importance of managerial institutions and managerial leadership to the achievement of trust in a society.*[14] Jaques argued that managerial organizations have become the most important social institutions in a modern free-enterprise democratic society.[15]

According to Dr. Jaques, everyone's ideas about human nature at work are clouded by ubiquitous, invasive, and serious misconceptions.[16] These misconceptions have continuously fueled the development of poorly designed managerial leadership systems. Dr. Jaques argued that liberty and freedom are basic conditions of individuals living and working together in social systems. If these social systems are to flourish, they must be organized requisitely to provide for the trust and justice required for effective interpersonal dealings. Dr. Jaques goes on to state that bureaucracy is the only structure that truly fits human nature. Free enterprise democracy is essential for healthy working institutions, for it places these institutions firmly in the position of having to understand social needs to be able to compete and satisfy them in order to survive.[17] Bottom line, the question of how to organize today's institutions requisitely should be of major concern to today's senior executives.

---

14 Jaques, Elliott. Requisite Organization. Arlington, VA: Cason Hall Publishers, 1996, page pair 15.

15 Ibid., 2.

16 Ibid., 134.

17 Ibid., 134.

Starting in 1951, Dr. Jaques authored over twenty books, many of which were seldom read or referenced in organizations throughout the world. In 1964, he first proposed the idea of *time span*, essentially surmising that the higher up an individual is in an organization, the longer their outlook or time horizon should be. He proposed that by measuring an individual's time span of work, researchers could ascertain at what level of work (i.e., complexity) the individual was performing.[18] Dr. Jaques began exploring, testing, and researching this theory in the years to follow while working at Glacier Metals in the United Kingdom. It was there that he first began to study the number of levels of management in an organization; which he called "strata." He explored the nature of those levels and their impact on the organization, its people, and its attendant work station. Much of this early work was published in *A General Theory of Bureaucracy in 1976*.[19]

Dr. Jaques's book eventually caught the attention of Sir Roderick Carnegie, who as the chief executive officer (CEO) of CRA (a large Australian mining firm) was looking for someone in the management field to help improve the company's competitive effectiveness. Sir Roderick had spent twelve years with McKinsey Consulting observing how the best companies in the world achieved productivity and efficiency. Sir Roderick found that having sound objectives, well-executed personnel practices, and well-implemented management practices motivated highly talented people. (In his work with McKinsey, Sir Roderick developed the strategic business unit structure that was first implemented in GE, and remains so today.)

According to Sir Roderick, Elliott Jaques brought five fundamental beliefs to organizational improvement:[20]

> 1. A belief that management practices are seriously flawed and that they are based on erroneous assumptions about human behavior and dependent on faulty measurement indices, such as medicine in the fifteenth century. Thus, they offer a vast opportunity for improvement.

---

18 Jaques, Elliott. General Theory of Bureaucracy. London: Heineman Educational Books, 1976.
19 Ibid.
20 Personal conversations with Sir Roderick Carnegie.

2. A belief that development of the time-span instrument was a significant discovery that now permits the objective assessment of the size of a job. To Jaques, this was the management equivalent of medicine's thermometer, which, when it was invented, dramatically changed the course of medical diagnosis. Discovery of time-span measurement was considered the first step in introducing scientific methods to the running of large-scale organizations.

3. A strong feeling that over the course of a number of years a set of universal principles would be discovered that would transform the field of management.

4. A belief that any long-term improvement requires the dedicated efforts and hard work of line managers at all organizational levels.

5. An intense feeling that any attempt at getting work done better had to be based upon the application of sound management principles. Jaques loathed so-called short-term quick fixes. To him, the only real solution was the systematic application of field-tested sound principles, and this was likely to require hard work over a longer period of time.

Dr. Jaques continued his work at CRA from 1978 to 1985. According to Sir Roderick, then chairman of CRA, Elliott had not yet fully developed his theory; what he had was a set of deeply held hypotheses. During this same period, Jaques was also involved in serious research with the U.S. Army. Jaques's research led him to what he called *Stratified Systems Theory*, a theory that organizations throughout the world could and should have no more than seven distinct layers of management between the worker and the CEO.[21] Jaques had previously discovered two organizations that in their natural state had a similar number of management layers for thousands of years. These two organizations were the Catholic Church

---

21 Jaques, Elliott. Requisite Organization. Arlington, VA: Cason Hall Publishers, page pair 10.

and the combat military. Thus, Jaques was interested in studying the U.S. Army, which had seven levels of command, or management. This concept of seven levels has existed in successful armies since the days of the Roman legion.

At this same time, one of the authors of this book, Dr. Stephen Clement, was developing the current policy and doctrine for the U.S. Army's leadership programs. Dr. Clement was assigned by the army to oversee the Jaques research project. The question Drs. Jaques and Clement began to explore was, why did the U.S. Army maintain seven levels of command in light of the fact that technology dramatically changed the combat power available to a commander at any given level? Drs. Jaques and Clement set out to test Stratified Systems Theory in the very unique test bed of the U.S. Army.

In 1989, Jaques published *Requisite Organization, which was the culmination of all of his past books and his more recent research at the U.S. Army and CRA.*[22] Dr. Clement, as Dr. Jaques's partner in the U.S. Army and CRA projects, coauthored *Executive Leadership published in 1991.*[23] The combined efforts of Jaques, Carnegie, and Clement were subsequently integrated into a set of working hypotheses, which ultimately were refined by Dr Clement into a comprehensive set of management principles.

In the twenty-plus years that have followed the publishing of *Requisite Organization and Executive Leadership,* countless books have been published in the field of organizational behavior and management thinking. However, we have failed to find a book or theory that has effectively reflected an all-encompassing organizational system theory that has withstood the test of time in the same vein that Jaques's theories (Stratified Systems Theory and Requisite Organization) have. In our opinion, the seminal value of Elliott Jaques's contribution is that he has presented us with the beginnings of a General Theory of Organizational Science.

The big contribution of theory is that it brings order out

---

[22] Ibid, 1996.
[23] Jaques, Elliott and Clement, Stephen D. Executive Leadership. Arlington, VA: Cason Hall Publishers, 1991.

of chaos: it provides meaning where it had previously not existed. Orderliness, however, cannot be provided unless the previously unrelated mass of facts has first been funneled through the mind of some thinking scientist.[24]
—Joseph R. Royce

Elliott Jaques was that "thinking" scientist. He was the first to provide us with the concept of organizations having a significant social role. His articulation that organizations (bureaucracies), if designed correctly, permit individuals to operate to their full individual capability and realize their full potential is a central tenet of meeting that societal obligation. Jaques was quick to point out that corporate work entities are built upon contracts with individuals and not with groups or teams. He also argued that for leadership to flourish in any organizational environment, the structure has to be right. Too many organizational layers often result in managers suffocating subordinate efforts because there is insufficient distance between the two parties, manager and subordinate. As described previously, Jaques's research suggested that the modern corporation need not have more than seven managerial layers from the bottom to the top-most layer, later expanded to eight to reflect even larger and more complex organizations.

Jaques also spelled out the need to clearly define the nature of lateral working relationships in terms of their underlying accountability and authority base. Once the correct structure has been clearly established, it is then necessary to ensure that individuals with the correct working capacity are selected to fill all roles in the structure. Finally, Jaques argued that it is then essential to ensure that all managerial leadership practices support getting work done efficiently and effectively, such as compensation practices—pay people correctly for the level of work they perform, hold subordinates accountable to work to their full individual capacity, have managers perform all potential assessments two levels down, and so on. Given the breadth of the above concepts, it is our contention that Jaques pioneered efforts at developing a general theory

---

[24] Royce, Joseph R. Toward the Advancement of Theoretical Psychology. Psychological reports, 1957, page 3 and 404. Reprinted in James Grier Miller, Living Systems, McGraw Hill, 1978, page 5.

of organizational science.

In the years since Dr Jaques's groundbreaking work, we believe we are now able to describe the foundational building blocks required to dramatically improve organizational performance and individual leadership. These building blocks are described in detail in the following sections of this book.

Chapter 4

Organizational Preparation and Situational Awareness

It All Starts with Customers

If strategy drives structure, then customers trump both. Without focusing on customers' needs and demands, an organization's strategy and structure will be flawed and its existence short lived. Meeting customers' needs must become a primary objective of every organization. And while many companies extol the value of organizing around customers' needs, the number of companies that actually tailor their design around these needs is much smaller. If customers are truly important, then references to them should be clearly stated in the company's mission statement.

Mission statements are important because they imply the presence of critical functions. These functions, in turn, form the foundation of an organization's structure. Merely referring to the importance of customers is not enough, however. For a company to remain relevant and maintain a competitive edge, it must develop a thorough and deep understanding of the customer. Such an understanding will subsequently have a profound influence on an organization's basic structure, its operating systems, and its key management processes. Analyzing and then fulfilling customers' needs, thus, must become a prime objective of every company.

This is an obvious statement for a business corporation competing in the marketplace. But it also applies to government and military agencies. Although not always understood or accepted, they too must identify and focus on their customers or they will become irrelevant—irrelevant in the sense that they may continue to exist but be underfunded or, in the case of the military, defeated. Our experience with many government and military agency senior leaders, during seminars, workshops, and personal conversations, is that you must convince them that they, in fact, have customers. When pushed to identify a specific customer, they frequently answer Congress or their funding source. For example, in the case of the U.S. Army Installation Management Command (a $12 billion dollar organization providing a variety of services to soldiers and their families, e.g., housing, electrical, child care services, recreational services, etc.), their customer is not the Chief of Staff of the Army or Congress; rather, their customers are soldiers and their families. The same question applies to the Department of the Interior (National Park Service): are their customers park visitors (tourists, campers, fishermen, etc.), environmental groups (Sierra Club, Greenpeace, etc.), or possibly even the environment itself (Mother Earth)?

Even when an agency does recognize that it has customers, it may not be apparent who its customers are. For example, in our military customer example, the ultimate customer may be army personnel, but a related question is, who is the immediate customer that receives value from the products or services being produced? Thus, is the real customer the consumer of a product or service or someone else? The Army Installation Command, offering day care services, has its consumer, a child, and its customer, the parents of the child. So identifying an agency's consumers and customers is a fundamental first step in designing a requisite organization. The distinction between consumers and customers is important because it has significant organizational structural implications. One the one hand, consumers are traditionally the focus of the marketing and product development functions (e.g., children, patients, etc.). On the other hand, customers are critical to the sales organizations and supply chain function because they represent specific groups buying discrete products and services (parents, medical insurance companies, etc.).

Organizational Preparation and Situational Awareness

Simply identifying your customers, however, is only part of the equation. We have observed in thousands of interviews in a variety of government agencies that agencies frequently correctly identify their customers but often do not have the work and processes in place to adequately fulfill their customers' needs. In other words, they know who their customers are, but all of their work, processes, and structure are really geared toward their funding source. For example, in the U.S. Army, an organization may claim that their customer is the soldier, but when you really analyze their work emphasis and resource allocation, it is clear that the customer is Congress (e.g., their funding source).

This is not a book about customers per se, for the literature abounds with detailed discussions about them. Nonetheless, obtaining intimate knowledge of your customers is one of the major accountabilities of an organizational leader. Customers impact *some components of every* role in the organization. Knowing the customer is a requirement of all positions in an organization. If a role in some way doesn't meet the needs of the organization's customers, then it should not exist. Bottom line, customers drive organizational structure and all of its dimensions—levels, positions, roles, accountabilities, authorities, working relationships, and on and on. And while customers are critical to any in-depth analysis or design of an organization, the presence of a principle-based theory is also critical to the design process.

The Importance of a Principle-based Theory

> *My client has 80 managers and with that, 80 different opinions and beliefs on how this company should be organized, when all they really need is 1.*
>
> —*A senior partner of an international consulting firm, commenting on his consulting experiences with large corporations to date*

As described previously, organizational structure has a powerful influence on how people act individually and in work groups and how they are motivated individually to work toward the goals of the organization. A properly designed structure is much more than wiring diagrams or rearranging boxes in organization charts; it should also include clearly documented accountabilities and authorities and clearly defined working relationships.

Organizational structure problems and their underlying pathologies are not the only background factors that affect human behavior, however. A person's internal beliefs and personal value system also affect how she is likely to react in a given situation. These beliefs and values tend to get codified into a person's underlying theory of human behavior. These internal theories (and the underlying principles associated with them) are important for a number of reasons. First, the presence of theory is ubiquitous. Everyone subscribes in one way or another to one or more theories. Theories are what guide most human behavior. The problem with theories is not that people have them (or subscribe to a particular one), but that many people don't realize what their theories are and how such theories actually shape their individual behavior. Second, people tend to hold on to their beliefs and theories tenaciously.[25]

The strong adherence to operating beliefs and the corresponding theories and principles that underpin them permit individuals to make sense of their environment. Without a theory or principle base, events are viewed chaotically, and individuals do not know how to react to uncertainty or fast-changing situations. Thus, most individuals aggressively challenge data that calls into question their beliefs and operating theory base. This is why people so adamantly resist change: it is the change itself that causes them to modify their personal beliefs and theory base. Not surprisingly, then, it is difficult for people to leave their comfort zones and behave differently. We believe that the way people will begin to accept change is to educate them first in new operating principles or theories and then to convince them that it is in their own best interests to embrace new knowledge in positive ways.[26]

One of the lessons we have learned over the past decade is that if organizational change is to be lasting, the change requires that organizational members accept the particular change. Accepting change,

---

25 Argyris, Chris and Schon, D. 1978. Organizational Learning; A Theory of Action Perspective. Redding, MA: Addison Wesley, page 16.
26 Ibid, page 17.

however, generally requires that individuals embrace new ideas or new concepts to replace existing concepts and theories. If those in workforce leadership positions don't embrace new operating principles, then it will be very difficult to achieve actual changes in workplace behavior. Therefore, it is important to start any change management initiative with an education module explaining the rationale and principles underpinning the change effort. By articulating a specific set of organizational design principles and an accompanying management philosophy, everyone in the company has a chance to at least understand the rationale behind the company's change initiatives. This understanding will prove very valuable in the long run as it will help each individual accept new ideas and new ways of doing business.

Preparing Your Organization for Analysis

These topics—customers, principles, and theories—are all discussed in much greater detail in later sections of the book. So why bring them up here? Simple, we want you to begin preparing yourself and your organization for the changes to come as a result of reading this book. If you plan to embark on an organizational project, you need to ensure your organization is beginning to seek an understanding of your customer base. At the end of the day, any organizational project begins with customers. And finally, it is important for leaders to begin thinking of ways to institutionalize the principles in your organization. To do so may require that you challenge all employees' personal theories of how your business should be organized.

Chapter 5

Principle #1: Organize around Levels of Work

Organizational Levels of Work and Complexity

Organizations are established to get work done, which is what they are all about. And work gets done by individuals who occupy roles in some sort of organizational structure. The nature of work expressed in terms of its underlying complexity is important because it sets the architectural standards for designing an effective structure. The importance of structure has been described previously. The tasks and goals that make up an organization's work flow naturally from the organization's basic mission and the functions inherent in carrying out that mission. Figure 5.1 depicts how an organization's mission and strategy define the functions and the attendant tasks it needs to perform to accomplish a given mission. These functions should be organized both vertically and horizontally so that the work and decision making associated with them can be effectively and efficiently carried out. To do this, a requisite organization structure must be established—that is, a structure required by the complexity of the mission, functions, and the ensuing work that flows from those functions.

Principle #1: Organize around Levels of Work

The Relationship Between Mission, Functions and Tasks

External Governance Factors

- Public Law
- Stakeholder and shareholder needs
- Cultural Imperatives

↓

Organizational Mission

Business Unit Functions

Mandated Directives
- Recruiting
- Training
- Overseeing
- Environmental

Generalized Activity
- Administering Medicare program
- Community involvement or good corporate citizen

↓ Tasks   ↓ Tasks   ↓ Tasks

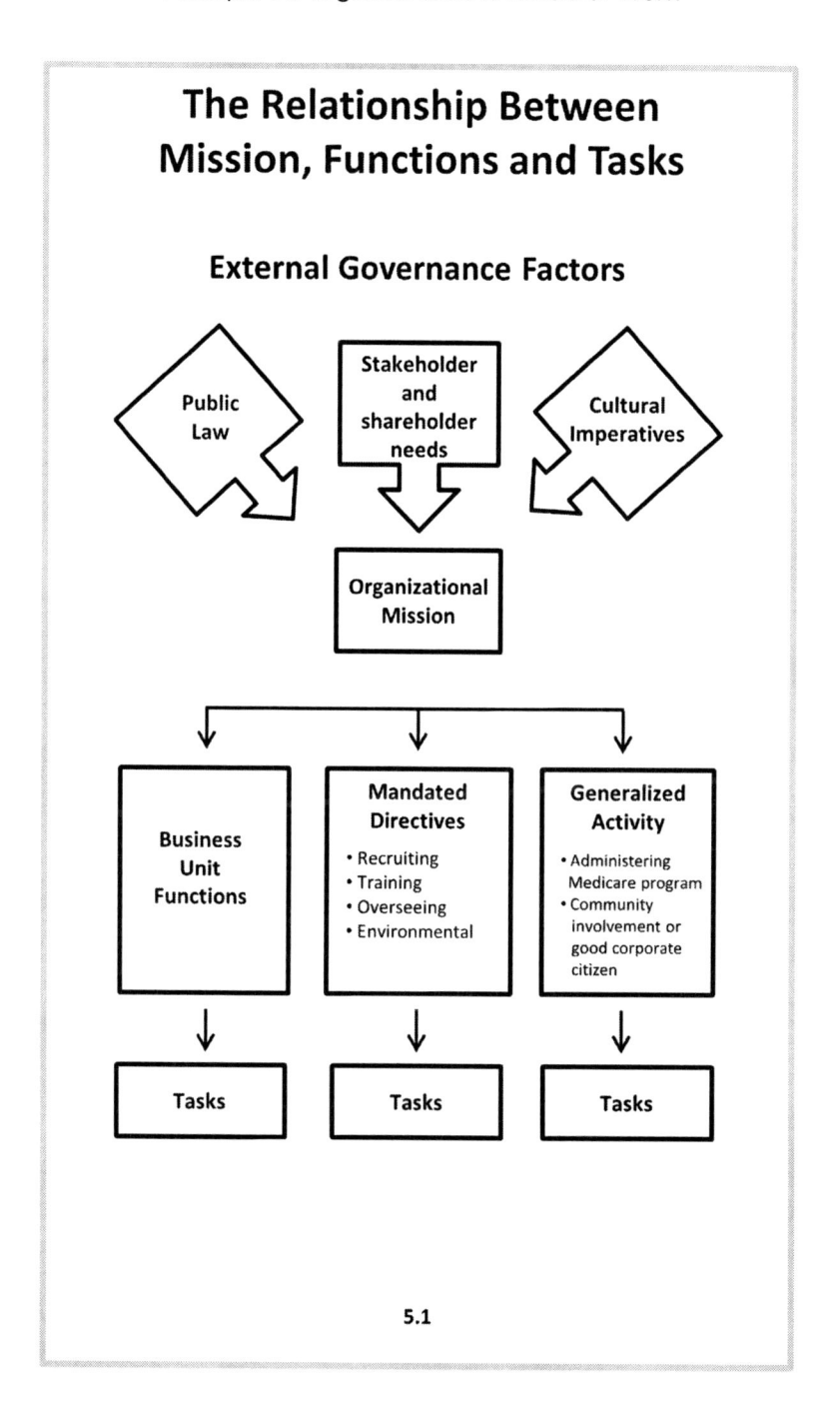

5.1

MISSION: A SHORT FORM AL WRITTEN STATEMENT OF PURPOSE

- *Pepsi*—"The world's premier consumer products company focused on convenient foods and beverages"[27]

- *The U.S. Army*—"Win the nation's wars"[28]

FUNCTION: A grouping of related tasks, supporting a basic organizational function or need or an externally imposed directive or generalized activity

- The training function includes conducting a front-end job task analysis, identifying critical tasks, designing training programs to master task performance, setting training standards, and evaluating training performance.

TASK: An assignment to produce specified outputs (including quantity and quality) within a targeted completion time, with allocated resources, and within specified limits

- The marketing function includes gathering and analyzing marketing data, evaluating consumer behavior and identifying new products or service needs, and developing new methods or procedures for communicating company solutions sets to meet such needs.

The general principle that structure follows strategy was first popularized by Alfred Chandler in 1963.[29] At the time, Chandler said that companies should organize around what matters most. This concept

---

27 http://www.pepsico.com/Company/Our-Mission-and-Vision.html
28 www.army.mil
29 Chandler, Alfred Jr., Strategy and Structure, Chapters in the History of the American Enterprise. Cambridge, MA: MIT Press, 1963.

Principle #1: Organize around Levels of Work

has subsequently been explored extensively by Jay Galbraith.[30] Galbraith argued that there are five dimensions of structure: function, product, market, geography, and process, with the correct dimension being dictated by a company's strategy. Building upon these concepts, Michael Raynor suggested that structure matters because it reflects a firm's strategic priorities.[31] Raynor astutely points out, however, that structure has generally been defined solely in terms of horizontal differentiation. Optimizing an organization's structure from a functional differentiation perspective reached its peak in the sixties when the McKinsey consulting firm developed the business unit (BU) model for the General Electric Company (GE). The BU model was designed to contain the optimum mix of functions needed to aggressively attack a given market segment. At the time, the BU model was only peripherally structured around vertical levels. The notion of a five-level BU emerged as a result of concerns over how best to develop people in a large corporate enterprise. This issue was first addressed by Sir Roderick Carnegie in his work as a senior McKinsey consultant in Australia.[32]

The hierarchical (vertical) nature of organizations has subsequently been exhaustively studied by Jaques. His findings have been published in two seminal works, *In Praise of Hierarchy*[33] and *Requisite Organization*.[34] According to Jaques, hierarchical layering was a breakthrough human discovery on a par with the discovery of fire or the wheel. It was a major event that fostered the transition from the tribal type of society to the broader, more widely dispersed type of society we now take for granted. Hierarchical layering stems from the manager-subordinate role relationship, which is precisely what organizational layers are all about. Those in one layer are in roles where they delegate work to others, called subordinates, in the layer immediately below, and they can be held accountable (by someone in the next layer up) for the output of those

---

30 Galbraith, Jay. Designing Organizations: An Executive Guide to Strategy, Structure, and Process. San Francisco: Josey-Bass, 2002.
31 Raynor, Michael, E. The Strategy Paradox. New York: Doubleday, 2007.
32 Personal conversations between the authors and Sir Roderick Carnegie, 2009.
33 Jaques, Elliott (1990 HBR Article), In Praise of Hierarchy, Harvard Business Review, 1990.
34 Jaques, Elliott. Requisite Organization. Arlington, VA: Cason Hall Publishers, 1996.

subordinates.[35]

The big finding about organizational layering, according to Jaques, is that there is an optimum pattern of organizational layering in which there is one layer for each quantum step in task complexity.[36] Task complexity was a crucial concept to the structure issue. The actual number of layers required in an organization is a product of its mission. Mission sets the long-term vision, and that in turn creates the overarching planning outreach and tasks that have to be performed. According to Jaques, hierarchical layering was a function of time; managers at successively higher layers had to cope with longer and longer time horizons if they were to be viewed as having added value to the work being done by people operating at lower layers.[37]

The optimum pattern that Jaques discovered was related not only to time (as expressed by different planning horizons) but also by the inherent complexity of the tasks, problems, and information that had to be dealt with at successive layers. These tasks, problems, and information were found to vary in terms of their underlying complexity. Complexity is determined by the number of variables, the clarity or uncertainty of these variables, the rate of change, and their interdependence. The higher one goes in an organization, the more complex the work.

The proper number of layers in any organizational structure must be such as to encompass successive categories of work-related complexity. Jaques' extensive project work found that work varies significantly from one layer to the next. This variation reflects a quantum shift in the nature of that work at successive layers as opposed to a simple change in scope. Jaques was able to identify eight distinct shifts in the nature of work.[38] Thus, we are now able to report that any large commercial enterprise should have no more than seven layers in their structure and that the very largest of these organizations should contain no more than eight layers from the top to the bottom. [39] As described previously, Jaques

---

35 Jaques, Elliott and Clement, Stephen D. Executive Leadership. Arlington, VA: Cason Hall Publishers, 1991.

36 Ibid page 114.

37 Ibid, page pair 40–41.

38 Ibid page pair 41.

39 Ibid, page pair 41.

Principle #1: Organize around Levels of Work

noticed that there were two organizations in the Western world that had the requisite number of organizational layers—the combat military and the Catholic Church. These two organizations had existed for two thousand years.

In the case of the combat military, the very nature of their mission is aptly reflected in the following workplace slogan: "Adapt or die." Not surprising, the military tends to not tolerate non-value-adding work (and layers), especially in combat situations that can result in soldiers actually losing their lives. Getting the right number of layers in their structure has been a central concern of military leaders since the time of the Roman legion.

Figure 5.2 depicts a sample of companies based on size and the corresponding proper number of organizational layers that should exist for those companies.

The key to determining the proper number of organizational layers is to begin by thoroughly analyzing the work to be performed by the company or agency. As described previously, each layer is made up of a unique pattern of key work-related variables. A full range of variables that apply at a given layer is outlined in figure 5.3 (note, not all roles contain all of these categories, i.e., some roles are not managerial leadership roles). A detailed description of each variable contained at each organizational layer is beyond the scope of this book. However, the following condensed discussion is offered to provide the reader with a broad overview.

Requisite Number of Organizational Layers

Organizational Layers

Layer	Examples
VIII	Government Departments Dept. of the Army Dept. Veterans Affairs
VII	PepsiCo; Rio Tinto Whirlpool; Ashland Chemical ConAgra Foods; Army Major Command
VI	Iron Ore Operations – Rio Tinto European Appliance Division – Whirlpool Pepsi - Independent Franchise Army Corps/Joint Task Force
V	Hippotronics (small stand-alone company) BU in large Corporation (Kitchenaide – Whirlpool) Army Division
IV	Whirlpool Factory; Mine site (Rio Tinto) Chemical Plant; Army Brigade
III	Real Estate Office; Large Retail Store Army Battalion; Macaroni Grill (Restaurant)
II	Small Chain Store McDonalds Franchise Army Company
I	

Size: Small   Medium   Large   Humongous

5.2

Key Work Variables by Level
(Generic Work – General Responsibilities)

- Task Complexity
- Information Complexity / Processing Characteristics
- Resources
- Planning and Decision Making
- Problem Solving Requirements
- Leadership Requirements
- Working Relationships
- Time Horizon (Time Span)
- Staff Role Requirements

5.3

This overview begins by analyzing work at the lower three layers. The first three layers in an organization represent the primary point of contact of the organization with its customer base. This is where the bulk of a company's employees work, and these three levels constitute how well or how poorly a company executes the critical functions inherent in their assigned mission. If a company gets the work done efficiently and effectively at the front line, then the company will likely be profitable and successfully carry out its primary mission. Alternatively, if the company is not successful at the front line, then trouble is not far away.

As described previously, the nature and magnitude of the mission determine the complexity of the work that occurs in the first three layers. For example, if an organization or organizational unit's mission is to issue passports or licenses, then its work is relatively simple: validate, print, and issue certificates. The organization will have a back-office operation of validating and printing and a front-line office to issue the certificates. People will be organized as workers, supervisors, and a manager. We now have the first glimpse of the vertical dimension of our structure—a vertical dimension consisting of level I workers, level II front-line managers, and a level III unit manager. This is the front-line production unit of most organizations. If management can get these bottom three levels right, they stand a good chance of being successful.

Tactical Work

In the first three levels, there are generally few, if any, support positions, perhaps a maintenance specialist, a work-flow expediter, or a process engineer, if it involves manufacturing or production activities. Strategy or staff positions generally do not exist at these front-line levels. The first three levels of an organization are often referred to as the *tactical* level of work. There is very little uncertainty inherent in the work carried out at these three levels. Stated quite simply, three levels of hierarchy are sufficient to accomplish the mission.

The first three levels in an organizational hierarchy involve face-to-face interaction between the manager and his or her subordinate(s). To be optimally effective, the front-line manager (level II) should personally know all of his or her subordinates, understand what is going on in their personal lives, recognize family issues that could potentially affect their

Principle #1: Organize around Levels of Work

ability to do their job, and so on. There is a finite limit to the number of subordinates a manager can know in this sense. This limit, in turn, is also affected by the complexity of the tasks the subordinate has been asked to carry out.[40] Consequently, the front-line manager (FLM) can effectively manage somewhere in the range of three to sixty subordinates. If the work is exceedingly complex, as in a nuclear power plant, then the number will be toward the lower end of the scale. Alternatively, if everyone is doing the same basic work, as in a call center, then the proper number will fall toward the upper end of the scale, which is sixty. If the FLM is required to manage work across three shifts or at multiple work sites, he may need one or more assistants to help him. These assistants are called *supervisors* (or lead hands). In the military, these roles include several distinct ranks of sergeants. The full nature of this assistance role will not be described in this book. Suffice it to say, however, the essence of this role is that it assists the FLM in doing his job.

The work that occurs in the first three layers is described briefly in figure 5.4 and summarized below.

---

[40] Jaques, Elliott and Clement, Stephen D. Executive Leadership. Arlington, VA: Cason Hall Publishers, 1991, page 121.

Front-Line "Value – Adding" Work is <u>Tactical</u> in Nature

Critical Tasks

Level III

- Develop pathway and goals
- Develop set of options to achieve goals
- Design key processes to accomplish objectives
- Achieve Continuous Improvement goals
- Ask "what if" questions
- Provide unit level leadership
- Higher level selling
- Negotiate agreement with customers
- Risk and probability analysis

Level II

- Accumulate data – identify trends
- Identify critical facts affecting performance
- Develop and implement annual budget
- Interact with customers
- Identify continuous improvement targets
- Measure output
- Lead output team
- Anticipate problems – take preemptive action

Level I

- Produce direct outputs
- Perform discrete tasks
- Hands-on work
- Follow procedural manuals
- Apply specified procedures
- Follow problem solving procedures
- Use practical judgment
- Trial and error learning
- Suggest continuous improvement changes to process

5.4

Principle #1: Organize around Levels of Work

Level I:

The work at level I is concrete in nature—type this letter, machine this bearing, respond to this customer inquiry—and tasks tend to be hands-on. Workers at this level are expected to follow specified procedures (standard operating procedures). They process information as discrete data points, such as read dials on a machine, but they don't link data points together in order to identify a theme or trend. They solve problems by following proven problem-solving techniques. The planning horizon is short—one week to three months, at most. They are provided a plan (pathway) by their manager and expected to follow it. They execute budgets according to preestablished plans, and their learning strategy is based on a trial-and-error approach.[41]

If a level I worker runs into a problem that she cannot solve on her own by following prescribed problem-solving procedures, then she will likely turn to her boss(manager or supervisor) for help. Even though level I workers are provided specified procedures to be followed in carrying out their tasks, this does not mean that they are not capable of identifying new ideas or revising existing steps so as to improve existing work procedures. Thus, they can play a key role in any continuous improvement process. Today, in developed countries, many level I tasks have been engineered out of the work system. Consequently, the direct output is often delivered at level II. For example, this is the level where an entry-level accountant functions or a financial analyst carries out her work. Thus, the front-line manager in these situations is the level III manager. Nevertheless, despite attempts at using technology to eliminate level I work, most organizations still retain a modicum of level I workers, such as administrative staff, warehouse workers, receptionists, and so on.

Level II:

At level II, tasks become more abstract: they are not completely defined. Individuals operating at this level can string data together and identify trends and then take preemptive action to overcome potential problems. This is also the level of the first-line manager. The planning horizon is up to one year, which includes developing an annual budget

---
[41] Ibid, page 24.

and conducting annual performance reviews. This is also the entry level for engineers and other staff specialists. Individuals at this level need to be able to identify and process critical facts that affect their business area; this capability is a precursor to trend analysis. Examples of level II roles are a nurse on a ward, a detective on a police force, a first-line manager, most sales representatives, a realtor, an insurance agent, a process or quality engineer, and a maintenance manager. Individuals at this level reason by accumulating data, which, in turn, allows them to identify trends and recognize behavioral or operating patterns that they can then use to make fact-based decisions. The essence of the first-line manager's role is that he is actually managing an output team consisting of a number of level I operators and is assisted by supervisory personnel, if required, while the manager operates at a level II.[42]

Level III:

Level III is the unit manager managing a number of FLM output teams. In the military, this is the battalion. In retail operations, it is the district manager who runs between ten and fifteen stores. The unit manager translates the planning process into pathways that she assigns to subordinate managers. Unit managers must be able to develop a set of options regarding their own pathway; these options represent alternative pathways to follow in the event that overwhelming obstacles block the preferred pathway. This is the world of what-if questions: what could possibly happen, what is the probability associated with a given scenario, and what is the downside risk. The absence of what-if thinking is crisis management. Continuous improvement project work emerges at this level, and the planning horizon takes on a longer focus—one to two years. Training and coaching become important people skills, and external relations become more important, especially with key customers. Level III managers must also be capable of working collaboratively with specialist advisors, such as process engineers, HR specialists, and so on.[43]

The first three levels in any organization are characterized by a sense

---

42 Ibid, page 25.
43 Jaques, Elliott. Requisite Organization. Arlington, VA: Cason Hall Publishers, 1996, page pair 26.

of personal involvement. Designed correctly, the numbers involved are small enough to reinforce a sense of personal knowledge about people. Even at level III, the manager should at least recognize all of the people as belonging to her operational unit. For many executives, it is this sense of personal knowledge that makes this level the last "fun" job in a managerial leadership sense. Here, when an order is given, people are seen to actually carry out the order. Ask any senior manager what her best job was, and chances are good that she will refer to her level III managerial leadership role as the best one.

The importance of the first three levels to long-term corporate or agency success should never be underestimated. If an organization can get the people operating at these three levels focused on the right issues and tasks, they will likely be successful in the long-term. For example, in a sales unit, if the level II sales rep is capable of accumulating sales information in order to identify changing sales trends, then he will likely be able to anticipate such trends and take corrective action to head off potentially negative effects. Similarly, if the sales unit manager is capable of assessing possible downside risks that could adversely affect sales operations and has thought through the challenges of shifting to an alternative course of action in the event of such an occurrence, the sales unit will likely avoid the appearance of a crisis response to constantly changing external events.

Operational Work

The work shifts dramatically above the first three levels. At levels IV and V, the sense of personal face-to-face interaction is replaced by a focus on operational tasks. A sense of anonymity begins to set in at these two levels. Tasks become less concrete and more abstract. The focus shifts to functions and the business unit as a whole. At level IV, the work focuses on achieving a fully integrated key BU or departmental function: sales, marketing, product development, production, HR, and so on. Level IV also encompasses continuous improvement (CI) project work and a concomitant awareness of the enterprise as a whole. Level V constitutes the stand-alone business unit or independent operating unit in many government agencies. While level IV represents the pinnacle of differentiation (each function being organized separately as a discrete entity), level V focuses exclusively on integration and synthesis. The BU president is accountable for running current operations as a single, fully integrated system. Figure 5.5 depicts the nature of work at levels IV and V.

Level IV:

Level IV is the head of a key operational function such as sales, marketing, production, finance, or HR. In government, it is the head of a key supporting function such as contracting or training. The focus here is on integrating multiple functionally oriented initiatives into a single integrated function. For example, a community hospital CEO integrates cost, quality, and access into a well-run medical facility. Complex program and project manager roles fall into this level, with the project or program requiring the careful integration of several independent activities into a single output: a sales or marketing vice president, a site general manager, a plant manager, senior business unit staff roles such as finance, HR, technical, and so on. Level IV is the beginning of enterprise thinking. Executives at this level should be the owners of key enterprise processes. Information overload also begins to occur at this level; hence, executives only want to know when data exceeds agreed-upon limits. They don't have time to process all relevant information. Pert charting and decision trees apply to this level. Individuals at the operational level interact externally with senior customer officials and buyers and key community leaders. Large continuous improvement projects are managed at this level, and multiyear plans are developed. An executive must be capable of parallel processing, handling multiple issues simultaneously while doing the trade-offs in his head. Manager-once-removed leadership requirements also emerge at this level. The planning horizon (time span) for individuals operating at level IV extends out three to five years.

Principle #1: Organize around Levels of Work

Business Unit "Value – Adding" Work is <u>Operational</u> in Nature

Critical Tasks

Level V – Business Unit President

- Strategy Implementation
- Identify Customer Needs
- Business Plan & Program Development
- Implement Continuous Improvement
- Integration and synthesis
- Manage Operational Unit(s)
- Manage Resources
- Integrate Cross-functions
- Create Supportive Climate
- Formulate Operational Unit Projects

Level IV – Functional Manager

- Program Execution
- Meet Customer Needs
- Implement Continuous Improvement
- Manage Resources
- Manage people, processes, activities, and resources to achieve goals & objectives
- Integrate discreet activities into a single function
- Differentiation
- Measure Customer Satisfaction

5.5

Level V:

Level V is the world of the stand-alone BU or agency department. The key focus here is integration: all separate (differentiated) functions are pulled together into a fully integrated operational unit. The BU is a total system where the whole is greater than the sum of the parts and focuses more on effectiveness than efficiency. The key metric at the BU is profit and loss (P&L) or customer service efficiencies in government agencies. At this level, innovation concerns cause the BU to shed legacy programs and products to make room for new services. The BU president is accountable for creating a supportive BU climate that reinforces desired workforce behaviors, for formulation of major BU continuous improvement projects; for managing cross functional working relationships; and for developing a five- to seven-year business plan that focuses on optimizing BU resources. External relationships become vitally important at this level as executives interact with major customers and local community leaders. Autonomous decision making occurs within policy parameters and agreed-upon limits. The BU provides key operational input to corporate staff as part of the policy development process. This input focuses on the likely impact of policy decisions on operating efficiency and effectiveness. Staff roles found in large corporations or government agencies generally function at level V. These roles tend to focus on a fully integrated support service activity (e.g., a large shared service function) or as the director of a complex staff activity, such as an integrated financial planning and analysis (FP&A) function. The planning horizon (time span) for individuals operating at level V extends out five to seven years.

A unique characteristic of work that occurs between levels I and V is that the flow of the work is generally downward. Direct output is produced at lower organizational layers and sent directly out to customers or consumers. This type of work is in stark contrast to that at the higher headquarters levels that operate above the BU. Here the work flow is upward—focused on helping the higher level manager do his or her work.

Strategic Level Work

Levels VI through VIII involve strategic issues or may represent enterprise support service activities. Work flows tend to go up the hierarchical chain supporting the organization as a whole. The higher levels in the corporate world support product or geographic groups or the corporation as a whole (e.g., corporate headquarters). In government and military agencies, the higher levels support service subagencies or the agency as a total institution. The higher levels may be stationed at separate locations with no work occurring below level IV at the location, except administrative support work. Lower level, operational work may be carried out at other geographic locations.

Work at the strategic level is much more nebulous and riddled with uncertainty (the subject of uncertainty will be discussed in detail later). At these levels, role incumbents deal with nonoperational issues such as strategy development, policy formulation and development, program analysis, resourcing, governance, envisioning the future, and so on. Work at the strategic level is described by most as less tangible and not as much fun as lower-level operational work. Figure 5.6 depicts the nature of work found at Levels VI-VIII. In those organizations containing only 7 layers, the CEO (or agency head) has to perform both the Level VII and VIII sets of tasks.

Corporate "Value – Adding" Work is <u>Strategic</u> in Nature

Critical Tasks

Level VIII – Corporate CEO (Fortune 100)

- Envision the Future
- Lead the Enterprise
- Secure & Allocate Resources
- Measure Enterprise Performance
- Create Enterprise Culture
- Manage Strategic Uncertainty
  – Create Strategic Options
- Manage the Talent Pool

Level VII – Corporate CEO (Fortune 500)/COO

- Envision the Future within their area of Responsibility (AOR)
- External Affairs
- Policy Application
- Governance
- Resourcing
- Set Structure, System & Processes
- Define Mission & Vision
- Establish Values
- Create Climate
- Formulate & Lead Enterprise Projects
- Initiate Change/Continuous Improvement

Level VI – Corporate EVP

- Policy Formulation
- Strategy Development
- Program Analysis & Integration
- Best Business Practices – Networking
- Secure Resources
- Maintain Global Awareness (Political, Environmental, Social, Technical Information)
- Manage Portfolios
- Allocate Resources
- Design Structure, Systems & Processes
- Prioritize Customer Needs
- Communicate Strategy to Lower Levels

5.6

Level VI:

The focus at level VI is strategy development, which, in turn, sets the context for the ongoing development of operational programs. Once a strategy has been articulated, this level then evaluates the efficiency of existing programs and determines their relevance to existing strategies. Policies are formulated at level VI that reflect input from lower organizational levels to ensure such policies are viable. Portfolio management becomes paramount as multiple business units are managed. Structure, systems, and processes are evaluated in terms of their continued relevance to enterprise goals. Worldwide networking becomes important as executives search for best business practices. Executives at this level function as the link between corporate headquarters and the lower-level operating units and political, social, technical, and information issues come into play. Typical roles include executive vice president (EVP) portfolio managers; senior corporate staff, such as chief financial officer (CFO), chief technology officer (CTO), HR, and so forth. Occasionally, level VI includes large stand-alone business units that simply contain too much complexity to be run as level V entities. The planning horizon (time span) for individuals operating at level VI extends out seven to ten years.

Level VII:

Level VII is the world of the CEO in most large organizations or a major agency head in a large government department. Executives at this level are concerned with external relations (shareholder communities or a political base). Balance sheet issues become primary as resources are allocated across major subordinate operating units. Policy application becomes important to ensure that the corporate vision gets institutionalized. Talent pool development issues become exceedingly important to ensure a proper flow of talent up the organization. Governance issues surface regarding CEO attention to ensure corporate behavior moves in the right direction: dealing with strategic uncertainty by developing viable strategic options that ensure the long-term survival of the company in the face of unprecedented world economic events, setting direction for the enterprise as a whole, and establishing a corporate culture to support desired corporate behaviors. The time horizon for CEOs is ten to fifteen-plus years. For example, CEOs need to be concerned about growing the next generation of managers so that they are capable of running the enterprise in the future.

Level VIII:

The roles at level VIII include the heads of the largest corporate entities (such as Walmart and Exxon) and the heads of major government departments such as the Department of Defense, Department of Veterans Affairs, and so on. The unique challenges at this level revolve around envisioning the future, securing sufficient resources to achieve a desired vision, and operating as a good steward of assigned resources. The time horizon at the very highest level is fifteen to twenty-plus years. Executives at this level must be concerned about the potential impact of Generation Z, which will ultimately replace Generation Y, and the corresponding effect that they may have on the existing corporate culture[44] At this level, one is not trying to predict the future but rather develop a set of strategic alternatives that allow the enterprise to survive no matter what happens in the future. For example, the Department of Defense must build appropriate wartime scenarios to permit rapid adaptation to deal with unprogrammed contingency missions; similarly, defense contractors must develop viable scenarios to permit enterprise survival in the event of massive funding cuts, such as the cancellation of a major weapon system . Other government agencies face similar budgeting challenges. The key to managing strategic uncertainty is to be capable of shifting to alternative courses of action; such a capability requires maintaining a careful balance between core and contingent capabilities (a contingent capability could be achieved by developing a strategic alliance with a key partner).[45]

The real challenge facing executives in large organizations is that they have to perform tasks relevant to both levels VII and VIII. This tends

---

44 Generation Z (also known as iGeneration , the Net Generation, or the Internet Generation) is a common name for the group of people born from a currently undefined point, defined variously as between 1989 and 2010, through to recent years, as distinct from the preceding "Generation Y/Millennials. http://en.wikipedia.org/wiki/Generation_z

45 Raynor, Michael, E. The Strategy Paradox. New York: Doubleday, 2007.

to consume most of their time and takes them away from day-to-day operations. Thus, it is easy for them to be perceived as aloof by people operating at lower organizational layers. The larger the company, the greater the organizational demands on senior executives, forcing them to spend less and less time on internal company issues.

This vertical architecture reflects the nature of work at varying organizational layers. Figure 5.7 shows eight levels of work, reflective of those in the largest corporate and government organizations.

As is evident from an examination of figure 5.7 (and reflective of the level-by-level work descriptions presented earlier), the nature of work at each level is qualitatively more complex than the layer below it. We define complexity as the number of variables, the clarity or uncertainty of those variables, the rate of change, and the interdependence of the variables.

Simply stated, work gets more complex the higher one goes in an organizational hierarchy. The center columns of Figure 5.7 are suggestive of the work (tasks) at each distinct level of the organization. The tasks are suggestive and based on the work we observed in extensive field projects conducted in numerous corporate and government agencies. Moving from the bottom to the top of the task column, the work and decisions become more complex, and their impact on the organization's time line lengthens. Also, on the right, note that the tasks become more strategic and policy focused as we move to higher levels in the structure.

Level VII Complexity
Managing Strategic Uncertainty

Level	Tasks		Time Horizon
VIII	• Envision the Future • Manage the Enterprise • Secure Resources	• Manage Strategic Uncertainty • Set the Direction of the Whole Enterprise	• 15 - 20 + Years
VII	• Envision the Future within AOR • Policy Application Resourcing	• External Affairs • Governance	• 10 - 15 + Years
VI	• Communicate Strategy to Lower Levels • Program Analysis & Integration • Best Business Practices (Networking)	• Strategy Development • Policy Formulation	• 7 – 10 Years
V	• Bus Plan & Program Development • Identify Customer Needs • Implement Continuous Improvement	• Strategy Implementation	• 5 – 7 Years
IV	• Implement Continuous Improvement • Meet Customer Needs	• Program Execution • Manage Resources	• 3 – 5 Years
III	• Implement Continuous Improvement • Produce Direct Outputs	• Manage to Budget • Interact with Customers	• 1 – 2 Years
II	• Implement Continuous Improvement • Production Planning	• Supervise • Product Direct Outputs	• 3 Months – 1 Year
I	• Implement Continuous Improvement • Hands-on Work	• Produce Direct Outputs	• Less Than 3 Months

Strategic Balance — Uncertainty — Commitment

Low I/III   High VII/III

5.7

Principle #1: Organize around Levels of Work

Uncertainty

Notice the base balance model in figure 5.7—uncertainty. In an exhaustive study of successful and unsuccessful companies, Michael Raynor concluded that successful companies survived not because they were managed in a fundamentally different way from those that failed but rather because they were better able to deal with "strategic uncertainty."[46] To Raynor, choosing and implementing a long-range strategy involved as much "luck" as it did careful strategic planning. He cites, as an example, Sony's near collapse because of the failure of their strategy in pursuing Betamax technology. According to Raynor, Sony did everything right in developing and implementing their strategy. Unfortunately, conditions emerged that simply made that strategy wrong.[47]

To Raynor, the underlying issue was how to deal with strategic uncertainty. Companies need to recognize that even though they have carefully developed what appears to be a well-thought-out strategy and long-range plan, it is nearly impossible to predict what may happen in the future that could cause that plan to quickly unravel. Raynor argues that companies need to develop and invest in strategic options to mitigate against the possible adverse effects of an uncertain future. (In some ways, the development of strategic options at levels VII and VIII is similar to the development of alternative courses of action at level III.)[48]

Raynor suggests that the real challenge facing senior executives is to properly structure the organization to deal with strategic uncertainty.[49] At lower organizational levels, the company is committed quite strongly to implementing a given program or plan. Front-line managers don't have the luxury of shifting from one program to another. At midlevels, uncertainty begins to become a more serious concern of operational managers; however, most BUs are still committed to executing a given base strategy and the underlying functions contained therein. At the top levels in most organizations, dealing with uncertainty becomes a primary concern of the senior executive team. This is where the development of

---

46 Raynor, Michael, E. The Strategy Paradox. New York: Doubleday, 2007, page 3.
47 Ibid page 44.
48 Ibid page 8.
49 Ibid, page 8.

strategic options becomes critically important.

Time Span and Time Compression

A key tenet of Requisite Organization Theory is use of the time-span measurement of the complexity of work.[50] According to Dr. Jaques, the time-span measure reflects the furthest forward in time that an individual is focused in terms of his or her current role. The higher an individual sits in an organizational hierarchy, the further forward in time she should be focused. Individuals at lower levels should be worried about this week's or this month's output, while executives at higher levels should be focused on what the company needs to do over the next five to ten years. To be valid, time-span measures must be obtained from an employee's manager. It is the manager who assigns tasks to subordinates; thus, it is the manager who is in the best position to set the time span over which a task must be accomplished.[51]

Level I work has a time span of less than three months and sometimes as short as one day. A front-line worker comes to work and plans his or her work for that day and, in most cases, does so in the context of the next full week's worth of work. The longest task that a front-line manager might assign to a subordinate operating at level I is ten to twelve weeks, assuming that the worker is an experienced operator. At the other extreme, the Secretary of the Army or a large corporate CEO must make decisions and set the strategic direction of the organization that will impact the enterprise over the next twenty-plus years (e.g., weapons systems design or pursuit of global market strategies).

As important as time span is to Requisite Organization Theory, we have found in our ongoing field research that a phenomenon of time compression is occurring in more and more corporate environments. As described previously, time compression was originally observed in the military in wartime operations. In wartime situations, characterized by rapid change, high degrees of uncertainty, and the need for continuous adaptation, military staff at all levels became focused on much shorter

---

50 Jaques, Elliott. Requisite Organization. Arlington, VA: Cason Hall Publishers, 1996, page pair 38.
51 Jaques, Elliott. Time Span Handbook. London: Heineman Educational Books, 1971.

time horizons. For example, a four-star general, who during peacetime would be concerned with issues extending ten to fifteen years into the future, found his focus in wartime on a much shorter five- to seven-year perspective. Wartime campaigns become the equivalent of five- to seven-year corporate business strategies. Battle plans equate to three- to five-year business unit operating plans, and tactical operational plans represent operating year responses to fast-changing competitive situations.

Over the past decade, our work with senior army combat leaders has allowed us to measure their length of wartime time horizons and contrast this data with time-span data gathered from senior leaders in the noncombat areas of the army. This comparison also allowed us to study individual time-span data from generals who happened to operate in both environments. Figure 5.8 summarizes our findings to date.

We also found, however, that wartime military leaders are not the only executives facing time pressures in today's rapidly changing environment. Most corporate executives also face similar pressures from their key stakeholders and marketplace competitors. Perhaps, you may recall the cola wars of the eighties and early nineties between Pepsi-Cola and Coca-Cola. Both companies were continuously battling each other for market share while simultaneously adjusting to steadily increasing social pressures attacking their traditional core business lines, such as the impact of carbonated beverages on children's health.

Time Compression
Wartime vs. Non-Wartime

	Wartime	Peacetime
General **Level VII** ★★★★	5-7 year time horizon • Training local militia • Nation building	**10-15 year time horizon** • Talent pool issues – development of next generation of leaders • Reconstitution and reset of the Institution
Lieutenant General **Level VI** ★★★	3-5 year time horizon • Strategic Training – transforming the Reserves into operational force • Build and nurture a relationship with local government officials	**7-10 year time horizon** • Policy Formulation – update policies to reflect changing social norms, e.g., women in combat roles • Strategy development
Major General **Level V** ★★	1-2 year time horizon • Involve local population in Nation building projects • Identify local reconstruction requirements	**5-7 year time horizon** • Budget development (POM) • Procurement of new weapon systems

5.8

Principle #1: Organize around Levels of Work

More recently, you can see in business literature and media the widespread use of words that one might expect from a general, not an EVP/VP. Words such as *battle plan, beating the competition, rapid adaptation, war room, strategic engagements, competitive attacks,* and *instant results* are spoken in today's executive suites throughout the country. The use of these words in and of themselves really has no bearing, but rather might be an indicator that business leaders and corporate CEOs are under intense time pressures to get results. In thousands of interviews, within all manner of organizations, we have seen a dramatic shift in the last few years in executives' stated time horizons. Whereas we would expect a level IV VP to have at least one task or project with a three- to five-year horizon and expected outcomes consistent with that time horizon, we are seeing in many companies that the longest task is usually twelve to eighteen months. While we have not studied this time compression issue in a formal research setting, we have consistently observed it and can only offer anecdotal reasons as to why time compression may be occurring.

One of our observations is that organizations are experiencing unprecedented levels of uncertainty not previously seen in our organizational history. In addition, uncertainty is seemingly coming from many different directions: market uncertainty (consumer shifts), government uncertainty (regulations and taxes), and global pressures (global economic declines and changes). This uncertainty, in turn, has a cascading effect on small businesses as large corporations alter the products, services, and pricing standards that are used by small business to create their products and services. Compounding this uncertainty is the dizzying pace of change driven by technology. What today may be a novel new product or service seems to be status quo, or old school, within months. Technology is driving large changes in consumer behavior as well. Consumer expectations now hover near instant gratification simply because many consumers have received instant gratification from the products and services of other companies: "If Amazon can get me X by tomorrow, why can't your company?" Our point in the above is simple: managers (and Organizational Development practitioners) should use caution in simply relying on time span as a singular measure of the level of work.

In our project work, we did not rely solely on time span in determining the complexity of work at various levels in an organization. We also used in-depth interviews and task analysis to validate a position's level in the structure. We combined our own experience, interviews, task analysis, and time-span measurement in constructing an agency's organization chart. This organization chart, with organizational layers superimposed in the background, provided us with a rational blueprint for subsequently analyzing and evaluating an organization's structure in greater depth.

Headquarters Work Differs from Operational Work: Headquarters Work Flows Up While Operational Work Flows Down

As described previously, we have differentiated work at the tactical, operational, and strategic levels of work. Work at these levels (I–V) tends to be produced and sent out at lower organizational layers. This type of work is called *delegated direct output (DDO):* tasks are delegated by senior managers to individuals occupying roles at lower organizational layers. Direct outputs are produced at these lower levels and then distributed directly to external customers. The outputs are generally not checked by senior management; however, the quality of that output is periodically reviewed by higher-level managers. [52]

When one moves to higher organizational layers ((levels VI–VIII), the work changes dramatically. Not only do the tasks change in context, the direction of the work flow also changes. At higher organizational layers, the nature of work is such that subordinates are often required to assist their boss in doing her work. This type of work is called *assisted direct output (ADO).*[53]

Figure 5.9 describes the nature of work at successively higher organizational layers. Note that one of the critical tasks found at level VII is to develop and promulgate enterprise policies. These policies are central to the development of an effective enterprise governance system. They are necessary because they set corporate-wide limits that control the behavior of employees in a given area. Without corporate policies, individuals would be free to behave in a variety of different ways. This variability would make it virtually impossible to get the whole organization moving in a common direction.

---

[52] Jaques, Elliott and Clement, Stephen D. Executive Leadership. Arlington, VA: Cason Hall Publishers, 1991, page 158.

[53] Ibid, page 158.

Principle #1: Organize around Levels of Work

The XYZ Organization
(The Impact Of Operating Across Multiple Organizational Layers)

The Principles That Apply

- People generally have trouble grasping the nature of work two (or more) layers above their current position; it seems abstract and unreal; they don't see how it is relevant; **the VP cannot understand nor explain it**

- People can understand the meaning and the work at the next higher organizational layer, but they cannot operate at that level; **the VP can understand it but neither do it or explain it**

- **People work at any given time utilizing the most complex cognitive mechanism they can use;** but they cannot explain nor articulate how they do the work; **the VP can do it but not explain it**

- People can explain and articulate how to work with the cognitive mechanisms at the next lower organizational level; **the VP can both do it and explain it**

The Tasks That Apply

Pres
1. Envision the future
2. External affairs
3. Policy application
4. Secure resources
5. Manage strategic uncertainty
6. Talent pool management system

EVP
1. Policy formulation
2. Strategy development
3. Program analysis and evaluation
4. Best business practices
5. Set structure, systems and processes
6. Create culture
7. Initiate change

BU President (GM)
1. Strategy implementation
2. Business plan and program development
3. Customer development
4. Continuous improvement projects
5. Integrate cross functions
6. Create supportive operational unit climate

VP
1. Program execution
2. Meet customer needs
3. Manage resources
4. Implement continuous improvement projects
5. Integrate functions
6. Measure customer satisfaction

5.9

The development of effective policies is not a solitary task to be performed by the chief executive in isolation. For any policy to be effective, it must reflect the realities of its potential impact on employee behavior at lower organizational layers. For example, if a policy seriously erodes the discretion and decision-making authority of a front-line worker in interacting with customers, such a policy needs to be carefully scrutinized to ensure its positive benefits offset its potentially negative effects. Thus, the development of policy needs to be thoroughly vetted with operational personnel before being finalized. The vetting process must involve getting operational input as a routine part of any policy development process. This input process constitutes ADO work.

Work that flows down and the associated products and services produced at lower organizational levels in a corporate organization or government agency is intuitive, but work flowing up is less obvious. A way of looking at work at levels VI and VII is that people at these levels are doing the work of their boss or doing work for their boss. The head of an agency is accountable for securing resources for the agency. This may mean appearing before congressional committees, investor relations briefings, and briefings on programs and then accounting for funds awarded to the agency. The head of the agency is accountable for securing resources but assigns all of the tasks associated with his resource accountability to managers and subordinates at levels VI and VII. They are doing the boss's work or doing work for the boss, and their work product flows up to the CEO or agency head. Headquarters work is in contrast to operational work at levels V and below. Work at level V and below directly supports design, production, and delivery of an organization's products and services.

Senior executives operating at levels VI–VIII often need assistants to help them do their work. Collectively, these assistants make up the headquarters' staff in most large organizations. Because staff roles by design help a boss do her work, the capacity of the individuals assigned to the staff should also be considered in constructing an effective staff organization. First, staff assistants must be able to understand the nature of the work that the principal (boss) is attempting to carry out. This means staff assistants must have sufficient cognitive capacity to assist the staff principal in doing her work. Generally, this capacity requires high-level individuals with both the experience and the background sufficient to support the staff principal. Figure 5.9 depicts the underlying ability of an individual operating at one level versus her capacity to work at successively higher organization levels.

If one were to apply these principles in a typical corporate headquarters and especially in most large government agencies, one would find an inordinately large number of personnel assigned to headquarters-level organizations. This happens because most HQ organizations are inappropriately involved in operational work. In other words, they tend to have too many people doing work that is downward focused. And additionally, many throw large numbers of resources (i.e., people) to compensate for insufficient capability at HQ and higher-level roles.

For the purpose of comparison, let us contrast the size of the HR headquarters staff in a large international mining company with nearly fifty thousand employees with a similar-sized appliance company. In the mining company, there are two level V executives (equivalent to a BU president) and four level IV vice presidents assisting the level VI EVP-HR with his work. These level IV and V executives are involved in developing compensation policies, labor relations interaction with high-level union leadership, design of training and development programs, succession planning, and organizational development initiatives. Each VP has one full-time assistant, and the total staff consists of twelve people

Alternatively, the appliance company has nearly two hundred people assigned to the HR function. This includes five senior executives involved in organizational development, compensation, talent pool management, industrial and labor relations, and so on. The big difference between the two companies is that the appliance company has a large personnel management organization engaged in the day-to-day provisioning of personnel services such as hiring, benefits, management, firing, recruiting, and so on. The mining company also had substantial service personnel providing a variety of HR services. This staff, however, was not assigned to the headquarters. Rather, it was consolidated into a service-providing organization located within each stand-alone BU.

The important point to remember is that the mining company distinguishes between strategic HR work and HR service work. Failure to differentiate between these two different types of HR work results in large HQ organizations. The adverse consequences of having a large headquarters staff involved in both strategic and tactical HR work is that the senior manager will naturally tend to focus on and be pulled down to work on the latest HR personnel crisis. We call this tendency to be pulled down the *gravity effect*. The important teaching point is that the present always drives out the future.

In our work at the Department of the Army, the aforementioned finding was further reinforced. Most department level staff organizations (level VI entities) contained an operations unit called a direct reporting unit. These operational units actually managed the day-to-day activities of a number of operationally oriented support functions. In other words, the staff organizations were engaged in both high-level staff work as well as operational support work. Because of the presence of this operational work (lower-level work), the size of the organization resulted in much larger headquarters staff organizations (on an order of magnitude of ten times larger). Most government agencies suffer from being overstaffed at the headquarters level because they fail to clarify the nature of work that should be done within headquarters. As an example, several years ago we witnessed the Defense Department Health Affairs (HA) organization grow unconstrained while each service department Surgeon General (Army, Navy, Marines and Air Force health organizations) was concurrently reduced in size. In analyzing the nature of work that the Health Affairs personnel were involved in, it became readily apparent as to why such growth occurred. HA staff members were involved in monitoring the day-to-day provisioning of health care services at military treatment facilities (military hospitals) worldwide. Not only did the HA staff develop health care policies, they actively managed the execution of such policies. This latter work clearly was the responsibility of the respective departmental health care delivery facilities.

In fact, over the past decade, staffing levels at the defense and service levels rose dramatically as more and more operational work was managed at the *secretariat level*. Much of this work allowed the staff element to inappropriately stay involved in the provisioning of necessary support services. This work also duplicated similar work being done in the field. Further, this type of work and the monitoring associated with it frequently resulted in HQ staff asking for more and more operational data (data calls) that placed an additional burden on field personnel. This proliferation of HQ work is a natural outgrowth of a failure to clearly define the work to be done by HQ personnel from the work being done elsewhere. The work then gets exacerbated in large government bureaucracies and leads to unmitigated growth of agency HQ organizations.

In the absence of true market forces, government agency HQ organizations have grown substantially larger than their civilian corporate counterparts. From time to time, Congress and the Office of Management and Budget (OMB) impose manpower limits to HQ staff organizations. However, most government departments have become very innovative in getting around these ceilings. Large commercial corporations need to periodically explain to their shareholders why their HQ organization has grown so large. Government agencies do not face such pressures.

The fact is that the past decade of research has convinced us that nearly all government agencies need to seriously reduce their overhead costs. The most requisite way to reduce these costs is to dramatically reduce the size of their HQ by refocusing HQ work on the appropriate tasks relative to their respective organizational level. Our experience, however, is that such agencies, when faced with funding cuts, tend to offer up highly needed services for cuts rather than attack their existing bloated overhead structures. That is why we strongly recommend that steep dollar cuts be imposed externally on those HQ organizations in order to force them to reduce their HQ size. The adage that applies here is, "The hog won't butcher itself!"

Chapter 6

Principle #2: Clearly Define Accountabilities and Authorities for All Roles

Clarity is a recurring theme in establishing an effective organization: clarity of structure and reporting lines, clarity of levels, clarity of roles, clarity of accountabilities, and clarity of authorities. But clarity of accountability and authority is paramount if the goals of an organization and the aspirations of the people in the organization are to be met. No matter how well-designed an organization's structure, people in an organization will be unhappy or unmotivated if they don't know what is expected of them and for what they will be rewarded. This principle sounds simple, but in reality, blurred accountabilities and authority are a frequent cause of individual discontent and fractured working relationships.

Background

All social relationships take place in some sort of social structure. There is no such thing as interaction between people without social structure. If relationships were totally unstructured, people would not know what to do, how to act, or how to respond in a given situation. In short, they would be confused, and their behavior would be erratic and unpredictable. It is the social structure that exists in a given relationship

Principle #2: Clearly Define Accountabilities and Authorities for All Roles

that sets the limits and basic concepts of how people behave toward one another.[54] Even casual contacts, such as standing with a stranger in a cafeteria line, takes place within strict limits that are structured by law or culture and that we have to learn and know to live comfortably with one another. This fact of the existence of a structure that provides the context for all social interactions by means of setting limits regarding them is especially important for leadership. Roles set the limits and expectations on the behavior that is required if we are going to be able to work effectively with people.

Structure reflects the pattern of relationships among the roles in any organization, no matter how big or small. All roles in any relationship are vested with two main properties: accountability and authority. Knowing what each person is accountable for in a relationship and with what authority each has been vested with respect to others is the absolute foundation for effective human relationships of any kind. Lack of clarity about what is required of each person by virtue of his or her role and about what each person is authorized to require each other person to do is a recipe for confusion and role conflict.[55] Without such clarity, human interaction is strained, and having a basic foundation is not enough. We need to build not just any kind of accountability into the roles but the proper kinds of accountability and authority.

Let's begin with a definition of accountability and authority.

> ACCOUNTABILITY: Accountability encompasses those aspects of a role that dictate the things that the occupant is required to do by virtue of being in that role.
>
> AUTHORITY: Authority encompasses those aspects of a role that enable the person in the role to act legitimately in carrying out the accountabilities with which he or she has been charged.

To discharge accountability, a person must have the appropriate authority to use resources or materials that make it reasonably possible

---

54 Jaques, Elliott. Requisite Organization. Arlington, VA: Cason Hall Publishers, page pair 77.
55 Ibid, page pair 77.

to do what needs to be done.

Accountabilities normally describe the work that is to be performed by a role incumbent. Previously, it was shown that the work of a given role flows naturally from an organization's mission—a short formal written statement of purpose of why the institution exists in the first place. This statement of purpose (mission) encompasses a number of key functions, and these functions, in turn, are made up of discrete tasks. Thus, a role incumbent is held accountable by her manager to perform these functions and tasks. Because clarity is essential to promoting good will and commitment on the part of most subordinates, the aforementioned functions and tasks should be specified in clear terms as to quantity and quality standards. In fact, the definition of a task accomplishes just that:

> TASK: A task is an assignment to produce a given output or to achieve a given goal (a what-by-when) with allocated resources and methods within prescribed limits. (See Figure 6.1 for more information.)

There are two different types of tasks. The first type comprises those tasks that are directly assigned by one's manager. The second type of task comprises those that are triggered as a result of a general responsibility that has been assigned by one's manager. A *general responsibility* is an instruction that applies indefinitely (unless amended) and specifies conditions, which, whenever they arise, require a person to take appropriate action within prescribed limits, such as answering a request for information or responding to a customer request.[56] Distinguishing between the two different types of tasks is important because the task-assigning process is different for each. Both types require the manager to set context, but while the manager must set a specific context for each and every single task that he assigns, he need not do so for each of the tasks generated by a general responsibility, only for the general responsibility itself. Clearly bounded general responsibilities release initiative and creativity because the boundaries are clear. Unclear boundaries and a lack of adequate limits always stifle initiative because people do not know how far they are free to push new ideas.

---

56 Jaques, Elliott and Clement, Stephen D. Executive Leadership. Arlington, VA: Cason Hall Publishers, 1989, page 106.

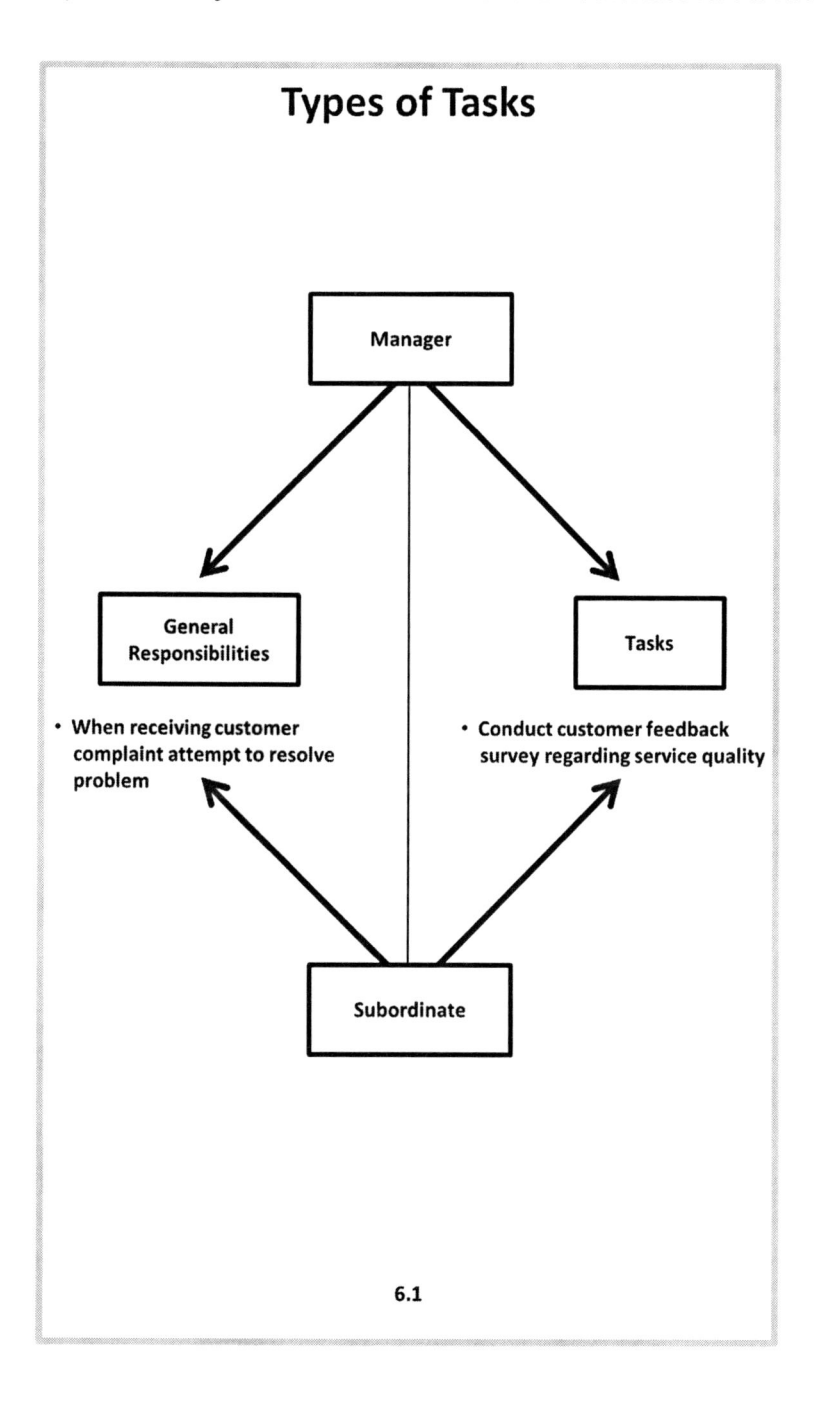

Principle #2: Clearly Define Accountabilities and Authorities for All Roles

Types of Tasks

```
                    ┌─────────┐
                    │ Manager │
                    └────┬────┘
              ┌─────────┴─────────┐
              ▼                   ▼
     ┌──────────────┐        ┌────────┐
     │   General    │        │ Tasks  │
     │Responsibilities│      └────────┘
     └──────────────┘
```

- When receiving customer complaint attempt to resolve problem

- Conduct customer feedback survey regarding service quality

```
                  ┌────────────┐
                  │ Subordinate│
                  └────────────┘
```

6.1

Tasks and general responsibilities are central to the development of viable role descriptions. If the tasks are not clear, then a role description will not be particularly useful. The sad fact is that most accountabilities are not clearly defined in terms of a "what-by-when."[57] Thus, most role descriptions are de facto job postings and descriptions that are used sparingly at best. A useful role description contains not only clearly defined accountabilities but also specifies the primary outputs to be produced by a role incumbent, defines key working relationships required to produce those outputs, and contains appropriate metrics to effectively measure the role incumbent's performance. When role descriptions are properly defined, they become an important element of an organization's existing governance system. In addition, clearly written role descriptions also inform an organization's performance appraisal system, such as the outputs required of role incumbents specified in clear metrics.

Thus far we have used the term *general responsibility* in a rather specific fashion, as it is tied to a specific role. Unfortunately, there is widespread use of the broader term responsibility that is often used interchangeably with the concept of accountability. The lack of clarity in definition and the corresponding confusion over terms leads to further problems. Consequently, we will provide the following description to differentiate between the terms accountability, general responsibility, and responsibility. For ease of differentiation, we will repeat our definitions of accountability and general responsibility provided previously. [58]

> ACCOUNTABILITY: Accountability encompasses those aspects of a role that dictate the things that the role incumbent is required to do by virtue of being in that role.

> GENERAL RESPONSIBILITY: a general responsibility is an instruction that applies indefinitely (unless amended) and specifies conditions, which, when they arise, require a person to take appropriate action within prescribed limits.

---

[57] By "what" we are referring to an assignment to produce a specified output and "when" the targeted completion time for that task

[58] Jaques, Elliott and Clement, Stephen D. Executive Leadership. Arlington, VA: Cason Hall Publishers, 1989, page 106.

Principle #2: Clearly Define Accountabilities and Authorities for All Roles

Responsibility, on the other hand, is more personal in nature. To be responsible is to accept personal accountability to act without guidance or someone telling us to act. In being responsible, the matter of how we conduct ourselves lies within each one of us and our own social conscience, our personal sense of what we ought to do under given circumstances where we feel that something or other should be done[59]. What we do influences what others think about us and how they regard us. But no one carries the authority, other than ourselves, to call us to account. Thus, responsibility has a fundamentally different feel from accountability.

Responsibility means taking personal ownership of an activity or a given situation: "I'll be responsible for cleaning the break room when it is in need of cleaning." Because of the personal nature of responsibility, there is no corresponding authority component to influence others to take any action. For example, a physician, while traveling on an airplane, witnesses a fellow passenger having difficulty breathing. The physician volunteers his or her assistance to airplane personnel in treating the passenger. The physician is acting as a responsible citizen in this situation. Airline personnel have no authority to order the physician to provide medical assistance. The decision to do so is a matter of choice by the physician: he was acting responsibly.

Accountabilities (and authority) associated with a given role are specified by superiors at higher levels in an organization. For example, the manager of the passport office or the day care center is accountable for carrying out a defined set of tasks, or outputs—what-by-whens. Accountability implies an outcome or output that is measurable in terms of quality, time, cost, or some other measurable result. To understand the difference between responsibility and accountability, ponder this statement: if you are a manager and aren't clear about your accountabilities, you need to take responsibility for finding out.

Distinguishing between responsibilities and accountabilities is especially important in government and military organizations because such organizations report to a legislative, executive, or judicial branch of

---

[59] Jaques, Elliott and Clement, Stephen D. Executive Leadership, Cason Hall Publishers: Arlington, VA. Page 106

government. The nature of this reporting relationship is often subject to widely varying interpretations. For example, if Congress is accountable to voters for overseeing military operations, what does this mean? Can Congress give orders to military units? Specifying the precise nature of this relationship in terms of accountability and authority is no simple task. Without clearly defined terms, individuals will be free to make up whatever rules suit them. This is a dangerous condition that ultimately leads to excessive Monday morning quarterbacking.

Accountability

Industrial hierarchies could perhaps be more appropriately called *accountability hierarchies* because managers in these organizations are held accountable for the output of subordinates.[60] To fully understand the nature of managerial accountability, it is first necessary to specify the true nature of the manager-subordinate relationship. Recall that this relationship is central to the concept of hierarchical layering.

First, let us define the fundamental nature of the manager role. Every manager is accountable not only for the work of subordinates but also for adding value to their work. Adding value does not mean the manager simply adds up the output of subordinates; it means performing work of a different level of complexity that either simplifies the subordinates' tasks or sets a proper context for the subordinates so that they can carry out their work more efficiently and effectively. Thus, managers are first and foremost accountable for doing their own work. Sometimes that work encompasses developing a broad overarching plan that sets the context for a given subordinate's tasks. And sometimes a manager's own work involves translating higher-level plans into shorter and less complex plans, or tasks, for subordinates or helping them to develop situational awareness regarding those tasks.

Second, each manager is also accountable for building and sustaining a team of subordinates who are capable of doing the work assigned to them by the manager. Finally, the manager must also set the direction for subordinates and get them to follow along with her enthusiastically

---

60 Jaques, Elliott. Requisite Organization, Cason Hall Publishers: Arlington, VA. Page pair 77

Principle #2: Clearly Define Accountabilities and Authorities for All Roles

and to move in that direction; that is to say, she must exercise effective managerial leadership. Subordinates are accountable for working to their full capability in producing their respective outputs. It is the manager, however, who is accountable for the quantity and quality of that output. The following discussion summarizes the above descriptions.

To make the carrying out of managerial accountability possible, it is essential to ensure that each manager has at least the minimum authority requirements to discharge the requirements of her role. Such authority must encompass the following implied actions:

Minimum Managerial Accountabilities:

In the context of organizational design and the workplace, a manager is a person in a role (a managerial role) that inherently carries the following minimum accountabilities:

1. Their own work

2. The output of others (subordinates)

3. Building and sustaining a team

4. Leadership—leading subordinates individually and as a team so they are capable of producing the outputs required by the organization

Minimum Managerial Authorities:[61]

VETO the assignment of an unacceptable individual to his team. If the manager is to be accountable for the output of a team, then he must have some say as to who is on that team.

ASSIGN tasks to subordinates consistent with the organizational level within which the roles are operative.

---

61 Jaques, Elliott and Clement, Stephen D. Executive Leadership, Cason Hall Publishers: Arlington, VA, 1989. Page 106

RECOMMEND rewards and punishments consistent with an individual's performance.

INITIATE removal of an individual from his or her team, after due process, whom the manager judges to be unable to do the work of the role.

Managers are accountable for results. Subordinates are accountable for their full commitment in carrying out the tasks necessary to produce the results. Because managers are accountable for results, they are also logically accountable for leading the individuals (teams) to produce the results.

We discussed earlier the necessity for clearly defined accountabilities to ensure that individuals in specified roles are working on the correct tasks. Our experience to date, however, in analyzing the accountabilities of most respondents in a substantial number of organizational studies is that they tend to describe their work in terms of loosely defined functions or activities. Rarely do they specify their accountabilities in clear terms of what they are supposed to do—what-by-when. More often than not, they describe their work in rather vague terms. Similarly, when comparing what managers state they are holding their subordinates accountable to do with what the subordinates describe themselves, the differences are striking. In many cases, managers truly believe that subordinates are working on tasks that may be clear to the manager but, upon further scrutiny, are unclear to the subordinate. Subordinates, in turn, report that they are busy working on tasks substantially different. If managers and subordinates don't agree on tasks to be performed, it is no wonder that desired outcomes are often not achieved. Further, because managers are accountable for the means and the ends, they must be given the authority and resources to produce outcomes for which they are accountable. Authorities will be the subject of the ensuing discussion.

Authority:

Authority and accountability go hand in hand with each other. They are like opposite sides of the same coin. One cannot be held accountable for something without being given the necessary authority to influence

Principle #2: Clearly Define Accountabilities and Authorities for All Roles

events in such a way as to effectively carry out a given accountability. Similarly, one cannot be given a certain level of authority without that same person exercising an appropriate level of accountability associated with that authority. Nearly everyone recognizes the relationship of accountability with authority. Few individuals, however, understand the corresponding relationship between authority and accountability.

For example, in many government agencies, senior-level leaders assert that they have oversight authority over various operating entities. But oversight authority is not passive in nature. It also entails a certain due diligence on the part of the overseer. That due diligence, in essence, encompasses certain accountabilities associated with a given authority, such as acknowledging the planning schedule of a subordinate. Unfortunately, many individuals don't readily accept the concurrent requirement to exercise appropriate accountability with a particular type of authority. The simple fact is that you can't have one without the other. The duality of this relationship will be discussed thoroughly in this section.

> AUTHORITY: Authority encompasses those aspects of a role that enable the person in the role to act legitimately in carrying out the accountabilities with which he or she has been charged. To discharge accountability, a person in a role must have appropriate authority to use the materials and financial resources as well as the authority with respect to other people that make it reasonably possible to do what is expected of him or her.[62]

This focus on authority is especially important to the leadership process in two ways. First, the roles we occupy in a properly structured organization must be vested with the necessary authority to do the work inherent in the role. This is commonly referred to as *role-vested authority*. We pick up that authority by virtue of our being in the role. We use the authority as we desire. It is this role-vested authority that allows us to require others to follow our orders or instructions. For example, in the manager-subordinate relationship, there is a fundamental difference, in

---

[62] Jaques, Elliott and Clement, Stephen D. *Executive Leadership*, Cason Hall Publishers, Arlington, VA 22202, 1989. Page 8

dealing with people from an authority perspective than in dealing with material things or financial resources. In the case of the latter, we do not have to earn the trust or the respect of material or financial resources. But human resources are different. Role-vested authority, by itself and properly used, is only enough to produce minimally satisfactory results by means of subordinates doing what they are role bound to do. What role-vested authority alone cannot do is to release the full creativity and cooperation of others. To achieve that type of behavioral response, the manager has to supplement his role-vested authority by winning the full personal support of those people by gaining what can best be called personally earned authority.

Role-vested authority and personally earned authority affect individual behavior from fundamentally different power bases. Role-vested authority is based on legitimate position power, where the role incumbent has the authority to order the subordinate to take specific action. Personally earned authority, on the other hand, represents a situation where the subordinate is influenced (persuaded) to take action by virtue of the strength of character or the personal qualities of the authority figure himself.

Character is an interesting mediating factor. Character refers to the type of person the influencer is. The concept of influence, in turn, can trace its roots to the Aristotelian concept of persuasion. According to Aristotle, a persuasive person is a person of good will, good intention, and logical thinking (ethos, pathos, logos). For example, if a manager is perceived to use subordinates to meet her own personal needs or to harbor ill will or poor intentions for subordinates, then the manager will not likely be perceived as persuasive or influential and not be able to win personally earned authority.

The dynamic of how personally earned authority can actually be won is perhaps best understood by viewing leadership as an exchange process. It should be self-evident that personally earned authority is a crucial issue for anyone in a role with leadership accountability. This authority should be built up over time and accumulated in the manager's social bank account for use in crises or when circumstances get tough.

Managers can build up their authority credits by

Principle #2: Clearly Define Accountabilities and Authorities for All Roles

1. Ensuring that their organization is properly structured with sufficient separation between manager and subordinate roles

2. Being operationally competent in the role so that subordinates have confidence in them

3. Discharging, with consistency, the managerial practices required to get work done effectively: task assignments, performance reviews, planning, recognition, rewards and penalties, coaching, training, and so on

4. Being their natural selves while at the same time exercising sufficient self-control so as not to behave in ways likely to be disruptive of required working relationships

5. Ensuring viable social exchanges occur between employee needs and management programs and benefits

The effects of authority on individual behavior are also mitigated by the quality of the corporate culture and operating climate as well as certain behavioral qualities of the authority figures themselves, such as their character and competence. These factors are depicted in Figure 6.2 as individual behavioral filters. They are symbolized as pulleys because they are part of the overall culture. Recall that for culture to have a positive effect on individual behavior, all of the cultural pulleys must move in the same direction. If the authority figure is perceived to be a good person with good intentions in mind for subordinates, competent in his role, and operating in a supportive culture and climate, then his subordinate will tend to behave toward the right of the horizontal axis as illustrated in Figure 6.2 (e.g., willing acceptance). Figure 6.2 depicts in total how the influence process is affected by all of the factors at play in the social exchange process between the manager and subordinate. Note that the behavioral outcomes at the bottom of Figure 6.2 represent management's workforce expectations.

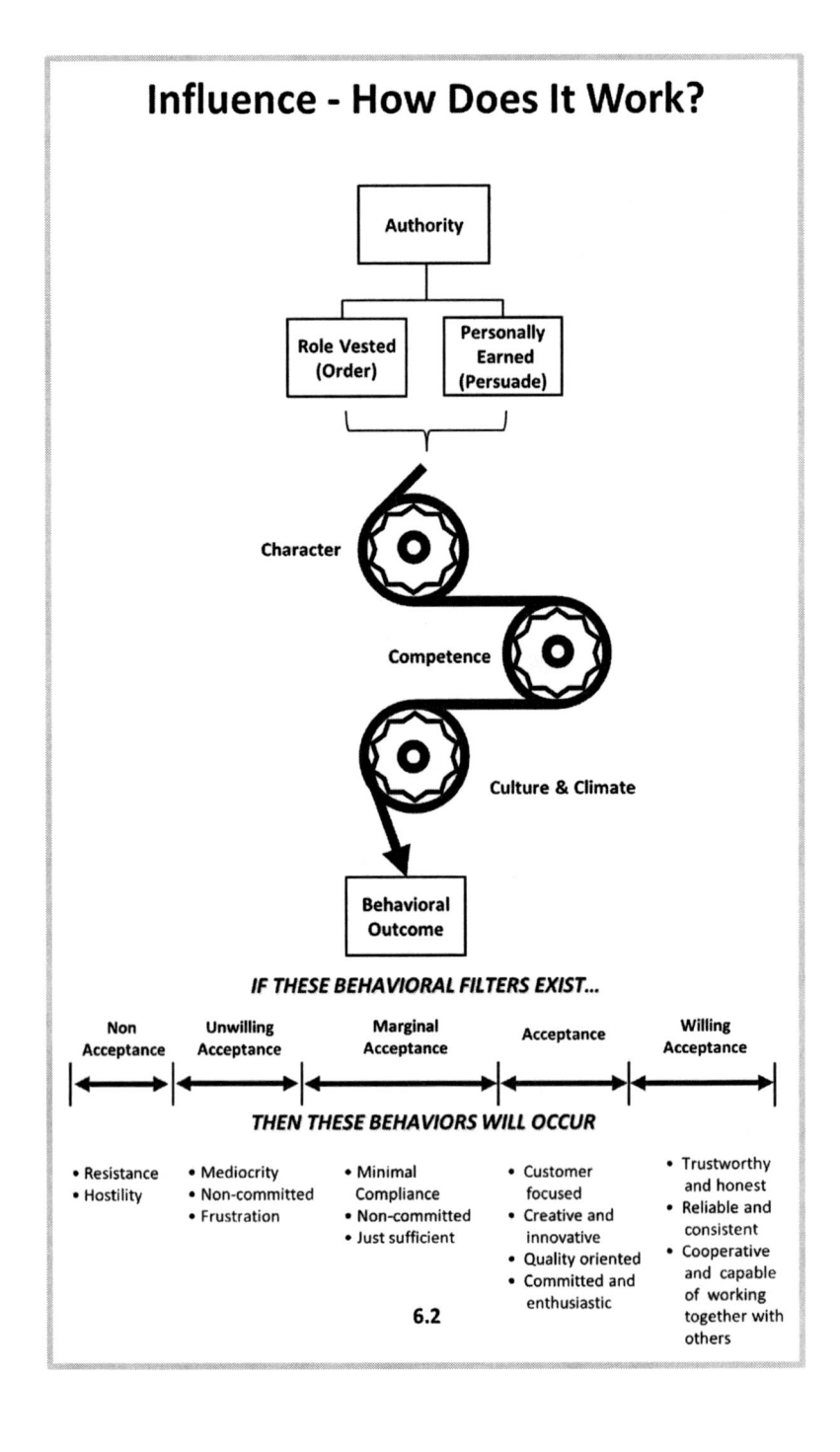

Influence - How Does It Work?

Authority
- Role Vested (Order)
- Personally Earned (Persuade)

- Character
- Competence
- Culture & Climate

Behavioral Outcome

IF THESE BEHAVIORAL FILTERS EXIST...

Non Acceptance	Unwilling Acceptance	Marginal Acceptance	Acceptance	Willing Acceptance

THEN THESE BEHAVIORS WILL OCCUR

- Resistance
- Hostility

- Mediocrity
- Non-committed
- Frustration

- Minimal Compliance
- Non-committed
- Just sufficient

- Customer focused
- Creative and innovative
- Quality oriented
- Committed and enthusiastic

- Trustworthy and honest
- Reliable and consistent
- Cooperative and capable of working together with others

6.2

However, as shown in Figure 6.3, even if a manager or leader has legitimate role-vested authority, if he is viewed as an incompetent manager or one who is of questionable character in so far as how he treats subordinates, then his influence on subordinate behavior will be seriously affected. Similarly, if the operating climate and culture are not viewed as supportive, these variables will also undermine the social exchange process described previously.

Figure 6.3 depicts the likely impact on subordinate behavior of a given manager's overreliance on role-vested authority coupled with severe character defects and corresponding climate issues. Note that in a situation that relies on role-vested authority exercised by a person of poor character or competence that is coupled with a perceived unsupportive operating climate and culture, the net result will be marginal acceptance and minimally compliant behavior. Alternatively, in a situation where the manager relies on personally earned authority backed up by a supportive culture and climate, willing acceptance and high performance can be expected as shown in Figure 6.4.

Character Counts

The aforementioned discussion is intended to clearly demonstrate to the reader that character counts. It is postulated that the old adage "what people do on their own time is their own business" is not entirely true. If a person is in a managerial leadership role where she will be called upon to influence others to work to their full individual capacity, then her overall character will have an effect on her persuasiveness. This is especially true in situations involving high degrees of stress or uncertainty. That is why character is so important to military leaders and why it is stressed so strongly in their leadership training and doctrine. But character is also important in other leadership roles, such as parental, clerical, and political roles. Simply stated, most people will not enthusiastically follow a leader of dubious character.

It's All About Work

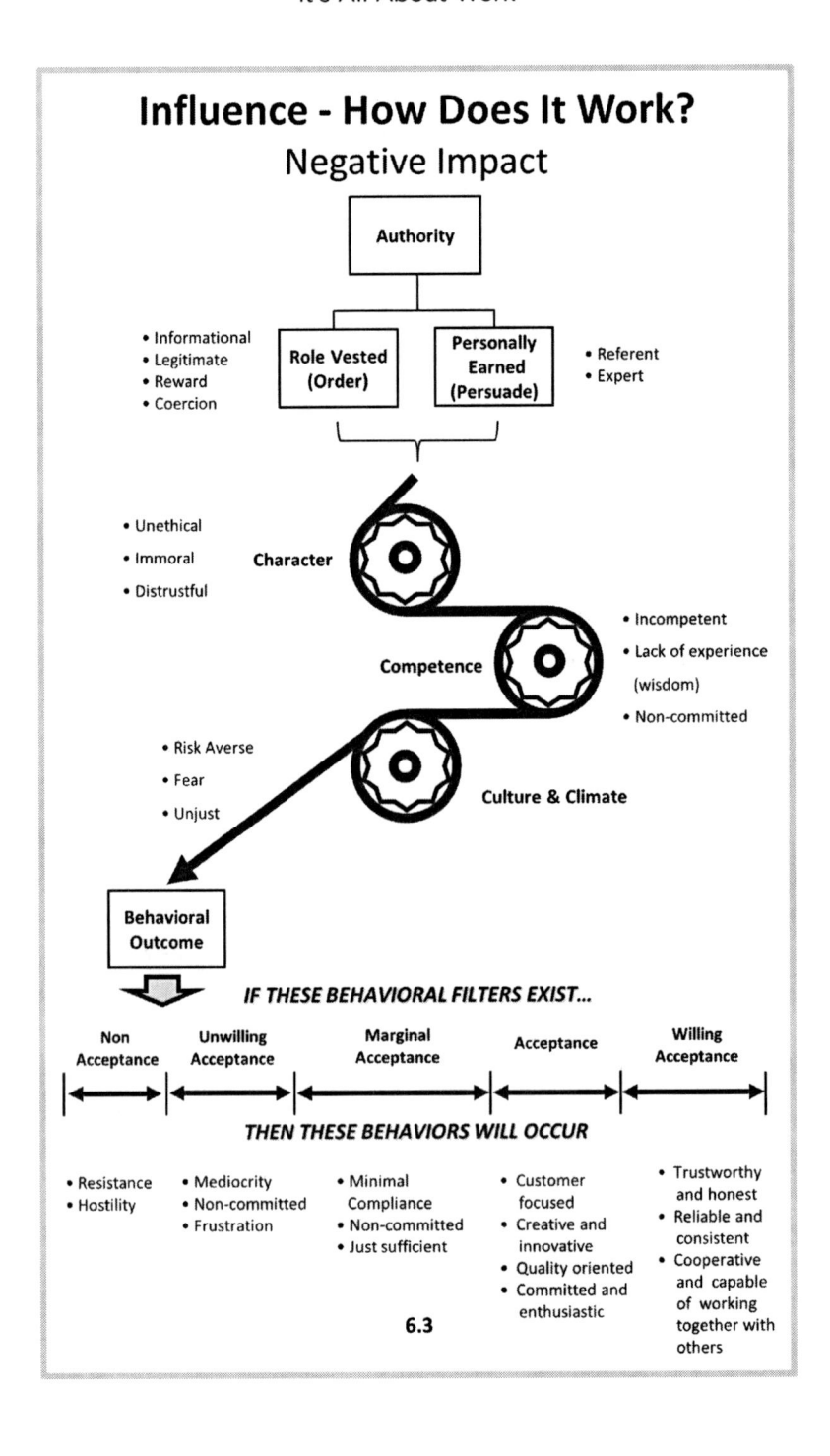

Influence - How Does It Work?
Negative Impact

Authority

- Informational
- Legitimate
- Reward
- Coercion

Role Vested (Order) | **Personally Earned (Persuade)**

- Referent
- Expert

- Unethical
- Immoral
- Distrustful

Character

- Incompetent
- Lack of experience (wisdom)
- Non-committed

Competence

- Risk Averse
- Fear
- Unjust

Culture & Climate

Behavioral Outcome

IF THESE BEHAVIORAL FILTERS EXIST...

Non Acceptance	Unwilling Acceptance	Marginal Acceptance	Acceptance	Willing Acceptance

THEN THESE BEHAVIORS WILL OCCUR

• Resistance • Hostility	• Mediocrity • Non-committed • Frustration	• Minimal Compliance • Non-committed • Just sufficient	• Customer focused • Creative and innovative • Quality oriented • Committed and enthusiastic	• Trustworthy and honest • Reliable and consistent • Cooperative and capable of working together with others

6.3

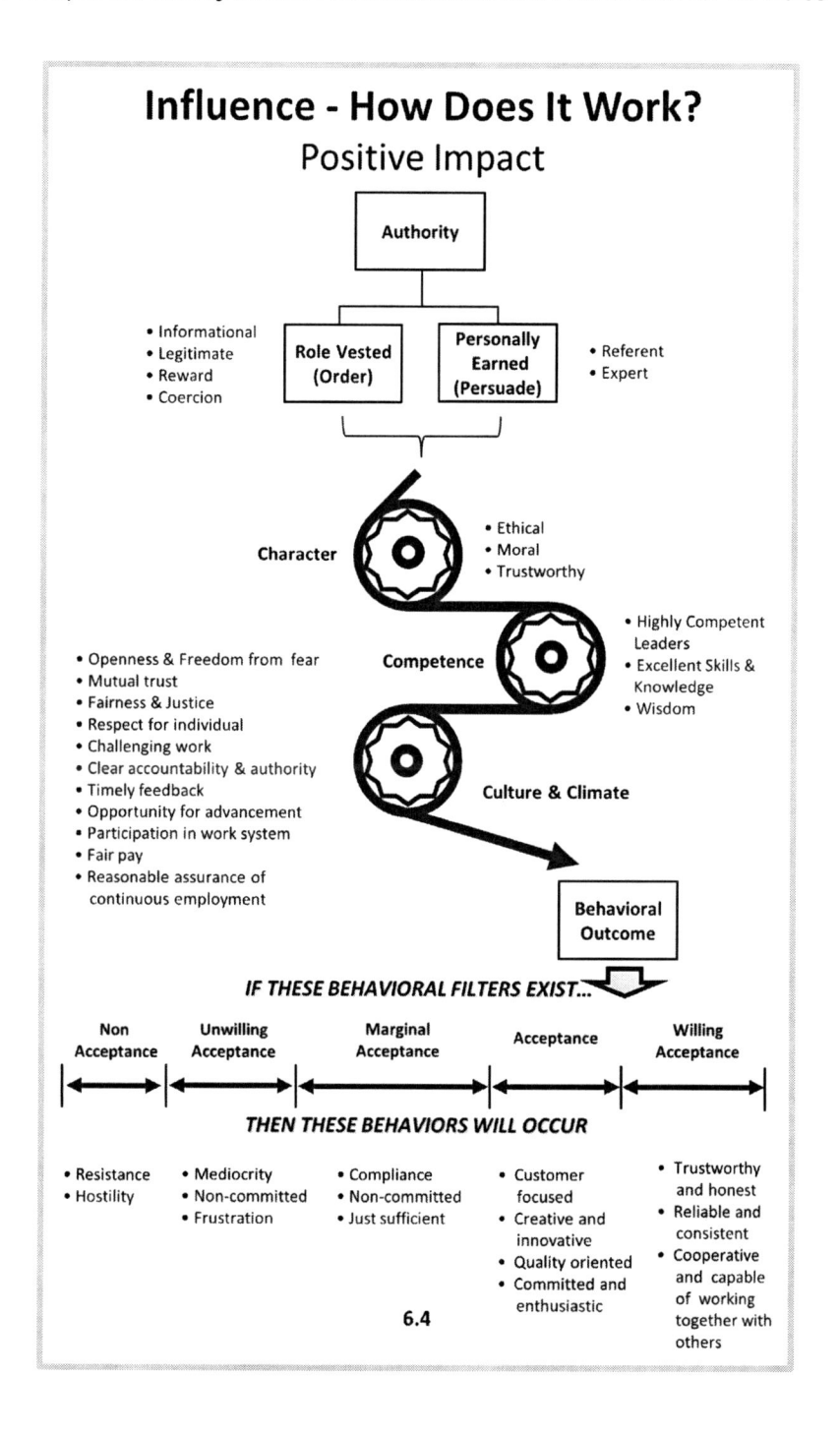

Principle #2: Clearly Define Accountabilities and Authorities for All Roles

Influence - How Does It Work?
Positive Impact

Authority

- Informational
- Legitimate
- Reward
- Coercion

Role Vested (Order) | **Personally Earned (Persuade)**

- Referent
- Expert

Character
- Ethical
- Moral
- Trustworthy

Competence
- Highly Competent Leaders
- Excellent Skills & Knowledge
- Wisdom

- Openness & Freedom from fear
- Mutual trust
- Fairness & Justice
- Respect for individual
- Challenging work
- Clear accountability & authority
- Timely feedback
- Opportunity for advancement
- Participation in work system
- Fair pay
- Reasonable assurance of continuous employment

Culture & Climate

Behavioral Outcome

IF THESE BEHAVIORAL FILTERS EXIST...

Non Acceptance	Unwilling Acceptance	Marginal Acceptance	Acceptance	Willing Acceptance

THEN THESE BEHAVIORS WILL OCCUR

- Resistance
- Hostility

- Mediocrity
- Non-committed
- Frustration

- Compliance
- Non-committed
- Just sufficient

- Customer focused
- Creative and innovative
- Quality oriented
- Committed and enthusiastic

- Trustworthy and honest
- Reliable and consistent
- Cooperative and capable of working together with others

6.4

93

Chapter 7

Principle #3: Clearly Define the Nature of Working Relationships

Working Relationships

Many roles contain specific accountabilities that an individual role incumbent simply cannot accomplish by himself. Such roles often require one individual to interact directly with another person to accomplish a specific task. For example, to ensure that corporate policies are being followed appropriately, Headquarters staff are accountable for providing expert advice to ensure that everyone in the company understands and interprets existing policies in the same manner. This means that HQ staff must have some form of working relationship with operating staff. In the case above, this relationship is advisory in nature. In other situations, corporate staff are sometimes required to monitor the quality of execution of specific company programs or processes. The intent of this monitoring effort is to ensure that accepted company rules and operating procedures are being properly followed and that the program or process is on track to achieve its assigned objective.

In the event that Headquarters staff members uncover a situation where policies are not being followed, what authority do they need to deal

Principle #3: Clearly Define the Nature of Working Relationships

with such a situation? Do they need the authority to stop the operator from taking further action or do they simply take note of the situation and notify the operator's manager? Note, as staff members they do not have full-scale managerial authority over any operating personnel. But what about their own accountability to their boss—the policy approver? What is the nature of this accountability? These and similar questions form the basis of the ensuing discussion.

In the absence of specification, especially about authority issues, individuals are free to make their own rules about what they can and cannot do in relation to one another. Some people may procrastinate while others throw their weight around. This can easily lead to a chronic undertow of unease and vague suspicion that can grow into downright mistrust. This has encouraged an unrealistic behavioral approach to organization in which conflict and inefficiency are explained in terms of the motives and personalities of the individuals concerned.[63] Organizational development is perceived in terms of quasi-psychotherapeutic approaches designed to change the attitudes and behaviors of individuals and how they cope with authority, power, and conflict[64]. The solution is to establish the required accountability and authority context for all roles and working relationships throughout the organization. Failure to clearly define the accountability and authority base relative to existing working relationships can lead to potential dysfunctional behavior as described in the following example.

In our detailed analysis of the Headquarters, Department of the Army governance system, a key element of the study was a thorough analysis of the nature of the working relationships within the HQ staff and between the staff and various operational commands. In analyzing the existing working relationship system in the Headquarters, it was found that there was no universally accepted language used in describing the nature of these relationships. Consequently, organizational staff elements and individuals within these staff elements chose whatever action verbs seemed to best fit their specific situation. The failure to clearly define the nature of these diagonal and horizontal working relationships led to the emergence of

---

[63] Jaques, Elliott. Requisite Organization, Cason Hall Publishers: Arlington, VA, 1996. Page pair 59

[64] Ibid. Page pair 59

eighty-four so-called action verbs. (See Figure 7.1 for a small sampling of these verbs.)

As one can see from the partial list contained here, organizations chose from a large number of loosely defined terms to describe their authority base. For example, some Headquarters staff elements reported that they had "tasking" authority over subordinate operations; that is, they could order subordinate organizations to carry out specific actions. Other staff reported that they had "directing" authority, or "convening" authority, or "delegating," or "assisting," and so forth. One of the most overused terms employed throughout Headquarters was "oversight." For example, several Pentagon employees in the Secretary of the Army organization stated that they were accountable to the Secretary of the Army for "overseeing" all programs developed and implemented by a subordinate command. Because there was no doctrinally accepted definition of *oversight*, these employees collectively chose to interpret this term as permitting them to task the subordinate command to take specific actions. Unfortunately, this interpretation of tasking authority sometimes conflicted with existing orders or instructions provided by the subordinate command's actual leadership. Defusing contradictory instructions consumed both time and energy on the part of all personnel and created an unhealthy atmosphere between HQ staff and the subordinate command's employees.

The above interpretation of what oversight means flows directly from the general definition that Congress uses to define their relationship with many government agencies, such as the Department of Defense, the Department of Homeland Security, and the Department of Commerce. According to the common use of the term throughout Congress, oversight means the ability to perform hands-on supervision of day-to-day operations.[65] Unfortunately, such an interpretation essentially makes the overseer a de facto additional manager of agency operating personnel. At best, such a relationship is confusing, and at worst it leads to dysfunctional meddling on the part of the overseer. What is needed is an agreed-upon definition of the concept that all parties can live with and of course the concomitant accountability that goes along with it. Congress loves to grant themselves authority, but try holding them accountable for the result! Of course, if it is a good result, they will certainly take credit (accountability) for it.

---

65 Headquarters, Department of the Army, Secretary of the Army, Briefing Charts, 2007.

Principle #3: Clearly Define the Nature of Working Relationships

Commonly Used Action Verbs

Abolish	Coordinate	Implement	Report
Accuse	Counsel	Influence	Research
Achieve	Create	Maintain	Retrieve
Advise	Decide	Measure	Review
Advocate	Define	Monitor	Select
Analyze	Design	Motivate	Serve
Approve	Determine	Negotiate	Set
Assess	Develop	Operate	Solve
Assist	Direct	Organize	Start
Coach	Distribute	Oversee	Summon
Command	Engage	Perform	Supply
Communicate	Evaluate	Persuade	Support
Compile	Extend	Prepare	Train
Compose	Finance	Prescribe	Transfer
Conduct	Formulate	Produce	Translate
Consolidate	Furnish	Promote	Undertake
Construct	Generate	Provide	Unite
Consult	Head	Recruit	Utilize

7.1

There are two major categories of working relationships in most organizations and companies: task assigning relationships (TAR) (manager–subordinate) and task initiating relationships (TIR), staff to line or staff to staff.[66] Task-assigning relationships are those relationships between a manager and his subordinates. In these relationships, a manager assigns work (tasks) to a subordinate and is held accountable by his manager to ensure that the subordinate delivers the agreed upon output. This specific type of work is called *delegated direct output*. The output is produced by subordinates at lower organizational layers and delivered to customers, distributed internally to other departments, or sent out externally to partners. The authority base underlying task assigning relationships is quite clear; it involves the following minimum authorities required to exercise effective managerial leadership. Recall the minimum managerial authorities:[67]

1. VETO assignment of an unacceptable subordinate to the managers' team
2. ASSIGN tasks to subordinates
3. REWARD differentially
4. INITIATE removal from role

Diagonal and Horizontal Relationships

The second major category of working relationship involves interactions between individuals across normal functional boundaries or across different organizational layers. These comprise diagonal and horizontal relationships as opposed to vertical ones. This category is called *task initiating because the role incumbent cannot assign tasks like the manager.*[68] Nonetheless, the role incumbent in such situations needs to interact with others to accomplish her own tasks. For example, a corporate staff member is accountable for ensuring that all offshore oil exploration and drilling initiatives meet approved safety and environmental standards. To carry out this accountability, the staff member must be in some form

---

66 Jaques, Elliott. Requisite Organization, Cason Hall Publishers: Arlington, VA. Page pair 60

67 Ibid. Page pair 24

68 Ibid. Page pair 60

Principle #3: Clearly Define the Nature of Working Relationships

of working relationship with those companies and organizations engaged in exploration activities. For this relationship to be effective, both the corporate staff member and the field operator must understand and accept the boundary conditions describing the relationship. The staff member is accountable to her boss to ensure that all exploration is done within corporate established limits. This means that the staff member must not only have access to exploration efforts but also exercise due diligence to ensure that all company personnel are operating within accepted limits. The exercise of due diligence is an accountability that goes hand in hand with the corresponding oversight authority. Just as one cannot be held accountable without the commensurate authority, one cannot be free to exercise an authority without also carrying out the associated accountabilities. For our purposes, we refer to this accountability as exercising due diligence. Figure 7.2 depicts the nature of this duality.

To exercise a given accountability (or authority), there are certain information rights that also must be met. For example, if an overseer is to exercise due diligence (e.g., conduct a surprise audit), then the overseer must have access to the normal production schedule of the organization he intends to audit. Without such information, it would be impossible for the overseer to properly schedule the audit or monitor operations to ensure that everyone involved is operating within prescribed limits. Failure to clearly define these critical working relationships can easily lead to recrimination and blame, such as what occurred in the aftermath of the catastrophic Gulf Coast oil spill of 2010.

In our field work to date with both government and corporate entities, we have been able to identify a finite number of (diagonal and horizontal TIR) relationships that must be defined to achieve reasonable clarity and understanding among workforce members. This finite number can be further subdivided into three major categories of relationships: diagonal, horizontal, and service providing. Within the diagonal category there are four different types of relationships: prescribing, oversight, monitoring, and advisory. The horizontal category consists of two different types of relationships: collaborating and coordinating. The final category could be viewed as either horizontal or diagonal, depending on the status of the two parties involved: service providing or service receiving. Each one of these types of relationships have been observed in a multitude of working situations, such as a monitoring role in a horizontal working relationship with two roles within the same organizational level. This classification of working relationships and role descriptions reflects a tailoring of an earlier taxonomy first developed by Dr. Elliott Jaques in 1989.[69] The tailoring was based on extensive fieldwork conducted by the authors in the U.S. Army from 2001 to 2008. This initial work was then followed by complementary fieldwork conducted in several corporate settings since then.

Figures 7.2–7.4 describe these relationships in greater detail. This listing of relationships varies in terms of their underlying authority base from strong to weak. Recall that this design parameter occurs because the task initiator is *not the immediate manager* but nonetheless relies on individuals in other organizational elements to get an aspect of her work done. Thus, they must be given some authority to do so, but such authority cannot exceed the authority that naturally exists between a manager and one of her subordinates.

As described above, the authority base depicted in Figure 7.2 varies in authority strength from high to low—with prescribing, oversight, and monitoring being high and advisory low. Whether an authority base is high or low depends on the nature of an individual's required response to a specific authority component. For example, if the initiator can cause another person to stop what she is doing, he has a high degree of authority. On the other hand, if the initiator can only advise another person to take specific action but it is up to the other person to decide whether or not to actually do so, the authority base is weak. Similarly, the horizontal relationships are also differentiated in terms of their respective authority base. Service providing and service receiving are unusual in that they could represent either a horizontal or diagonal relationship. The following section contains a more detailed description of these terms.

---

69 Ibid. Page pair 60

Principle #3: Clearly Define the Nature of Working Relationships

Advisory Relationships

Relationship	Advise	Monitoring	Oversight	Prescribing
Accountability	To provide expert advice on processes, programs or outputs	To Track program or function process execution & outputs	To ensure program or function process execution & outputs are within policies & standards	To take corrective actions in specific situations where failure to act could lead to serious consequences
Authority	To PERSUADE	To DELAY work	To STOP work	To ORDER specific actions
Due Diligence Actions	• Maintain situational awareness of program or function	• Assess information on process or outputs (does NOT include performance audits) • Identify issues and/or develop improvements	• Assess information on process or outputs (can include performance audits) • Identify issues and/or develop improvements	• Maintain situational awareness regarding possible emerging situations • To provide experts to make external checks
Information Rights	None	To request the monitored regularly supply some subset of regularly maintained operating data / information	To agree with the overseen on regular reporting requirements	To have access to routine process execution information
Responses	• Inform the advisee • Attempt to Persuade	• Inform the monitored of issues • Attempt to Persuade • DELAY work	• Inform the overseen of issues • Attempt to Persuade • Delay Work • STOP work	• To step in and take control of emerging situations

7.2

Service Providing and Service Receiving Relationships

Relationship	Service Provider	Service Receiving
Accountability	To **provide** specified services to authorized service receivers when requested	To **receive** specified services from authorized service providers when requested
Authority	To PROVIDE services	To REQUEST Service
Due Diligence Actions	• Select customer satisfaction data • Identify customer needs • Identify issues and/or develop improvements • Analyze cost data (transfer pricing or competitive cost data)	• To periodically evaluate customer service quality • Maintain situational awareness of service providers capabilities and/or capacity limitations
Information Rights	• To request customer satisfaction data • To have access to customer production schedule service meetings • To periodically request customer utilization data to understand service needs • To collaborate with customers to improve services	• To be timely informed of potential service capacity issues • To understand service providers priority scheme
Responses	• Provide requested services on time and to quality standards • To inform customer of possible service delays	• To inform service receivers of possible delays or service issues • To inform manager of service capacity shortfalls

7.3

Principle #3: Clearly Define the Nature of Working Relationships

Collaborating Relationships

Relationship	Coordinate	Collaborate
Accountability	To assemble a team	To attempt to resolve issues
Authority	To PERSUADE	To PERSUADE
Due Diligence Actions	• Assemble the team • Guide the team • Inform the team	• Assemble the team • Guide the team • Inform the team
Information Rights	• None	• None
Responses	• Attempt to Persuade • Inform supervisor of any impasse	• Attempt to Persuade • Inform supervisor of any impasse

7.4

The relationships are described in terms of the accountabilities and authorities held under each relationship as well as the actions undertaken to exercise due diligence under the relationship and the normal response expected by the parties involved in a given relationship. Figure 7.5 shows two manager-subordinate pairs (A-B and D-E), ostensibly from two organizations, although A and D may share a common manager. Managers A and D work at the same organizational level; that is, they are colleagues, and both are expected to produce specific outputs. Neither A nor D have task assigning authority over the other. Manager A and subordinate E work at different organizational levels, and while manager A may have a working relationship with subordinate E, manager A is not accountable for E's output (E's manager is D). For example, A is accountable to ensure that E's output is within approved limits. A is not accountable for E's output because E is a subordinate to D.

The following descriptions discuss the diagonal and horizontal relationships in terms of these individuals.

Prescribing

> APPLICATION: A prescribing relationship is the strongest of any potential diagonal relationship between two individuals. It nearly rivals the normal relationship between a manager and her subordinates because a prescriber has the authority to order an individual to take specific actions. Recall that a manager has the authority to assign tasks to a subordinate. In the situation depicted in Figure 7.6, A has the authority to prescribe certain actions to be undertaken by E, even though A is not E's manager. Because of the underlying strength of this relationship, it should be rarely used as it could easily undermine the formal manager-subordinate relationship and put E in the untenable position of essentially having multiple bosses. Consequently, prescribing authority is generally found in serious safety or dire financial situations where failure to act could lead to serious consequences or dangerous outcomes. Similarly, prescribing authority may be required under certain conditions (such as financial or emergency situations) where failure to act may result in disastrous outcomes (financial collapse or bodily harm).

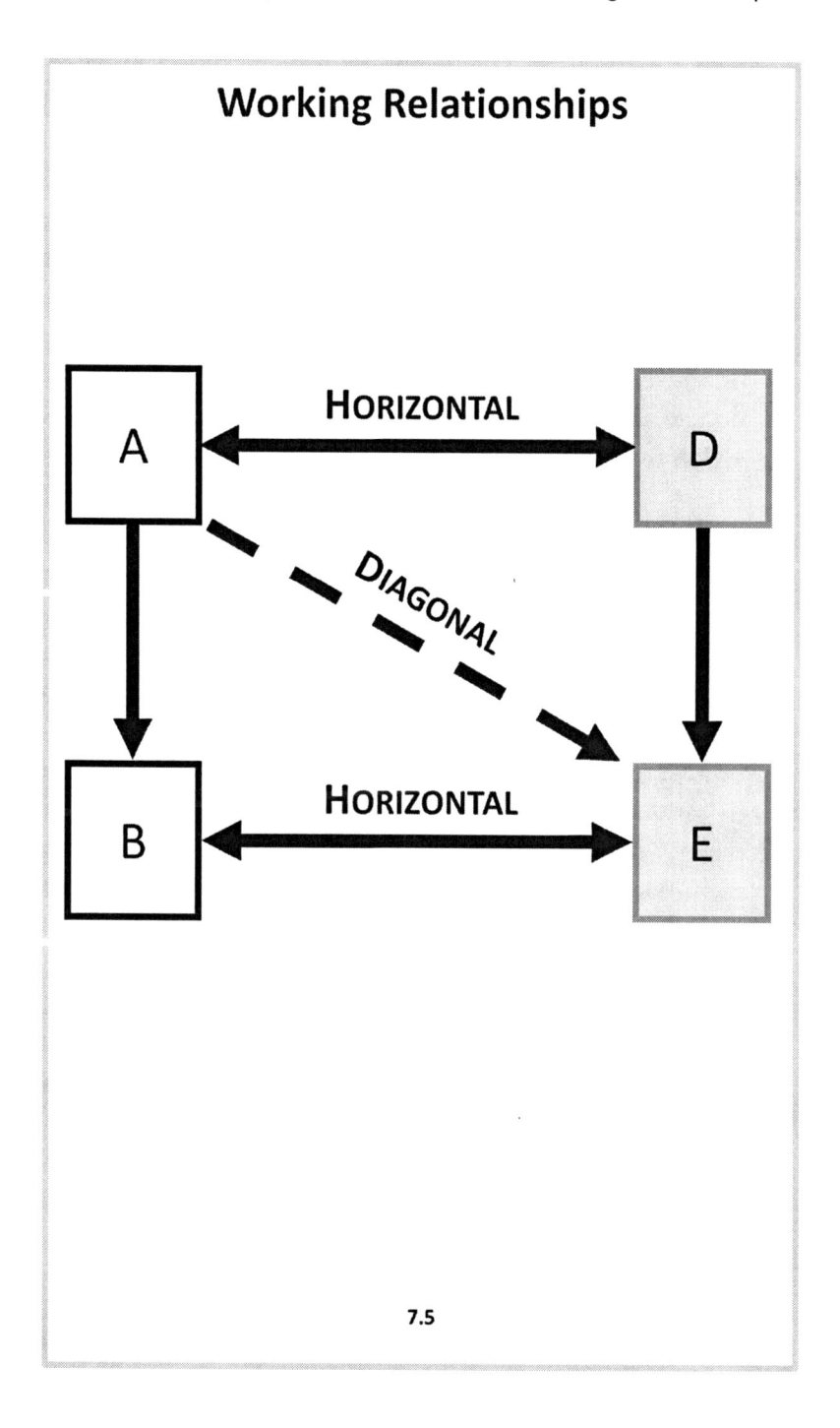

Principle #3: Clearly Define the Nature of Working Relationships

Working Relationships

```
    A  ◄——— HORIZONTAL ———►  D
    │  ╲                     │
    │   ╲  DIAGONAL          │
    ▼    ╲                   ▼
    B  ◄——— HORIZONTAL ———►  E
```

7.5

ACCOUNTABILITY: An individual is accountable for maintaining reasonable situational awareness such that they are in a position to detect serious safety violations or other situations, such as a financial situation, where failure to step in and order corrective action could lead to possible injury or dire consequences for one or more individuals affected by the situation. It is critical that a prescriber have greater expertise in the matter at hand than the responder. Managers and senior executives should always be on the lookout for potential dangerous situations, know what to do if such situations arise, and be prepared to take appropriate action to alleviate the danger in such a situation.

AUTHORITY: An individual (A) has the authority to require (E) to do something, and (E) must do it (but can raise questions afterward if he or she is dissatisfied with (A's) prescription).

DUE DILIGENCE ACTIONS: Everyone must maintain situational awareness of events going on around them so as to be able to detect possible emergency situations that could result in serious consequences if appropriate remedial action is not taken. When such situations are prevalent, it is essential that the organization provide for experts to make external checks on the work being done.

INFORMATION RIGHTS: E must provide A regularly maintained data or information. In an audit situation, E must provide A with all specifically requested data or information.

RESPONSES: When there is a difference in opinion between A and E, A must be the one to decide. In all prescribing situations, it is the prescriber who is accountable for the prescription, but it is E's manager who is accountable for ensuring that E is capable of carrying out the prescription.

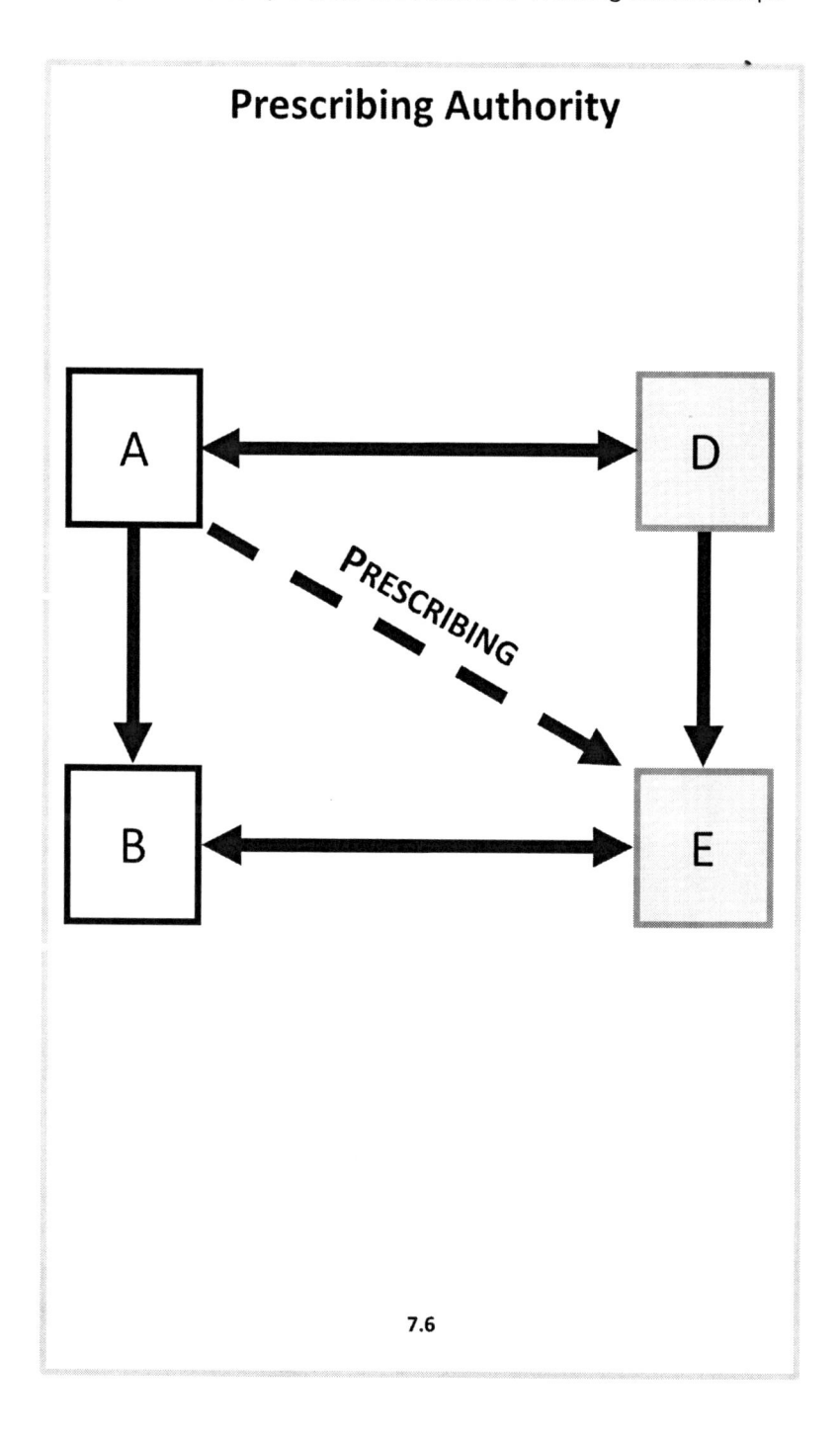

Principle #3: Clearly Define the Nature of Working Relationships

Prescribing Authority

```
A  <──────────>  D
│         ╲        │
│     PRESCRIBING  │
▼            ╲    ▼
B  <──────────>  E
```

7.6

It's All About Work

EXAMPLES: A Doctor has the authority to prescribe orders to a nurse on a ward, and the nurse must follow the orders even if he disagrees with them. (The nurse may raise questions about the orders afterward). The nurse does not report to the doctor but to a nursing manager.

Oversight

APPLICATION: Policies and processes constitute important elements of any organization's governance system. They set limits that are used to control individual and organizational unit behavior. Some roles in an organization's headquarters hold a headquarters staff individual accountable for *ensuring* that the process execution of some function or program remains within established policies, standards, or tolerances. When programs or functions are executed by organizations outside such an individual's direct chain of command, that individual must have oversight authority over the executing entities.

ACCOUNTABILITIES: To ensure that the quality of programs and processes are operating within specified limits, these limits may be set by company policies, legal statutes, or accepted cultural practices. Examples include financial procedures or limits, product tolerances, quality standards, and operational procedures.

AUTHORITIES: An individual (A), in an oversight role, has authority to stop another individual (E), one or more levels below (A), from performing work because the work being done is outside the rules, regulations, policies, tolerances, or other limits governing it. The overseer (A) does not have the authority to instruct the other individual (E) on what to do to remedy the problem or to task (assign work) the overseen (E). There is no timeline associated for the overseer to issue the stop order: it may be immediate or delayed while awaiting other information or actions.

Principle #3: Clearly Define the Nature of Working Relationships

DUE DILIGENCE ACTIONS: To meet her accountabilities for ensuring that program or process execution meets policies and standards, the overseer (A) must have reasonable visibility over program outcomes or performance standards. This visibility may occur as a result of periodic performance audits or routine access to performance data.

INFORMATION RIGHTS: There may be performance data required by the overseer that is not a routine element of the program manager's normal performance assessment (scorecard). This is because the overseer may have different priorities for assessing the health of a given process or program than the program manager. In such a case, the overseer needs to work closely with the program manager to see whether such data should be a routine part of the program information reporting system.

RESPONSES: In exercising due diligence of oversight, the overseer (A) may identify problems or develop ideas for improving a process or program. When this occurs, the overseer (A) should inform the overseen (E) of the issue or improvement and attempt to persuade E that some action is in his best interest. In persuading E to undertake some action, E's supervisor (D) must also be informed and persuaded because D must agree to any changes in E's workload. At this point, if a satisfactory solution cannot be agreed upon, a delay or a stop in work may be ordered by the overseer (A) while further actions are taken. Further, actions may include coordination with other individuals or organizations, studies, pilot tests, or third-party audits. A consequence of these further actions may include data calls to support such actions.

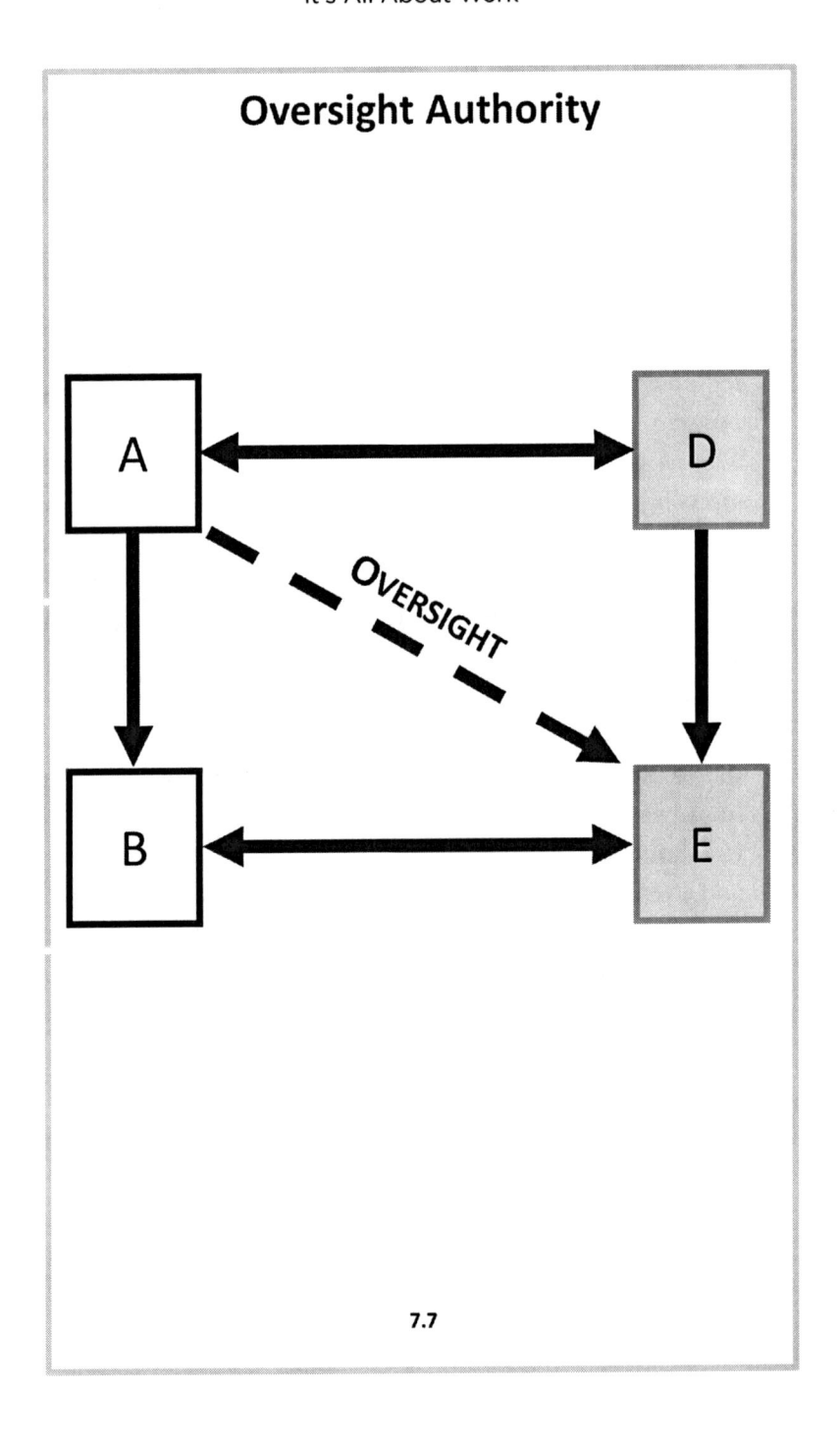

Oversight Authority

```
A  ←——————→  D
|      ＼       |
|    OVERSIGHT  |
↓        ＼    ↓
B  ←——————→  E
```

7.7

EXAMPLES: The company controller has oversight authority over the day-to-day expenditure of funds throughout the company. Legal counsel has oversight over contracts and contractual language regarding business ventures company personnel are about to engage in.

Monitor

APPLICATION: There are times when it is important that an organization ensure that its people are following agreed-upon plans and behaving within company-specified limits. For example, it is important in today's Sarbanes-Oxley world that everyone within a company conform to legally prescribed financial reporting requirements. Thus, it is necessary to ensure that financial reports are being submitted on time and meet an agreed-upon schedule.[70]

ACCOUNTABILITIES: Some roles in an organization's headquarters hold an individual specifically accountable for *tracking* the efficacy of programs or *tracking* the work of other individuals or organizations because they provide inputs to the individual's work or represent central steps in an overarching planning system. In these cases, the individual is granted the authority to monitor the work of those other organizations (or individuals). The monitor cannot be held accountable for the success or failure of the monitored operation. However, he may be held accountable for not keeping his superiors aware of the state of the monitored operation or for being ignorant of the state of that operation. A monitor is accountable for identifying potential problems and discussing possible solutions to those problems with the monitored individual (or organization).

---

70 Ibid. Page pair 74

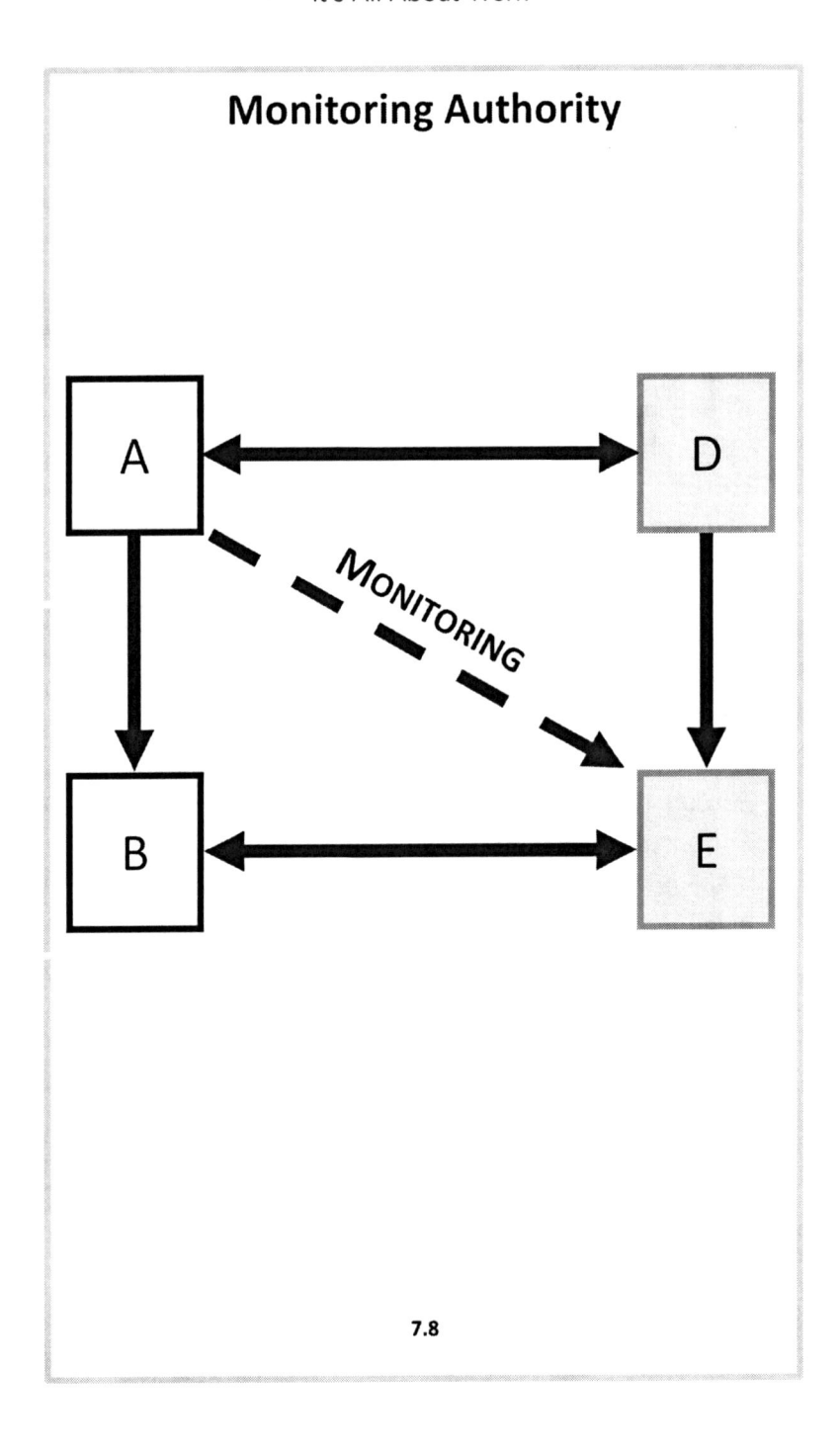

Monitoring Authority

7.8

AUTHORITIES: An individual (A) monitoring another individual (E), one or more levels below A, has the authority to order a delay of the actions and to report deficiencies to E's superior (D). The monitor does not have authority to stop E's actions indefinitely. In order to exercise monitoring authority, the monitor must have access to routine operational information pertaining to the activities of those being monitored. When a monitor identifies problem areas, she has the authority to attempt to persuade the monitored individual (or organization) to take appropriate corrective action. If the monitor is unable to persuade him to change his procedures or practices, then she has the authority to order a delay of further action and to report deficiencies to her manager. Monitoring is in the middle of the overseeing-monitoring-advising authority base because a monitor cannot stop work.

DUE DILIGENCE ACTIONS: To meet his accountabilities for tracking program execution, the monitor (A) must be able to assess and evaluate information about the program. As a result of program analysis, the monitor should identify emerging issues and possible improvement opportunities. The monitor (A) is not accountable to ensure compliance and may not audit the performance of E. The monitor (A) does not have the right to task E.

INFORMATION RIGHTS: E must supply her regularly maintained data and information to A. A cannot demand that E track information other than what E already does as part of his established management work.

RESPONSES: In exercising due diligence of monitoring, the monitor (A) may identify problems or develop ideas for improving the program. In persuading E to undertake some action, E's supervisor (D) must also be informed and persuaded because D must agree to any changes in E's workload. At this point, if a satisfactory solution cannot be agreed upon, a delay in work may be ordered by the monitor (A) while further actions are taken. Further actions may include consultation with other individuals or organizations or with higher headquarters. Note that the monitor does not have the authority to order studies, develop pilot tests, or request third-party audits; however, a consultation with a higher headquarters common to both A and D may result in that higher headquarters ordering these actions.

EXAMPLES: Human resource specialists have monitoring authority over operating managers to ensure that they are conforming to existing personnel policies. A quality engineer will be monitoring production operations to ensure that they meet all quality standards.

Advise

APPLICATION: There are many incumbents in an organization who require expert advice in order to accomplish their assigned work. For example, production personnel often need to call on process engineers or maintenance specialists for expert advice. Similarly, most company personnel require human resource advice from HR specialists to deal with many personnel management issues. Thus, nearly every company needs to ensure that unique expertise such as the aforementioned specialists are readily available to everyone throughout the company.[71]

---

71 Ibid. Page pair 72

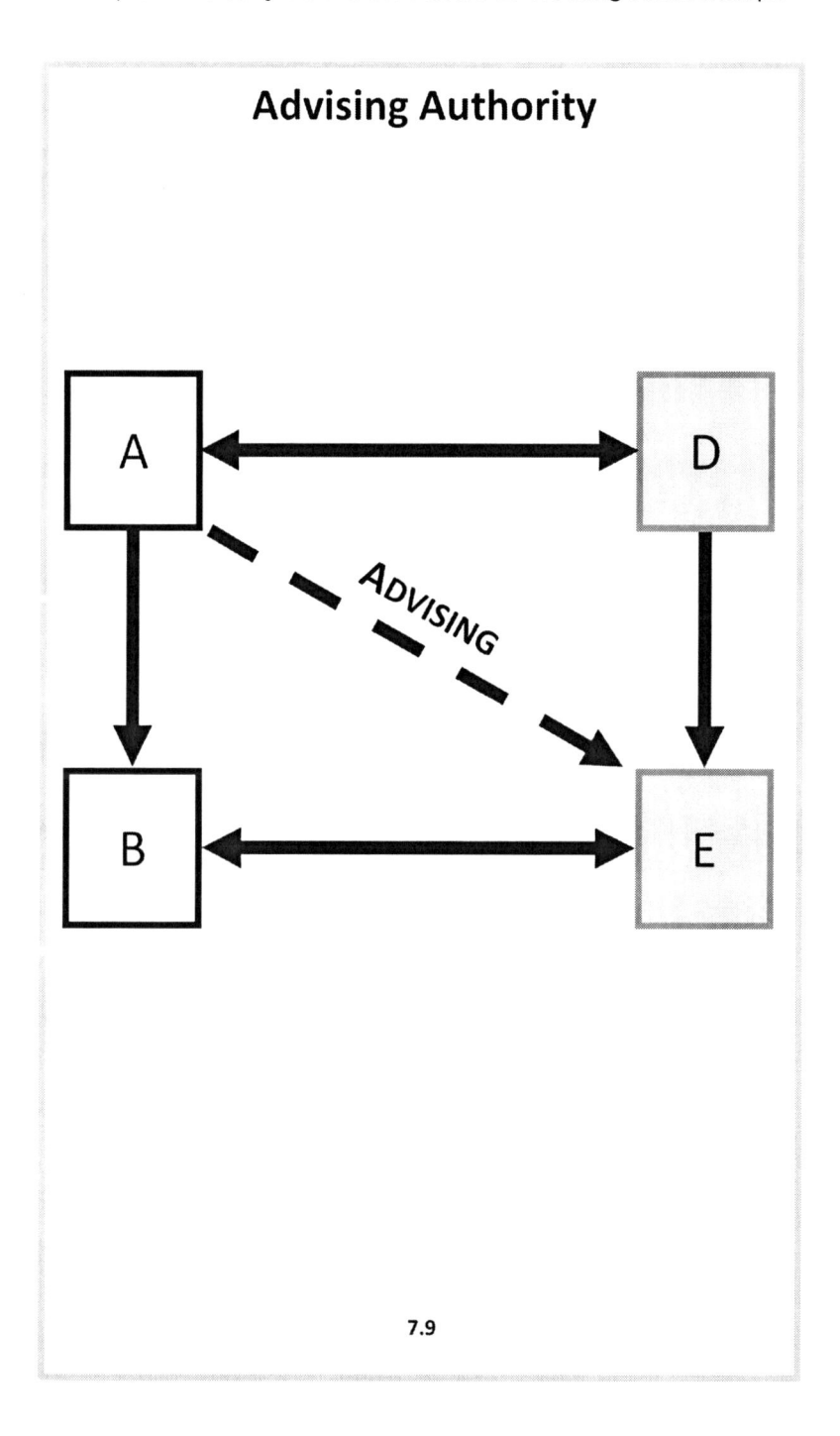

Principle #3: Clearly Define the Nature of Working Relationships

Advising Authority

7.9

ACCOUNTABILITIES: A specialist expert who has been given advisory authority by the organization will need to take the initiative in identifying individuals in the company who could benefit from her expert advice. The expert is then accountable for approaching a potential advisee and presenting information that may be of use to him. This means that the expert cannot sit back and wait for the advisee to solicit needed input.

AUTHORITIES: An individual (A) offers an opinion or suggestion to another individual (E), who may be at any level relative to A, and documents that the advice has been offered. The advisee (E) may accept or reject the advice of the advisor (A). The advisor has no formal recourse if the advice is rejected. Advising is the least authoritative level of the overseeing-monitoring-advising authority base.

DUE DILIGENCE ACTIONS: The advisee has the responsibility to maintain situational awareness of programs or functions for which he possesses specialist knowledge. In the case of technical specialties such as law or engineering, this situational awareness may include maintaining professional standards or certifications.

INFORMATION RIGHTS: The advisor (A) is not entitled to any information maintained by the advisee (E). However, in the course of receiving advice, it may be in the best interest of the advisee (E) to share information in order to get the best possible advice from the advisor.

RESPONSES: The advisor (A) has no response recourse beyond providing pertinent information and advice and attempting to persuade the advisee (E) to take some action. If the advisee chooses not to take the advice, that is her choice. In the event that problems occur as a result of not following an expert's advice, senior-level management must first assess the quality of any proffered advice. Second, the advisee's manager

Principle #3: Clearly Define the Nature of Working Relationships

must attempt to understand the circumstances explaining why the advice wasn't taken by the subordinate and take appropriate action, if any is necessary.

EXAMPLES: Maintenance engineers are authorized to provide specialist advice to production personnel on how they might reduce maintenance costs. Company lawyers offer legal advice to operating managers on interpretation of contracts with outside vendors.

Collaborate

APPLICATION: In today's rapidly changing world, companies often have to establish cross functional teams to attack complex multifunctional problems. Teamwork is an essential element of good corporate behavior. Such teams are often made up of colleagues. Colleagues who work together at the same level are expected to try to get along with one another and work together to accomplish common goals.

ACCOUNTABILITIES: Individual's who work at the same level in an organization, usually for the same manager but not always, are generally held accountable to work together. These individuals are expected to collaborate with one another. Colleagues generally should have a good idea of what needs to be done in a given situation because they should mutually understand the overarching context of the work expected of them. Collaboration is the most basic of working relationships. If colleagues simply can never seem to get along, then their manager is well within his or her rights to consider replacing one or both of them.

AUTHORITIES: Colleagues have no authority over one another. They are expected to try and persuade one another to take appropriate action.

DUE DILIGENCE ACTIONS: Colleagues are expected to

understand the context of the work (or project) within which they are expected to collaborate with fellow team members. Colleagues are expected to accommodate one another's needs within that context. Team members are expected to share pertinent information with other team members.

INFORMATION RIGHTS: While colleagues are expected to share pertinent information with one another, they have no rights to demand or order information from one another.

RESPONSES: If colleagues cannot resolve a problem, they should first attempt to agree on what their superior would expect them to do and refer back to their superior only when they cannot agree.

EXAMPLES: Colleague functional managers (e.g., production, marketing, sales, finance, etc.) are expected to work together to achieve business unit goals. Colleagues chosen from across the company are expected to cooperate and work together on a corporate-wide project.

Coordinate

APPLICATION: Cross functional coordination is useful when developing new programs or capabilities that require the input of individuals from multiple departments. To achieve such coordination, it is often necessary to *assemble a specific team to accomplish the aforementioned work.*[72]

ACCOUNTABILITIES: An individual is designated as accountable for assembling the proper mix of skills and representatives to achieve cross functional coordination. The coordinator should propose how tasks should be approached, keep the group informed as to ongoing progress, and help overcome problems and obstacles encountered in the effort.

---

72 Ibid. Page pair 75

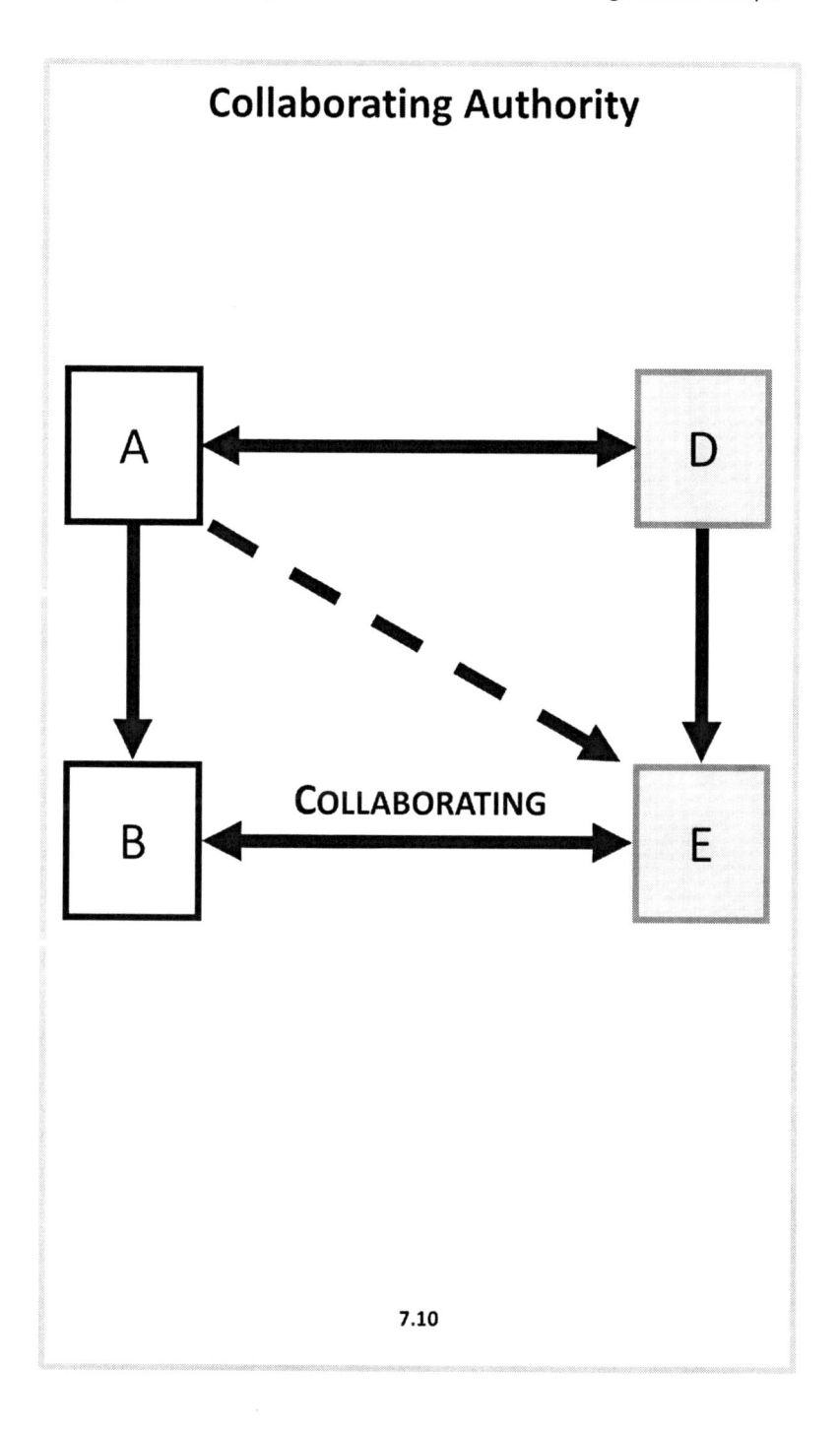

Principle #3: Clearly Define the Nature of Working Relationships

Collaborating Authority

A ⟷ D

A → B

A ⇢ E (dashed)

D → E

B ⟷ E COLLABORATING

7.10

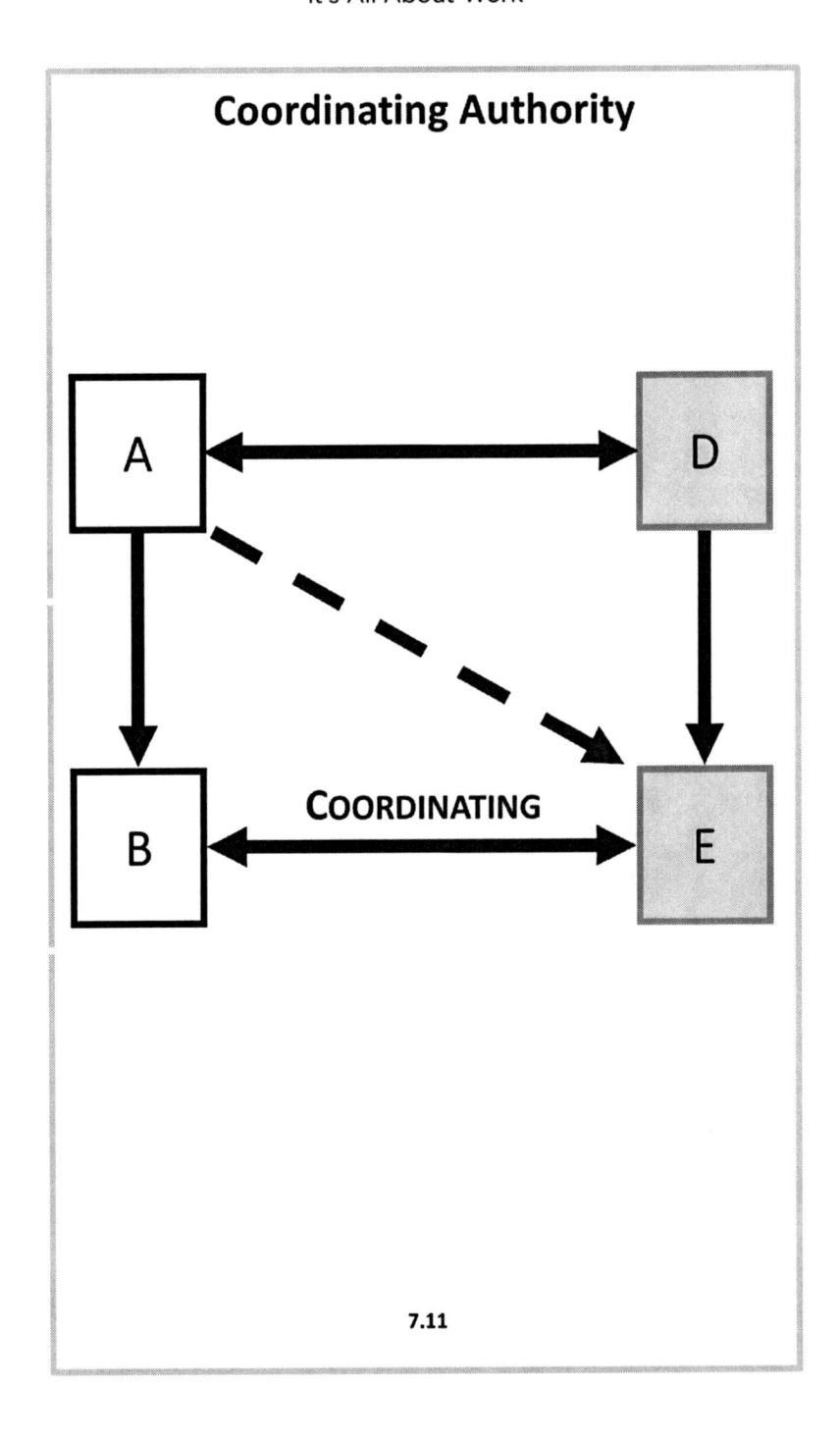

Coordinating Authority

COORDINATING

7.11

Principle #3: Clearly Define the Nature of Working Relationships

AUTHORITIES: An individual, who acts as a coordinator (B), assembles a group of individuals, usually at the same level of the organization (B and E) to work together. The coordinator (B) and the individuals whose efforts are to be coordinated (E) will be identified by their superiors one level higher (A and D). The coordinator (B) has the authority to try to persuade the others (E) to act in concert toward some end, but does not have the authority to issue overriding instructions in the case of disagreement. The coordinator (B) has the authority and accountability to take disagreements to his superior (A) if he fails to settle a problem to his satisfaction.

DUE DILIGENCE ACTIONS: Because the coordinator does not have task assigning authority, he must rely on his individual persuasive skills to get his team to act collectively to implement actions. Because persuasive authority is very different from role-vested authority, the coordinator must take appropriate actions to ensure that he optimizes his persuasive abilities. For example, being widely known as extremely competent in his own role builds up expertise. Being aware of team members varying needs and trying to meet them in a responsive and timely manner and behaving as a person of good character will also enhance a person's persuasive power. The coordinator acts as the group's representative outside of the team and exercises due diligence by keeping all team members informed of developments and status of the team's efforts.

INFORMATION RIGHTS: The coordinator has a responsibility to establish, for the group, an agreed-upon information system to facilitate the project, but he has no rights to demand information from the team members.

RESPONSES: In the case of disagreement or an impasse where the team cannot reach a consensus, the coordinator reports this to his supervisor (A). It is then the A's responsibility to collaborate with his peers to attempt to resolve the impasse.

EXAMPLES: An office manager brings together all functional heads to allocate office space. A product development project chief synchronizes the work of the research and development (R&D) staff with marketing and production personnel. Team leaders and committee chairs also have coordinating authority.

Service Providing and Service Receiving

APPLICATION: Individuals and organizations throughout the company need to be able to request and receive services that they need to get their work done. These services may be provided by inside personnel or outside contractors. Getting the service component to work smoothly is essential to increasing operating effectiveness. Failure to be clear about this process often leads to recrimination, hostility, buck-passing, and blaming.[73]

Accountabilities:

SERVICE PROVIDER—The service provider must know what services she is accountable to give and to whom. In addition, she must be aware of the resources and time available to complete assigned services and tasks.

SERVICE RECEIVER—The service getter must know what services he is authorized to receive and from whom. If the service getter is unhappy with the quality or responsiveness of the services he receives, he is accountable for notifying his manager of perceived service shortfalls.

Authorities:

SERVICE PROVIDER—The service provider cannot decide that she will not give an authorized service; however, if the service provider is overwhelmed because of unforeseen circumstances or she does not have sufficient resources or time to provide agreed-

---

73 Ibid. Page pair 73

Principle #3: Clearly Define the Nature of Working Relationships

upon services, she must be able to decide not to do so. In such situations, it is incumbent upon the service provider to suggest alternatives or to delay the provisioning of services until she has the necessary capability.

SERVICE RECEIVER–It is up to the service getter's manager to deal with sustained service failures by negotiating better service arrangements with the service provider's manager or by seeking permission from higher headquarters to seek such services from an outside vendor.

Due Diligence:

SERVICE PROVIDER—When an individual is accountable for providing services, problems often arise over priorities. The service provider must discuss this possibility in advance with her manager and agree upon a system for prioritizing such services. The service provider's manager must, in turn, discuss this prioritization system with his colleagues to avoid recrimination and blaming in the future.

SERVICE RECEIVER—The service receiver must ensure that he has adequately identified all service requirements in advance. The service getter must then program when he desires such services and discuss the program requirements with the service provider. Potential conflict situations should be discussed and plans established to amicably resolve such situations when they occur.

Responses:

> SERVICE PROVIDER—The service provider must seek periodic feedback from customers as to the quality and responsiveness of her service activity. When such feedback identifies potential areas of improvement, the service provider should discuss possible corrective courses of action with the service receiver.
>
> SERVICE RECEIVER—The service receiver should always keep the service provider informed as to any changes in service requirements. Similarly, if the service getter is able to identify ways to improve the quality or responsiveness of the service, he should discuss this issue with the service provider.
>
> EXAMPLES: The IT Department is accountable for providing timely and responsive help-desk services to all IT users. Maintenance staff are expected to provide routine maintenance services to the production team in accord with agreed-upon maintenance plans. Emergency maintenance services are to be provided in as timely a manner as possible, even if routine services have to be postponed or rescheduled.

Working Relationships Are Quite Dynamic

Working relationships don't always occur within the same level or next lower level. For example, a monitor may have the accountability to exercise this authority on roles at higher levels in the organization, sometimes spanning two or more levels. In fact, all of these working relationships and their accompanying accountability and authority base can be found (and defined) in a myriad of ways in large organizations: up and down levels, diagonal, horizontal, and even with outside vendors and partners. For example, a quality manager in a production plant might have monitoring authority over an outside vendor and its incoming product (raw materials) that feeds the production line. The quality manager may not have the authority to terminate the vendor relationship in the event of quality problems, but he does have the authority to *delay* incoming shipments of raw materials from that vendor until the raw material meets the agreed-upon quality standards or another solution is found.

When Dr. Jaques began to explore accountability and authority in working relationships, he focused mostly on the roles rather than the tasks. However, in our experience with implementing these working relationship concepts, we have found that the accountability and authority relationship often vary by specific task. For example, two colleague managers, an HR manager and a sales manager, normally have the relationship in which the HR manager has advisory authority over the sales manager. If the sales manager has a sales associate that is struggling with her performance, the HR manager can only attempt to persuade the sales manager to take a particular course of action as it pertains to that associate (e.g., terminate, increase one-on-one time, etc.). That is a task that we might call performance coaching, and the HR manager only has advisory authority as it pertains to that task. With a separate task, however, such as sexual harassment training, the HR manager might have oversight authority. The HR manager is accountable to oversee that all sales associates and team members attend this training by a certain date. This gives the HR manager more authority to meet his oversight accountability.

It is not necessary to define every single task in this way; that would simply be too cumbersome and overwhelming. We suggest that you define the working relationships only for the five to ten key tasks of a given role. However, as new tasks emerge (such as project work), we suggest you immediately have the working relationship conversation as soon as these tasks are defined. If you (or the accountable manager) do not define these new tasks and working relationships, you will most certainly see the individuals involved define it themselves. This would put you on the path to self-defined roles and the concomitant detrimental effects to efficiency and effectiveness such actions tend to cause.

Chapter 8

Principle #4: Assess the Working Capability of a Person and Match That Capability to a Given Role

The Challenge

Perhaps the most difficult challenge facing any company today is to ensure that it has sufficient management capacity coming up the organizational pipeline to effectively carry out the anticipated future work of the company. Critical to meeting that challenge is a concomitant requirement to periodically assess the working capability of the existing talent pool. This chapter talks about the concepts and principles that underpin any successful assessment process. As will become evident, these principles will challenge many commonly held assumptions about working capability, including what key variables combine to define it, how these variables mature and at what rate, and how a manager can utilize this knowledge to dramatically improve the accuracy of individual assessments.

Principle #4: Assess the Working Capability of a Person

Failure to Meet the Challenge

Everyone who has ever worked in a modern corporation, government institution, or even a small organization will have had the dubious experience of working for a manager who was not effectively greater in capability than themselves.[74] This manager was therefore likely to be perceived by the subordinate as unable to provide effective managerial leadership. This situation may have come about because the manager may have been promoted above his level of capability; or he may have been brought in from the outside as a new hire or political appointee, in the case of a government agency; or he may have simply slipped through the selection process, perhaps on the basis of his broad experience, the force of his personality, or who he knows (the good ol' boys' club).

Irrespective of how the manager got there, his leadership suffers because he cannot set an adequate context, he gets involved in too much detail, he tends to breathe down the subordinate's neck, he seems to be more comfortable in doing the work of the subordinate, his day-to-day work contributions do not add any value, or he exhibits a leadership style where he takes all the credit for what goes well and tends to blame subordinates for everything that goes wrong.[75] Regardless, the outcome of the aforementioned experience is unpleasant, unmotivating, and a morale buster. Its widespread occurrence is a major social disease in contemporary organizations. Left untreated, this disease undermines the overall productive effectiveness of any work unit and will eventually erode the morale and spirit of the entire institution.

As bad as the above situation is, even worse is to have a manager whose level of capability is lower than that of the subordinate. This circumstance occurs more often than people might surmise. It also is a destroyer of morale and a disastrous producer of stress and conflict. The manager in such cases drags the subordinate down to the manager's level of capability. The specific limits that define the manager's work space are, in turn, imposed on the subordinate. The presence of these confining limits stifles her opportunity to apply her initiative and judgment. All hopes for creativity and innovation are likewise suppressed. The subordinate

---

74 Jaques, Elliott and Clement, Stephen D. Executive Leadership, Cason Hall Publishers: Arlington, VA. Page 42

75 Ibid. Page 42

may find it difficult to even go to work for she knows that the manager's approach to certain tasks, emerging problems, and decision-making requirements will be insufficient to achieve the goals of the organization. As the subordinate struggles to deal with this negativity, she will in all likelihood become disengaged. Failure will not be far behind. It is a powerful testament to the strength and resilience of human nature that some of us are able to get any work done at all in some of our managerial hierarchies or under the dysfunctional leadership practices of some of our current managers.[76]

By contrast, many of us have had the experience of working for a manager whose level of capability was sufficiently greater than our own, enabling him to set clear context around our work and the task assignments inherent in that work, to be helpful when problems arise, and to be confident enough in the existing work situation to focus on his work, thereby leaving subordinates free to pursue their own work. Our experience, therefore, suggests quite strongly that an absolute minimum condition for achieving constructive managerial leadership is to ensure that the managerial leader is one full step higher in capability than his or her immediate subordinates.[77]

Further, we have found that leadership competence is a matter fundamentally of competence in each and every role that carries leadership accountability.[78] What do we mean by competence in role? What are its elements? We argue that if a person has the competence to handle the role of general manager of a manufacturing plant, director of regional sales operations, or command of an army battalion and that person values functioning in the role of general manager, sales director, or battalion commander, then she will be able to exercise the leadership accountability in role in relation to her subordinates regardless of the possession of any unique personality traits or characteristics.

Jaques and Clement called this personality "T" for temperament.[79] They believed as long as an individual's emotional makeup (temperament) did not have a severe negative impact on working relationships, then the

---

76 Ibid., page 43
77 Ibid.
78 Ibid
79 Ibid., page 79

type of temperament wasn't important. Thus, you need to ensure that those personality characteristics are of a quality that will not severely damage or disturb working relationships with others. At the end of the day, your people will lead in a multitude of different ways, each with a substantially different style, and all will be effective so long as they are not suffering from a socially debilitating psychopathology (e.g., total closed-mindedness, excessive narcissism, etc.).

The conclusion that we shall offer is that effective leadership demands four straightforward conditions:[80]

1. Requisite organizational conditions—the right structure.

2. People in roles who have the necessary competence to carry the requirements of those particular roles.

3. Individuals who are free from any severely debilitating psychological conditions that interfere with interpersonal relationships.

4. Freedom to use their own styles, thereby allowing them to use the full and free expression of their natural selves.

This brief discussion of how capability affects leadership is presented here to set the stage for a more comprehensive discussion of the leadership subject in chapter 9.

Working Assumption: Most Individuals Want to Work to Their Full Individual Capability

The importance of working capacity is straightforward. We believe that most people naturally want to work to their full individual capability. These people feel uncomfortable or stressed if they are put into a position where they are required to work on tasks beyond their current capability; they feel overstretched. Similarly, they get frustrated and unhappy when they are forced to operate at too low a level where

---

[80] Ibid., page 28

they are not challenged. Because we believe people want to work to their full capacity, they will do so either on the job or somewhere else. This capacity issue explains why you give your toughest task to your busiest subordinate. In all likelihood, that subordinate has the greatest unused capacity. Intuitively, you know that, and, hence, continue to assign him additional tasks until you overload him. If you continue such practices, over time you stand a very good chance of losing that subordinate.

In a similar vein, if an individual is underemployed, she might put herself in situations outside the workplace that fully challenge her capacity. For example, while conducting an organizational study in a Pepsi bottling plant, the authors noted that the plant engineer was also the president of the local school board, president of the Kiwanis Club, and head of the local soccer league. This was an indicator that this individual had untapped capacity to do more complex work.

In numerous studies over the years, we have found that cognitive capacity is not directly tied to age. In several situations, we observed a young, high-potential individual who was clearly ready for a bigger job despite the individual's youth and so-called lack of experience. We also know from our time doing project work at the senior levels of the U.S. Army (three- and four-star General level) that some of the best leaders surrounded themselves with hand-picked younger officers that demonstrated high capacity despite their junior grades. For example, General Max Thurman (then the Vice Chief of Staff of the U.S. Army) relied on a small group of highly competent majors (level III) to work special projects for him. He used to say, "I have no problem being the 'dumbest' guy in the room."[81] In effect, what General Thurman was doing was intuitively selecting and challenging underutilized individuals and taking full advantage of their excess working capacity.

The ability to work is one of the most important of human capabilities. Thus, how we spend that time and what we do while we are working is central to our sense of self-worth, our personal feelings of importance and value to others. Most of us spend the bulk of our available time at work, so our work is a very important part of our lives. It is through our work that we earn the resources required to procure the necessities of life, to provide for our families, and to pursue our hobbies. Therefore,

---

[81] From a personal conversation with the author.

Principle #4: Assess the Working Capability of a Person

working capability is central to the development of an individual's self-confidence.

One of the seminal discoveries of Dr. Jaques was that not only did work vary proportionately in terms of its underlying complexity from level to level, but so also did a human being's capacity for doing that work.[82] To Jaques, the perfection of this match suggested a sound explanation for the emergence and tenacious hold of hierarchical organizations as a means of getting work done. This form of organization was a reflection and expression of the hierarchical property both of work and the corresponding cognitive working capacity found in human beings. It also meant, however, that there was one, and only one, correct system of organizational layers.[83] Chapter 5 described the underlying nature of the tasks associated with these organizational layers (a requisite system). These same layers describe the basic nature of human capability that will be discussed in this chapter.

Establishing the right structure is the easy step because it is does not involve the human dimension. The real challenge is finding an individual with the internal capacity to perform the work associated with a given layer. In other words, the individual's ability to do the work assigned to a given role. That is the hard part because it involves making judgments about a given individual's cognitive capacity, that is, their ability to get their arms around the complexity of work in a specific role or at a given organizational layer. In essence, the real challenge is putting a face in the space.

Synchronizing individual capacity with work requirements is central to achieving sustained competitive effectiveness in any organization. The common technique for doing so is trial and error. Most companies utilize position descriptions to describe underlying role requirements (e.g., skills, knowledge, experience, etc.). A person is then selected or assigned to a given role and later evaluated as to whether or not he has successfully accomplished the work of the role. If the individual is successful, the work of the role gets done, and the individual is later evaluated to see if he could continue to do more and more complex work. If the individual

---

[82] Jaques, Elliott and Clement, Stephen D. Executive Leadership, Cason Hall Publishers: Arlington, VA, 1991. Page 114

[83] Ibid. Page 116

is unsuccessful, however, then the organization is left in a position where the work assigned to the role does not get done. This situation, in turn, results in someone else having to step up (or down) to do the work that is not getting done. This outcome is dysfunctional because it creates an imbalance in the work system that is unfair to everyone involved. Unfortunately, skills, knowledge, and experience are not the only variables that affect working capacity. As will be shown, success in a role also depends on an individual's cognitive capacity. And cognitive capacity is unique in that it is not distributed uniformly throughout the population.[84]

There is a better way than trial and error to synchronize individual capacity with requirements, and that is to make a more realistic comparison between the two. To make such a comparison, however, it is first necessary to clarify the nature of work and its underlying complexity at successive organizational layers (recall the discussion in chapter 5). This step allows the senior leader of the organization to ensure that every layer adds value to the work of the next lower layer and that the proper number of layers exist to get the work done in order to accomplish the organization's basic mission. The real value of this detailed specification of tasks by organizational level is that it can then serve as a baseline for making a more reliable judgment about a person's capacity to actually do a specific type of work.

Properly synchronizing structure with individual capacity to perform work inherent at a given organizational layer takes us into the realm of human capital management. This is where organizations are forced to confront the difficult challenge of dealing with individual differences. In most Western democracies, there is a tendency to think that all people should be free to pursue roles at any organizational layer. This right is considered essential to developing a sense of fairness in the workplace. The truth, however, is that individuals vary dramatically in their capacity to work at successive organizational layers. Simply stated, some people can handle greater and greater complexity as they naturally mature while other people seem to peak out at an earlier age.

Unfortunately, most organizations tend to promote people to the next

---

[84] Jaques, Elliott. General Theory of Bureaucracy, Heineman Educational Books: London, 1976.

Principle #4: Assess the Working Capability of a Person

higher organizational level based on their performance at the current level. While this promotion process meets the fairness test, it doesn't necessarily meet the capacity challenge. We all know of individuals who were promoted to a level beyond their capacity. Such individuals were commonly referred to as products of the "Peter Principle."[85] What was missing in these situations was a more thorough understanding of the nature of individual working capacity and how that capacity matured differently among individuals. The ensuing discussion describes this natural variation in greater detail.

Individual Working Capacity:

An individual's working capacity is determined by several key factors. Some of these factors are constitutional in nature while others are not. For example, Dr. Jaques believed that the ability to process information, make decisions, and overcome problems appeared to be innate in a given individual and a natural part of his or her makeup.[86] Jaques observed numerous individuals in his consultancy work in all walks of life who naturally rose to the top of their social organization.[87] He witnessed this phenomenon in street corner gangs, uneducated natives in third-world societies, and large corporate entities. This capacity seemed to be inborn and was maturational in nature as opposed to developmental. In other words, this capacity matured predictably along one of several possible maturational paths. Some people peaked at an early age, while others continued to grow in this capacity until they eventually died.[88]

Why is matching an individual's working capacity with the actual

---

85 The Peter Principle is a belief that, in an organization where promotion is based on achievement, success, and merit, that organization's members will eventually be promoted beyond their level of ability. The principle is commonly phrased, "employees tend to rise to their level of incompetence." In more formal parlance, the effect could be stated as: <u>employees tend to be given more authority until they cannot continue to work competently. It was formulated by Dr. Laurence J. Peter and Raymond Hull in their 1969 book</u> The Peter Principle, a humorous treatise, which also introduced the "salutary science of hierarchiology.". www.wikipedia.com

86 Jaques Elliott and Cason Kathryn, Human Capability, Cason Hall Publishers: Falls Church, 1994

87 Ibid.

88 Ibid.

complexity of the work to be performed important? First, achieving a proper match will set the stage for getting work done efficiently and effectively. If an individual has sufficient capacity, she will tend to get the work done on time and within budget parameters. Individuals with excess capacity tend to get the work done even earlier and under budget. *Second,* if people have excess capacity, they may choose to utilize this capacity on the job or off. Thus, if an individual is fully challenged, she will likely be more fully committed to the enterprise.

Interestingly, however, cognitive capacity is a necessary but not a sufficient condition for getting work done. There are several other factors that we have found that also affect working capability. These will be described in greater detail in the next section of this chapter. These other factors, however, are more developmental in nature. They are subject to change and proportional to the amount of developmental effort put into them. As an example, skill and knowledge acquisition is directly affected by the amount of training undertaken or the quality of job experiences one is exposed to. Just because an individual has the capacity to get his arms around the full-scale complexity of work at a given level does not necessarily guarantee that he will do that work effectively. For example, if a person does not value a particular type of work, he will not likely put his heart and soul into it. Most people tend to commit themselves to work they truly value. (Values are used here in a motivational sense as opposed to their more classic use as statements of importance.) Let us now turn our attention to working capability in more detail.

Working Capability: Cognitive Capacity, Values, Skill and Knowledge, Wisdom and Temperament

First, let us define some key terms that are central to this discussion:

> CURRENT WORKING CAPABILITY (CWC): Current working capability is the maximum level of work-related complexity a person could currently handle given an opportunity to do so and within the confines of reasonably favorable working conditions. These conditions include an assumption that the work is of inherent value to the person and takes into consideration full awareness that the individual has

not had a previous opportunity to acquire the necessary skills or knowledge to perform this specific type of work.[89]

FUTURE POTENTIAL WORKING CAPABILITY (FPWC): Future potential working capability is the maximum level at which a person will be capable of working in one, three, or more years in the future.[90]

COGNITIVE CAPACITY: Cognitive capacity is the maximum amount of task complexity, information processing, and problem-solving skill that a given individual can handle or apply at any given point in her development.[91]

As described previously, cognitive capacity constitutes a necessary, but not always sufficient, precondition for successfully accomplishing the work assigned to a given role. If a person does not have the capacity to get his arms around a given set of tasks, to solve problems that naturally occur at a given organizational layer, or to process information relative to that layer, then he is likely to experience difficulty in getting role-related work done on time and to established standards. Such individuals are often described as being over their heads or victims of the Peter Principle.

But capacity is simply a necessary but not sufficient condition for getting work done. There are several other variables that also affect *working capability,* such as skill, knowledge, experience, values, wisdom, and temperament. Unfortunately, none of these latter variables develop according to a predictable maturation process.[92]

Total working capability is a function of all of these attributes as depicted in figure 8.1.

---

[89] Jaques, Elliott and Clement, Stephen D. Executive Leadership, Cason Hall Publishers: Arlington, VA, 1991. Page 45
[90] Ibid. Page 46
[91] Ibid. Page 49
[92] Ibid. Page 69–81

Individual Working Capacity

Working Capacity (f) =

Information / Problem Solving Capacity

   X Values

       X Skills/Knowledge

          X Wisdom

             X Temperament

8.1

VALUES: Values are those things an individual wants to do or to give priority to doing.

SKILL: Skill is the routine application of facts and procedures that have been learned through practice: for example, producing a financial analysis report, designing a weekly production schedule, working with spreadsheets, solving simultaneous equations, machining a bearing, drilling a blast hole, or riding a bicycle. Once acquired, skills generally remain in one's inventory, and some are relatively resistant to decay, such as riding a bicycle, while others require periodic updating, such as solving mathematical equations.

KNOWLEDGE: Knowledge is objective facts, including procedures, that can be stated in words, formulae, models, or other symbols that one can learn, in the sense of being able to pass examinations or tests about them. Knowledge is useful in that it can be applied to specific situations to resolve problems and make decisions. Examples include knowledge of market factors, competitive intelligence, and knowing the impact of incentive awards.

WISDOM: Wisdom is soundness of judgment about the nature of people and the world around us.

TEMPERAMENT (T): Temperament is the tendency for a person to behave in given ways. These traits, or characteristics, give emotional color to personal interactions and add personality and style.

Many leadership experts focus on personality traits and qualities with the aim of developing and assessing leaders. Jaques and Clement believed that this focus on personality was misguided.[93] In the English language there are over 2,500 personality variables, some positive (passionate) and some negative (heartless). Those variables that are positive simply

---

[93] Ibid. Page 80

need to stay within reasonable limits before they become detrimental. For example, if a person is reflective to the point of indecisiveness, then this personality variable becomes detrimental to getting work done. For all variables, positive and negative, it is the duty of the manager to judge whether the subordinate's behavior has moved to an unacceptable degree. However, it is our contention that is not the role of the manager or the organization to attempt to change an employee's personality. The organization and manager need be concerned with an individual's personality only if it becomes overly detrimental to getting work done. Unfortunately, many companies spend an inordinate amount of time and resources trying to deal with the personality issue.

Our research, however, especially within the Army, concludes that trying to change an individual's basic personality is difficult at best and likely impossible under conditions of high stress. While some people can modify their personality to a limited extent, as stress increases, these same individuals are likely to revert back to their natural inclinations. Put simply, most people will be unable to dramatically change their basic constitutional makeup. Further, it is not the manager's job to practice psychotherapy. In the event a given subordinate suffers from temperament issues, the manager should point this out to the subordinate and suggest that he get professional help if such problems are severe enough.

The Assessment Process

Jaques was able to demonstrate that cognitive capacity (mental-processing and problem-solving capacity) matured predictably along one of several natural maturation bands.[94] The evidence he provides to support this assertion is voluminous and will not be repeated in this book. The essence of it, however, is simple and straightforward. Not all people contain the same innate cognitive capacity, nor does that capacity necessarily mature at the same rate or to the same end points. Intuitively, most managers would agree with that assertion. They may argue about whether or not there are seven distinct bands, but they will generally be in agreement with the concept as a whole.

94　Jaques, Elliott. Requisite Organization, Cason Hall Publishers: Arlington, VA, 1996. Page pair 50.

It is the maturation process of cognitive capacity that makes it possible for the evaluation of where a person might develop in terms of their future potential capability and where that person's potential is likely to be in the future, perhaps in one, two, or three years' time. It does no good to try to focus much beyond three years. From a capacity point of view, that period of time is simply unreal to most people.[95]

An effective assessment process provides data regarding each individual's future working potential. Future working potential is the potential capability a person will have at various times in the future as a result of the ongoing maturation of her cognitive capacity (mental-processing capacity) and, consequently, her job experiences. Jaques borrowed the term *potential* from the natural science field of mechanics where it refers to the amount of energy (mental) currently available for use. The assessment data is a judgment of a given person's cognitive (mental) capacity to perform the type of work that exists at a specific organizational layer.[96]

Given Jaques's background as a psychoanalyst, he originally studied and researched most of the then available cognitive tests routinely cited in the psychoanalytical literature to measure or determine mental-processing capability. Tests such as the California Personality Inventory (CPI) and Minnesota Multiphasic Personality Inventory (MMPI) were unable to accurately predict future working capacity, neither was the Meyer-Briggs personality inventory. Jaques and Clement found, however, that a manager in a properly structured hierarchical organization was clearly capable of rendering a valid and reliable judgment about a given individual's mental-processing capacity to handle task complexity, solve problems, and process information of a particular kind relative to a given organizational layer.[97] They originally hypothesized that judgment was better than any tests. For their research, they both tested individuals and asked managers to make judgments of these same individuals. They then plotted and followed the careers of many managers, sometimes in excess

---

95 Jaques Elliott and Cason Kathryn, Human Capability, Cason Hall Publishers: Falls Church, VA, 1994.

96 Ibid.

97 Jaques, Elliott and Clement, Stephen D. Executive Leadership, Cason Hall Publishers: Arlington, VA, 1991. Page 247.

of ten years, to study whether tests or judgment was the better predictor of future capability. The results of this study confirmed their original hypothesis.

In a related study of career army officers, a large number of officers were assessed at the U.S. Army War College, utilizing a variety of instruments. Predictions were then made as to who would go on to be general officers and who would not. The data was put away, and the careers of these officers progressed normally. After fifteen years, the natural careers of these officers were analyzed and matched with the original assessment data. Remarkably, the judgment data accurately predicted future success. Because of the sensitivity of this project and the Army's concerns over predestination issues, this study was never formally published. Nonetheless, the study did confirm the efficacy of Jaques's other published findings. Dr. Clement was originally assigned by the then Vice Chief of Staff of the Army to monitor these ongoing studies. Throughout this period, he worked closely with the army researchers that were involved in this project work. Consequently, he has firsthand knowledge of the results. The results of this project work and Jaques's other work collectively allowed us to conclude that a manager's judgment of an individual's future capability was far more successful than any other test available then or now.

While conducting their research around assessing capability, Jaques and Clement also looked at *who should do the actual assessment*. They discovered that the manager's manager, the person Jaques called the "Manager-once-Removed" (MoR), was the ideal candidate to perform this task.[98]

New Organizational Role: Manager-once-Removed

Results from the aforementioned research showed that the position most capable of assessing future potential is the next highest manager in the managerial hierarchy, the manager's manager. Many terms have been used to describe this role, such as skip-a-level manager and senior rater. The term that we shall use to describe this role is the *Manager-once-Removed*. The MoR role has been successfully employed by a number

---

[98] Ibid. Page 240

of civilian organizations in describing talent pool management and succession-planning issues; hence, there is ample available experience to draw upon regarding use of the term. Executives in these firms have readily adapted to use of the MoR nomenclature. This term was also selected because it applies to both the civilian workforce and the military and government population.

Figure 8.2 depicts the MoR role. Note that this role spans three organizational layers. The topmost role is called the MoR, the middle role is the immediate manager, and the bottom role is the Subordinate-once-Removed (SoR). The great importance of the requisite role of the MoR has not been generally recognized.[99] There are, by and large, no solid terms of reference for talking about the role. However, failure to be clear about the full range of accountabilities associated with the role of the MoR undermines all other efforts at improving organizational effectiveness. Given a lack of clarity, many of the accountabilities that should be associated with the role of the MoR get piled on to the immediate manager's role. And because there should be one level of difference in capability between the manager and the MoR, tasks inadvertently assigned to the immediate manager will simply not get done effectively. The full range of accountabilities associated with the role of the MoR are outlined below:[100]

- Assess the current potential of SoRs and match their individual career aspirations (career development) with organizational requirements.
- Mentor SoRs with respect to the use of their potential capability.
- Ensure that the quality of managerial leadership effectiveness of subordinate managers is satisfactory. Select, coach, and train immediate managers.
- Establish candidate slates at SoR level.
- Build and sustain three stratum-level teamworking.
- Ensure the equitable allocation of resources, both good and bad, across subordinate roles.

---

99 Ibid.
100 Ibid.

The Manager – once – Removed Role

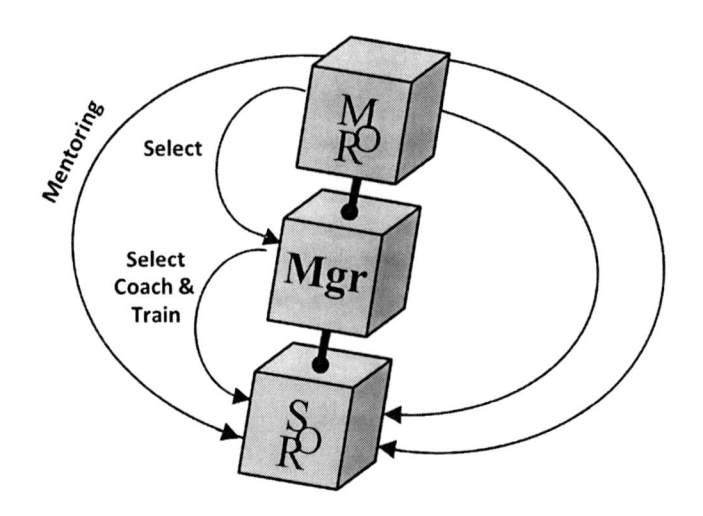

Mentoring

Select

Select Coach & Train

MoR

Mgr

SoR

- **Equitable allocation of resources**

- **Establish three level team working**

- **Establish SoR candidate slates**

- **Evaluate Mgr-Sub leadership relationship**

- **Assess SoR potential and plan career development**

8.2

As described above, one of the major accountabilities of an MoR is to make a judgment about a SoR's current potential capability, that is, the highest level at which a SoR would be capable of working.

Why Should the MoR and Not the Immediate Manager Make This Assessment?

1. Better judgment is generally reflected by the MoR's greater wisdom and experience.

   - The MoR plays a key role in the business planning and managerial succession-planning processes. Because the MoR is more than one organizational layer removed, he is more likely to view the match between the SoR's future capability and the organization's future needs more objectively. He sets the overall planning context and integrates and approves planning goals for subordinate work units. Thus, the MoR is in a unique position to assess future potential against future work requirements.

   - Because the MoR has likely occupied a number of roles at the manager's organizational layer, he is likely to have a larger experience base upon which to judge an SoR's possible future success.

   - Because the MoR operates one full organizational level above the immediate manager, he is in a better position to fully describe specific work requirements appropriate to the immediate manager's organizational level.

2. Managers should not be authorized to promote to their own organizational layer.

   - While a manager should naturally be able to recommend a subordinate for promotion consideration, especially because she has firsthand knowledge of the subordinate's current performance, she should not be able to approve such an action. Managers need the requisite authority to *veto* appointment of any individual to their team that is not acceptable to them; however, they do not need the accompanying authority to nominate or select anyone of their choosing. The authority to establish candidate slates must rest with the MoR (and her corporate-level colleague managers) as a natural part of her responsibility for managing the corporate talent pool. Thus, the promotion process in any company should begin with the senior management group meeting to establish a slate of candidates for a specific vacancy. This slate of candidates is then presented to a hiring manager who subsequently interviews each applicant and then selects a specific individual or rejects the entire slate.

- The reason the hiring manager selects potential subordinates and not someone else (either the departing incumbent manager or personnel department manager) is because it is only the hiring manager who can clearly articulate what he expects of an incumbent in roles subordinate to him and because it is the hiring manager who ultimately assigns tasks to that subordinate. More importantly, it is the hiring manager who is accountable for the output of the individual to be placed in any open roles.

- Finally, there is a tendency on the part of managers to select people like themselves. High-potential individuals are often difficult to manage because they tend to do more than is required because they prefer to operate to their full individual capacity. If they happen to have more capability than their manager, they are sometimes seen as a threat and held back or disparaged by their manager.

3. MoRs can take a more detached view of the assessment process.

- The MoR is not as likely to be compromised by prejudices or unmet expectations that occur naturally in the immediate manager-subordinate working relationship. For example, the MoR is not as likely to be unusually impressed or completely

Principle #4: Assess the Working Capability of a Person

disenfranchised as a result of recent performance outputs as an immediate manager might be. The MoR is more likely to look at the entire performance picture rather than the most recent episode.

4. Maintain a broader perspective on business needs.

- The MoR is able to view the SoR's present performance in the larger context of the immediate manager's overall leadership and task-setting qualities. The MoR is also able to compare a given SoR's performance with her peers operating within different work units but all at the same organizational layer. In this way, the MoR can evaluate that performance from a broader work-related perspective.

- Because MoRs are likely to be concerned with the longer-term business needs of the company, their judgment tends to avoid a situation where a person's career depends entirely on a single relationship with his or her immediate boss.

The MoR role focuses on the future, such as future potential and future development needs, whereas the manager role focuses on meeting current needs, such as assigning tasks, conducting performance reviews, and applying rewards. Both roles are required for the long-term effectiveness of a company. The following two key managerial processes reflect these differing perspectives.

Performance Review (Immediate Manager):

- An ongoing process, formalized at least annually.

- Focus is on outcomes and judgments of how well an individual worked to achieve those outcomes.

- Accountability rests with the manager.

Potential Review (MoR):

- Sometimes a less frequent event.
- Focus is on approaches to tasks and capacity to handle more complex work.
- Accountability rests with the Manager-Once-Removed.

The immediate manager must always have access to provide input to the MoR on all issues affecting the SoR (including potential assessment). For example, the immediate manager should inform the MoR of ongoing performance data relative to the SoR and any coaching or training efforts that he may have scheduled to address performance issues. The immediate manager is also in an ideal situation to offer a judgment as to whether or not he feels that an SoR is ready for more complex work, either at the same organizational level or at the next higher level. The MoR does not have to accept the manager's input, but at the very least she should carefully take it under consideration. After all, the immediate manager does in fact work very closely with the SoR; hence, it is not unusual for him to develop some strong opinions about the potential of that individual. While these opinions must be carefully evaluated by the MoR, they must not constitute the only input that the MoR has regarding the SoR.

Whatever the MoR's final assessment, she must inform the immediate manager of that assessment and coordinate any subsequent managerial actions closely with the immediate manager. For example, successful development actions often need to be carried out in partnership with the immediate manager.

The MoR-SoR relationship constitutes a very strong personal relationship. This is so because the MoR is directly involved in many critical long-term career decisions regarding an SoR. The essence of the relationship between the MoR and SoR is personified by the potential assessment process. To carry out an assessment properly, it is imperative that the MoR listen to the SoR's career aspirations and carefully weigh such aspirations in reaching a final judgment and in formulating a follow-on development program.

Thus, it is important that the MoR be proactive in getting to know an SoR. A once-a-year casual conversation is simply not good enough. The failure to spend adequate time with an SoR sends a powerful message to the SoR that the issue is simply not important enough to the MoR to warrant sufficient time to discuss the SoR's career needs. In addition, the failure to spend adequate time on mentoring and career development issues operationally communicates a lack of caring, minimal concern for individual growth and development, and a general lack of concern on the part of the MoR for promoting a sense of trust and fairness throughout the work unit. To attempt then to build commitment and loyalty among subordinates in such an environment is virtually impossible (see Figure. 8.3).

Notwithstanding the importance of the MoR-SoR relationship, there are some very real concerns that the MoR must consider in interacting with an SoR. First, the MoR should clear all contacts pertaining to an SoR with the immediate manager. There should be no surprises regarding these interactions. Such interactions are not an attempt to spy on the immediate manager. In fact, it is imperative that in any discussion with an SoR the conversation between the MoR and SoR never be allowed to focus on the immediate manager. MoRs should not accept any comments or views the SoR might have regarding the competency or behavior of the immediate manager. That is not a proper role for an MoR-SoR discussion. Further, MoRs should not get involved in coaching, training, or performance-review issues pertaining to an SoR. These types of issues require the presence, or acknowledged concurrence, of the immediate manager.

Potential Assessment

The actual assessment process should begin by focusing around an individual's competence in performing work in his current role and the likelihood that he could handle more complex work normally associated at the next higher organizational level, now or in the near future. That work may exist at the individual's current organizational layer or at the next higher layer. What makes assessing potential difficult is the natural tendency on the part of most managers to get bogged down in considering whether a given individual has the necessary skills, knowledge, experience, values, and temperament to do a specific job.

MoR - SoR Relationship
Strong Personal Relationship

- Be proactive and consistent in getting to know SoR's

- Skillfully and genuinely carry out potential assessments

- Ensure that development action is carried out

- Be open to discussion and to the initiatives of the SoR regarding his/her career development

- Demonstrate fairness and openness in promotion, transfers and dismissals

8.3

While these variables are important, especially from a job fit perspective, they do not measure potential working capacity. The ability to process more complex information, apply that information to problem-solving situations, and synthesize that information into one's decision making and planning is what potential assessment is all about. In other words, a person could have substantial additional potential yet lack specific skills and knowledge or previous experience to perform a specific type of work.

To facilitate achieving a valid assessment, it is useful to base one's judgment on whether a given individual is perceived to be capable of handling the complexity of work normally found at a specific organizational layer. Thus, knowledge of a baseline description of the key characteristics of work that applies at a given organizational layer should prove useful in making a valid assessment. For example, suppose a level IV manager was being asked to judge whether individual A, currently functioning in a level II job, had the potential to work at organizational level III. Figure 8.4 lists the key characteristics of work normally found at level III. Recall that the essence of rendering such a judgment is for the level IV manager to decide whether she feels that individual A can get his arms around the work normally found at level III (described in Figures 8.4 and 8.5).

Step I: Preparing for the Assessment

Prior to making an actual assessment, the MoR has some homework to do. First, she must gather essential data regarding the individual's current performance such as the performance review, ratings, surveys (customer and employee/subordinate), and key result areas (sales, margin, complaints, etc.), anything the company currently uses to measure the output of the role. Second, the MoR needs to solicit input from the immediate manager regarding the SoR's current performance (if the MoR doesn't already have this information). This information should center on how well the SoR is performing in his current job. Generally, most managers are well aware of how each of their subordinates are performing and will have no trouble answering the following question:

Nature of Work by Organizational Layer (Level III)

General Description:
Manager-of-managers; Manager of Mutual Recognition Units (200-250 employees); senior or chief engineers, staff specialists, lawyers or doctors capable of operating independently

Task Complexity	Information Complexity	Resources	Planning & Decision Making	Problems
• Pathway goals and plans must be developed	• Serial processing, adopt a linear approach to arguments	• Look across and synchronize multiple unit budgets	• Switch to alternative pathway as required	• Anticipate obstacles
• Tasks not clear	• Manage abstract concepts	• Archive CI goals	• Probability analysis	• Ask "what-if" questions
• Methods and procedures not fully developed	• Identify patterns in actual performance	• Integrate people, materiel and financial resources within context of a unified sub-system	• Risk analysis	• Develop options to overcome potential problems
• Develop a set of options to achieve goals	• String data together to extrapolate likely conclusion			
• Design key processes to accomplish objectives	• Resolve information overload by filtering data			

★ The individual works out a plan (with pathway) to accomplish a goal, conducts what-if scenarios, assesses risk and probability of alternative scenarios, develops pre-planned alternative paths to, switch to as required.

8.4

Principle #4: Assess the Working Capability of a Person

Nature of Work by Organizational Layer (Level III)

General Description:
Manager-of-managers; Manager of Mutual Recognition Units (200-250 employees); senior or chief engineers, staff specialists, lawyers or doctors capable of operating independently

Leadership	Relation ships	Time Horizon	Staff Work
• Provide unit level (MRU) Leadership	• Manage contacts at regional or corporate level	• 1 - 2 years	• Plan organizational changes in work-flow
• Establish project teams	• High level selling		• Plan for changing personnel requirements
• Last level of direct management /tactical leadership	• Collaborate with colleagues		• Maintain contact with corporate HR staff
• Create a supportive work environment	• Negotiate agreements with customers, suppliers and unions		• Specification of methods for filling orders
• Integrate output of multiple subordinate units			• Cost analysis of different methods
			• Modification of methods
			• Coordinates the production flow between units, supplies, production and services

﹡ The individual works out a plan (with pathway) to accomplish a goal, conducts what-if scenarios, assesses risk and probability of alternative scenarios, develops pre-planned alternative paths to, switch to as required.

8.5

It's All About Work

Is individual A (the SoR) experiencing trouble in his current job? ____Yes _____No

If the immediate manager's answer is no, the MoR should proceed to step II. If the answer is yes, the individual is having trouble, then the MoR needs to validate such an assessment. This validation can be done in one of several ways. First, the MoR can ask the immediate manager the following probe questions:

a. Does the SoR have trouble getting tasks done on time?

b. Does the SoR come back for help a lot?

c. Does the SoR ask a lot of questions?

Second the MoR can review critical information gathered during her career-development discussions with the SoR:

a. Does the SoR have upward aspirations? Does he feel he could handle more complex work?

b. Is the SoR aware of the immediate manager's assessment that there are or are not performance problems?

c. Has coaching or training taken place?

Third, the MoR needs to analyze the immediate manager's performance assessment pattern.

a. Do the assessments fit into a tough or easy pattern?

b. How do the immediate manager's assessments compare with his colleagues assessments?

c. Is there any evidence of personal bias because of the SoR's age, sex, prior experience, or education?

Having processed the above information, the MoR is now in a better position to evaluate the accuracy of the immediate manager's original assessment: yes or no, the SoR is having trouble in his current job. If the

MoR concludes that the SoR is not having trouble in his current role, then the MoR has to decide if there truly is a performance problem, a leadership shortfall, or a job fit issue. Once this decision is made, the MoR should then proceed to step II in the assessment process.

Step II: The Potential Assessment Process

As described previously, the biggest problem with trying to assess an individual's working capacity is that most assessors get hung up on the more tangible work-related factors such as previous experience and skill or knowledge sets. Thus, the assessor tends to view a given individual from a relatively narrow perspective. Such a view often results in an assessment that limits an individual's potential to a narrow, single-functional area. It is almost impossible to get a manager's rendering of an assessment to avoid this natural bias. There are, however, several techniques to help the manager avoid such a limited view. The first technique is to pose the following questions:

1. If the individual had several more years of experience working in this area, could she take on a bigger role or operate at the next higher level?

2. Suppose the individual had a modicum of skill training in the new area; could she successfully work in that area?

    a. In a cross functional move to the same level?

    b. Actually take on a bigger role?

A second technique that is useful in assessing future working capacity is to attempt to view the assessed individual further out into the future. For example, could person X ever fill your job (MoR two levels up)? Trying to view the individual in this light often brings her long-term potential into better prospective. The assessment of working capacity and future working potential is a significant part of the broader field of talent pool management. It is not the intent of this book to thoroughly cover this topic. (The authors have developed separate assessment instruments tailored specifically for large and small businesses to assist them in the assessment process.)

The following questions can assist an MoR in making his assessment. Each question requires the higher-level manager to exercise judgment in making his assessment. The questions relate to specific work characteristics found at a given organizational layer. Each topical area also contains a descriptive listing of specific properties and key elements inherent in each work category or area. This work description, in essence, becomes the baseline criteria for a given assessment.

It is important to note that any assessment of potential is a judgment call on the part of the MoR. Rather than shy away from rendering a judgment, the MoR is instead encouraged to do so. At the heart of the judgment is whether the MoR believes the SoR could actually do the work apropos to a given organizational layer. The MoR will have to work hard to avoid being biased by an SoR's lack of training (skills and knowledge) or experience for a given type of work. He needs to keep in mind this question: "If the SoR had this training or experience, could she get her arms around this work and perform it effectively?"

A key characteristic of high-potential individuals is that they are generally fast learners. As such, they can be expected to pick up whatever specifics they need rapidly. An MoR's inability to suspend his natural bias toward skill, knowledge, or experience generally leads to underassessments of potential. If an MoR prefers to be overly cautious in the assessment process to avoid either an under- or overassessment, he can always utilize special project work at the immediate manager's level to test out his assessment before making it final.

These questions relate directly to the level III work described in Figures 8.4 and 8.5. Note that the questions flow naturally from each broad category contained in Figures 8.4 and 8.5. The rationale for using Figures 8.4 and 8.5 is that it describes work categories normally associated with an individual operating at level III. This work description in essence becomes the baseline criteria for a given assessment.

Principle #4: Assess the Working Capability of a Person

Potential Questions: Level III Readiness (Currently in Level II Role)

1. **TASK COMPLEXITY:** Tax complexity is what-by-when. This is an assignment to produce a specified output, including quality and quantity, within a targeted completion time, within allocated resources and methods, and within prescribed limits (policies, rules, procedures). The output is the target or goal.

   The MoR must ask, Can you envision the SoR carrying out the following work?
   - Conducting operational reviews (production operations, sales operations, marketing analysis)
   - Designing or improving key processes to achieve objectives
   - Coping with tasks that are not completely specified and that might need interpretation (improving customer relations, improving quality indicators)
   - Achieving continuous improvement goals (e.g. 5 percent target improvement)
   - Producing a competitive analysis of key market players operating in a given area

2. **INFORMATION COMPLEXITY:** Information complexity involves aggregating data to solve problems and make decisions.
   - Does the SoR appear to have up-to-date situational awareness of critical facts affecting her business area?
   - Can the SoR string data together into a linear line of argument?
   - Has the SoR successfully accumulated data and identi-

fied trends?

- Has the SoR taken preemptive action to avoid obstacles?

3. **RESOURCE COMPLEXITY:** Resource complexity is the allocation and use of resources, tools, dollars, and time to accomplish a goal.

    - Do you see the SoR synchronizing multiple individual budgets?

    - Can the SoR utilize specialist knowledge appropriately?

    - Can you envision the SoR implementing and achieving continuous improvement practices?

4. **PLANNING AND DECISION-MAKING COMPLEXITY:** Planning and decision-making complexity is making a choice by using discretion and judgment for the commitment of resources.

    - Can you see the SoR constructing a plan to accomplish assigned goals?

    - Would you expect the plan to contain two or more options to handle possible contingencies (emerging obstacles, etc)?

    - Would the options be sufficiently thought out and detailed enough to achieve the plan's goals or would they likely be a simple afterthought?

    - Has the SoR shown any evidence of switching to alternative pathways when conditions require it?

    - Does the SoR argue her point by constructing a linear series of events with one leading to the next?

    - Does the SoR diagnose problems as part of decision making?

Principle #4: Assess the Working Capability of a Person

5. **PROBLEM-SOLVING COMPLEXITY**: Problem-solving complexity is the ability of an individual to handle complexity in solving problems.

    - Think of the typical problems that can occur at level III: for example, a plan disintegrates because of unforeseen circumstances, competitive action disrupts current plans, or new federal statutes require adjustments. Has the SoR asked himself what-if anticipatory questions?

    - Doe the SoR have an alternative course of action should unforeseen problems emerge?

    - Can the SoR do risk and probability analyses?

6. **LEADERSHIP COMPLEXITY**: Leadership complexity involves leading a group of subordinate units or leading a staff section.

    - Has the SoR successfully led a small operating unit or project team or served as a front-line leader?

    - Can the SoR successfully integrate the output of multiple subordinate units?

    - Does the SoR show evidence of being able to create a supportive work environment?

    - Has the SoR successfully established project teams?

    - Has the SoR demonstrated persuasive capabilities?

7. **WORKING RELATIONSHIP COMPLEXITY**: Working relationship complexity is how people work together in any organizational setting. These working relationships contain the volatile ingredients of interacting accountabilities

and authorities. Working relationships are both internal to the organization and external (customers, suppliers, etc.).

- Has the SoR demonstrated a capacity to function collaboratively with teammates on other teams or in other departments?

- Does the SoR demonstrate success in working on multiple teams?

- Does the SoR work effectively with corporate staff and outside key influentials (vendors, community leaders, customers, unions, etc)?

- Can the SoR negotiate agreements with customers, suppliers, unions, and the like?

8. **TIME HORIZON AND TIME SPAN:** Time horizon or time span is the level of work as measured by those tasks in the role with the longest maximum target completion times.

- Does the SoR envision key events and issues expanding from one to two years?

- Does the SoR currently have any tasks with a target completion time of one to two years?

- Time Compression: For individuals operating in a time compressed environment, SoR can envision and understand downstream consequences and impact out to 1 year and beyond?.

These questions are meant as examples for assessing the current capacity of an individual occupying a level II role. Assessment questions for higher or lower levels will be different. For more information, consult our website: www.organizational.com.

Career Development

Once you have completed the assessment of an individual's cognitive capacity, you must then make plans for what to do with this data. If the individual shows evidence of capacity to work at the next higher level, then what does the organization do next? The MoR and immediate manager must then look at the other components of working capability to decide if a development program is needed. For example, if the SoR does not have the necessary skills or knowledge, what is the training plan to assist her in gaining these attributes? If she is short on wisdom, how does the organization put her in positions or roles to gain experience and, subsequently, wisdom? We believe that skills, knowledge, and wisdom can all be part of employee development programs.

Every organization must devise a carefully thought out strategy that properly emphasizes and matches career development needs with future organizational requirements. In most organizations, such a process is generally referred to as *succession planning*. Too often, however, the process boils down to a few lucky individuals being taken under the wings of a senior executive who takes it upon himself to look after their careers. Such arrangements are fine for the lucky few, but what about the rest of a corporation's human resources? Are they left simply to fend for themselves? If so, then such organizations must be willing to accept potentially adverse consequences in individual behavior and morale.

In the absence of a planned strategy that involves all individuals within a company, an unplanned strategy is likely to emerge, which generally involves everyone looking out for themselves. This type of approach can rapidly deteriorate into an operating philosophy of careerism, as opposed to professionalism. Careerists tend to look out for themselves and shape their behavior appropriately, while professionals tend to do what is right, irrespective of personal consequences. A process that results in individuals focusing unduly on their own individual needs is likely to be at odds with and undermine the development of a more desirable set of corporate values. Thus, every corporation needs a planned strategy to ensure that all of its people are afforded the opportunity to "sit on a log" with a superior to discuss their careers, their continued growth in wisdom and experience, and their future in the enterprise.

These types of discussions form the basis of any successful career-development and succession-planning process. The organizational role best suited to take up this accountability is the MoR for two very simple reasons. First, it is the MoR, not the immediate manager, human resource manager, or HR team, who needs to be held accountable for succession-planning efforts. Second, it is the MoR, not the immediate manager, who is far enough removed from the SoR in terms of capability and experience to be able to meaningfully discuss the SoR's current potential and likely future career contributions. Every corporation's HR development strategy must firmly root this accountability in the MoR role. Here is a definition of the terms:

Mentoring

The term *mentoring* has become commonplace within the management field, but perhaps no concept has been so widely used yet so universally misunderstood.

> **MENTORING:** Mentoring is the process by which one individual (the MoR) helps another individual (the SoR) (1) to understand his work-related potential and how that potential could be maximized within the organization and (2) to grow in wisdom, good judgment, skills and knowledge, and temperament.[101]

Thus, mentoring offers the potential of achieving some real developmental benefits for a company.

Mentoring, if done right, is not a process that can be taken lightly, one that takes place if and when an MoR finds time. SoR development is too important to both the SoR and the company to be left to chance. Carrying out these accountabilities takes management time and must be done in earnest to be effective. Yet, managers need to be cautious that they do not establish unrealistic expectations within subordinates or promise development opportunities that cannot be delivered.

As an example, we believe that companies spend far too much time

---

101 Jaques, Elliott and Clement, Stephen D. Executive Leadership, Cason Hall Publishers: Arlington, VA, 1989. Page 89.

Principle #4: Assess the Working Capability of a Person

trying to change values and temperament. Unless you are a psychiatrist or mental health specialist, we think organizations should stay out of their people's heads. However, we believe leadership can influence (but not change!) behaviors in terms of bringing those personality traits within *reasonable limits* so they do not prevent work from getting done.

Let us take, as an example, our introspective person from earlier. Recall that this person was extremely introspective, almost to the point of indecisiveness. This personality trait exceeded the limits of reasonable behavior for this individual, even though the role itself may have needed a certain amount of introspection, such as a financial analyst role. It is the role of this individual's immediate manager to coach the SoR in getting this behavior back within acceptable limits. It is the role of the MoR, in acting as a mentor, to assist the SoR in adjusting her behavior over the long-term. The key point here is that it is incumbent on leadership to bring a subordinate's dysfunctional personality traits within limits but not to try and change the subordinate into something she is not. The aforementioned discussions are central to the following talent pool management process.

Talent Pool Management

> TALENT POOL: Career development and mentoring together feed a company's talent pool management system.

> TALENT POOL MANAGEMENT: The design and implementation of a talent pool management system identifies, assesses, and develops a sufficient pool of people capable of filling key managerial positions

Talent pool management in many companies is limited to succession planning. While succession planning is indeed dependent upon an effective potential assessment process, its integration into a comprehensive talent pool management system is a far more complex undertaking. True talent pool management requires that a company have in place a system that periodically matches future work requirements against existing workforce capabilities. Management development programs then become a key strategy for closing existing gaps or voids. An effective talent pool system must include all members of the workforce and focus on the larger needs of the company as a whole.

Because of the steady increase in work-related complexity, we believe that the current paradigm of succession planning is outdated. Tomorrow's replacements need to be better than today's role incumbents. Thus, we have chosen a new term to replace succession planning. The new term is *surpassion planning*.

> **SURPASSION PLANNING:** Surpassion planning is a succession planning system whose primary goal is to fill future open positions with individuals who have *greater capability and capacity than current incumbents.* [102]

Tomorrow's replacements have to be able to surpass today's incumbents. They must be better and capable of not just filling existing shoes but bringing bigger shoes to the equation. The importance of this topic to the assessment process should not be underestimated. (This subject is also discussed in greater detail in related follow-on training materials.)

These three outcomes—career development, mentoring, and talent pool management—of assessing capability and the role of the MoR require an entire book unto themselves. The people part of work is far too important to simply be tucked into a brief book aimed at addressing organizational structural problems. Look for more on this topic in future publications.

---

[102] From personal conversations with Michael Allen, former president of the Michael Allen Company, 1998.

Chapter 9

Principle #5: Provide Effective Managerial Leadership

Improving leadership in an organization is often seen as a crucial step in improving overall productivity levels. Thus, many companies spend considerable time and effort seeking the one sure pathway to improving leadership effectiveness. In their quest, they run into many purveyors of leadership programs that supposedly will meet their needs. As described in the opening chapter, however, many companies are unsuccessful in this endeavor. As it turns out, there is no single straightforward leadership development program that will produce lasting success, despite what the training community might argue. As will be shown, there are several preconditions that must be addressed first: for example, the correct organizational structure, clear accountability and authority, and the like. Once these preconditions are met, it is then up to the individual to carry out her role accountabilities to their fullest capacity. It is our contention that everyone can become a more effective leader with practice, so long as the necessary preconditions exist within the workplace environment.

Figure 9.1 depicts six key steps necessary for building and sustaining an effective leadership program that adds unique value at successive organizational layers. In Figure 9.1, note how values and culture permeate the development of an effective organizational structure, including the key underlying management systems and processes that operate in that structure and the overall quality of leadership at all levels.

But structure itself is only the first step in a larger process underpinning effective leadership. For structure to survive over the long haul, key organizational systems must reinforce and support it. As shown in figure 9.1, there are three distinctly different kinds of leadership that must occur in the company: direct (face-to-face or tactical), operational, and strategic (organizational). These three different types of leadership are not mutually exclusive. Interestingly, as an individual progresses up the organizational hierarchy, he must add additional leadership tasks to his workload. Thus, senior executives must exercise competent direct leadership with their immediate team, effective operational leadership with their operating units, and, finally, at the topmost levels, strategic (organizational) leadership with their whole organization. These concepts form the backdrop for the following discussion.

Direct Leadership (Face-to-Face or Tactical)

Good leadership is one of the most valued of all human skill sets. To be known as a good leader is a much sought after accolade.[103] It signifies the capability to bring people together, to get them to work with one another as an effective team, to cooperate and trust one another, and to rely upon each other as they strive toward accomplishing a common enterprise goal. The exercise of effective leadership is central to the long-term success of any organizational entity. Competent leaders deal daily with rapidly changing situations, high degrees of uncertainty, and steadily increasing complexity. How well they handle these challenges is central to the financial and operational success of any enterprise. Thus, it should come as no surprise that organizational effectiveness is a primary outcome of good leadership.

---

[103] Jaques, Elliott and Clement, Stephen D. Executive Leadership, Cason Hall Publishers: Arlington, VA, 1991. Page 3.

Principle #5: Provide Effective Managerial Leadership

Six Steps to Sound Organization and Leadership

"The Integrator" — CEO

- Mission & Functions
- Values
- Functional Alignment
- Culture
- Organizational Structure
- Information Planning & Control Systems
- Human Resources Sub-systems
- Leadership → Organization/Team Performance

STRATEGIC LEADERSHIP
- CEO — VII
- EVP — VI

OPERATIONAL LEADERSHIP
- GM / BU PRES — V
- VP / PROG MGR — IV

DIRECT LEADERSHIP
- PROJECT MANAGER DIRECTOR — III
- ENGINEER / MANAGER — II
- SPECIALIST — I

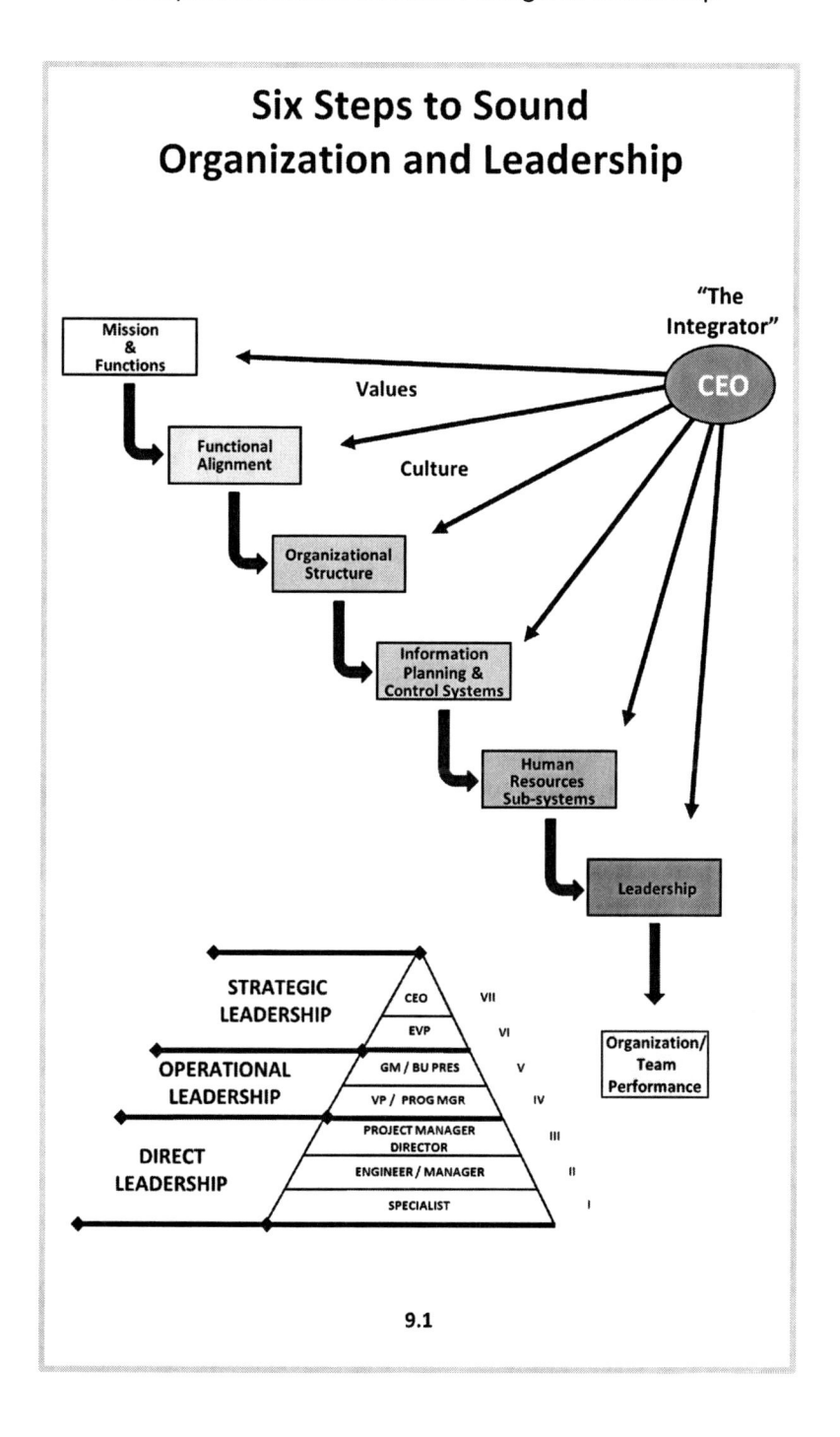

9.1

The cost of good leadership, however, is not free. It requires a substantial investment of management time to achieve desired outcomes. This time demand cannot be ignored because if sufficient time isn't devoted to the process, subordinates will likely feel that they are being used rather than being led. It is the nature and extent of these time demands that pose the real challenge to aspiring leaders, especially in today's hectic and frenzied work environment. Later, we will discuss the application of specially designed leadership arithmetic equations to address calculating the exact nature of leadership time demands.

Historical Perspective:

Good leadership has also always been seen as one of the most mysterious of human activities. Over the years, a number of separate and distinct views of the leadership process have emerged. One view was wrapped up in the notion of personality and charisma. According to this view, some individuals have been graced with divinely bestowed magnetism and talent that enables them—almost magically it would seem—to win the staunch devotion of others and to get them to work together. Such a view is discouraging because it fixes upon the notion that if you are born with only a limited amount of God-given leadership personality then you must rest content with giving only a limited amount of leadership in your lifetime.[104]

A second view suggests that some leaders are better suited for one situation than for another. While there is a kernel of truth in such a view, it is simply impractical if you happen to find yourself in a difficult situation to throw up your hands and walk away from the problem. When difficult challenges occur on the job, most individuals can't simply turn their backs and avoid the issue. The reality is that it is not the situation that is important but rather the fact that different situations encompass different role requirements. And, as will be shown, role competence is absolutely fundamental to the practice of effective leadership.

Third, there is a view that leaders need only focus on accomplishing assigned missions while simultaneously taking care of those individuals who happen to be involved in the process. It is hard to argue with this

---

[104] Ibid.

Principle #5: Provide Effective Managerial Leadership

recipe, but it doesn't really tell you much. The real challenges are how you go about accomplishing the mission and what do you do to take care of your people. In some situations, you have to be tough on your people to ensure that assigned goals and objectives are accomplished, while, at other times, there is ample room for considering individual needs, especially as they potentially affect the work situation.

Finally, there is a view that effective leadership is dependent on the mastery of a basic set of interpersonal skills. Proponents of this view espouse the value of skill training to the leadership process. By improving one's communication skills, it is argued that improvement in leadership will follow. This latter approach is not necessarily wrong, especially as it pertains to face-to-face leadership situations; however, not all leaders operate in such situations. Those individuals assigned to operational leadership roles, for example, are likely to find that they would be better served by mastering project management skills and practices (e.g., Lean Six Sigma training) rather than communication skills.[105]

To fully reconcile the above varying leadership views requires that one first understand and apply the following two basic organizational principles. The first principle acknowledges the fact that the concept of leadership has rarely been defined with any precision. Thus, some of the mystery surrounding the leadership concept can be attributed to varying definitions that permeate the literature. In his seminal work on the subject, noted leadership researcher Ralph Stogdill devoted an entire chapter to these varying definitions.[106] To alleviate the confusion caused by the wide variety and focus of these definitions, we adhere to the following definition:

> **LEADERSHIP** is that process in which one person sets the purpose or direction for one or more other persons and gets them to move along together with him or her and with each other in that direction while exercising their full individual competence, innovation, and commitment.[107]

---

105 Clement SD and Ayres DB, Leadership Monograph Series #8, A matrix organizational leadership dimension, US Army Administration Center: Ft Harrison, IN, 1976

106 Ralph Stodgill, Handbook of Leadership, Free Press, 1974

107 Jaques, Elliott and Clement, Stephen D. Executive Leadership, Cason Hall Publishers: Arlington, VA, 1991. Page 4.

This definition of leadership as a process is intended to express what leadership is about. It is not intended to describe how one goes about the process of achieving it or the mental characteristics and organizational conditions necessary for doing so. The second organizational principle, taken from the field of sociology, is that leadership is not a free-standing activity; it is one function, among many, that occurs in some but not all roles. As discussed earlier, roles contain specific properties such as accountabilities and authorities. These properties set the work context within which all individual behavior takes place. The proposition that leadership is associated with some roles in a social structure is important because it permits us to offer the following thesis: "Everyone is capable of exercising effective leadership in roles that carry leadership accountability, so long as they value the role and are competent to carry the basic requirements of that role, and so long as that role is properly structured and the organization has properly instituted leadership practices."[108]

The idea that leadership is a property associated with some roles but not others is significant because it permits one to get away from the concept of leadership as a stand-alone activity. One can then view leadership in the context of the existing social structure. Very few individuals in modern society exist totally apart from social structure. Nearly all of us work or play in organizational entities: business or government structures, church or social groups, family structures, and the like. Given our definition of leadership and our proposition that the practice of leadership is a property of specific role interactions in today's widely varying world of social structure, we believe that all managerial roles, parental roles, clerical roles, and political roles carry with them leadership accountabilities.

Perhaps the most important hypothesis that we shall offer is the following: The ability to exercise leadership is not some great "charismystery" but is, rather, an ordinary quality found in every person so long as the following two foundational conditions exist: organizational conditions for effective leadership and psychological conditions for effective leadership.[109]

---

108 Ibid. Page 44.
109 Ibid. Page 25–26.

Principle #5: Provide Effective Managerial Leadership

Organizational Conditions of Leadership:

This is the first key precondition of effective leadership. Requisite organizational structure is the absolute foundation for effective leadership. For example, clearly structured organizations are essential for managers at every echelon to be able to focus on value-adding work sufficient to accomplish a given mission. This dependence on organization is why the military has been intensely preoccupied with continual experimentation in organizational design from the times of the very earliest and greatest armies. Further, planning, information gathering (intelligence), communication, developing clear operational orders, and conducting regular follow-up reviews must be perfected to the nth degree for combat. Thus, the emphasis in the military lies upon the competent commander working in a sound organizational structure.

Psychological Conditions of Leadership:

The major psychological condition in managerial leadership roles is an individual's personal capability to exercise the functions and duties of the managerial role. If a manager cannot competently discharge all the functions of her role (i.e., cannot do her *own* work), then she does not stand a ghost of a chance of exercising effective leadership in relation to others because it is very unlikely those others will have confidence in her.[110] In the military, this translates into tactical and technical proficiency. If the military leader is not functionally competent, subordinates will be reluctant to follow him because they fear he might fail as a result of an inadequate operational plan. (In the army, inadequate plans could actually lead to death!) In industry, role competence encompasses the ability to carry out the technical aspects of one's role, be it an engineering role or a marketing one. How effective do you think an individual would be if he had *all* of the attributes from *all* of the leadership how-to books and yet was unable to solve the problems and challenges of his own role? Effective leadership starts with one's *own* work.

The other psychological condition relevant to managerial leadership roles is the ability to gain personally earned trust and respect from

---

[110] Ibid., page 42.

others.[111] To gain this trust and respect is mainly a matter of sensible and consistent application of requisite practices in how one goes about discharging the specific accountabilities of one's role, such as assigning tasks, conducting performance reviews, coaching and mentoring, and so forth.

Recall that working capacity is a necessary but not sufficient condition for getting work done. Just because an individual has the capacity to get her arms around the work inherent in a given role does not necessarily mean she will be successful in doing that work. She may not value such work and hence not put her heart and soul into it. She can do it, but she does not value it. Alternatively, even though one values the work of a role, if she does not have the innate capacity to handle the complexity of the work, she will not be able to get the work done efficiently or effectively, no matter how hard she tries.

Unfortunately, the leadership community has placed far too much emphasis on personality attributes and skill development than they have on the other key variables that affect role competence. While personality and skills are important variables in the working capability equation, they are, by themselves, insufficient to the overall process. Sometimes organizations subject their managers to personality assessment tests and classify them as introverted, extroverted, and so forth (e.g., Myers-Briggs testing). They then try to complement their personality styles with similar styles on their team. All of this has led to substantial investments in trying to make people and teams into someone that they are not.

Leadership is first and foremost a key role accountability. Some roles carry this accountability and some do not (independent contributor roles). All managerial roles carry leadership accountability. Recall that accountabilities are those aspects of a role that dictate the things that the occupant is required to do by virtue of being in the role. Accountabilities cannot be separated from authorities in a properly structured organization. Authorities are those aspects of a role that enable the person in the role to act legitimately in order to carry out the accountabilities with which he or she has been charged. To discharge accountabilities, a person in a role must have appropriate authority; that is, he must have the authority with respect to the use of materials and financial resources as

---

111 Ibid.

well as the authority with respect to other people, making it reasonably possible to do what is expected of him. (See the earlier discussion of the minimum authorities of a manager in Chapter 6)

As described previously, however, role-vested authority by itself will likely only achieve minimally compliant behavior. To inspire subordinates to work to their full potential in a committed and enthusiastic manner requires reliance on personally earned authority. This is the authority base the leader earns as a result of how she actually treats subordinates. Effective leaders treat their subordinates with respect and dignity, even though they may demand tough standards. Winning the respect of one's team is a crucial step in the leadership process. (For more details, see the section on personally earned authority in chapter 6.) Unfortunately, the price tag for achieving personally earned authority is management time. Hence, time is the Achilles heel of exercising effective leadership.

Direct (Tactical) Leadership (Front-Line Levels I-III):

Direct (tactical) leadership encompasses the first three levels in an organization. This is the level in which leadership is practiced face-to-face. Crucial to the success of any enterprise is the efficiency and effectiveness of the front-line operating units. The bulk of the people employed in an organization work in the first three organizational levels where products and services are designed, manufactured, and distributed. The first three levels of an organization encompass the majority of customer-facing activities that occur in most enterprises.

The clarity of roles that exist at these levels and the corresponding enthusiasm that incumbents apply to their work each day are critical to the long-term success of the enterprise. If the individuals who work at these levels in the organization perform their work effectively, then the total organization is likely to be an effective competitor. Only in this way can the strategic direction formulated by top management have any chance of successful implementation. By contrast, if deficiencies exist in the leadership of the front-line organization, the competitive performance of the company is likely to be in doubt, and long-term trouble is not likely to be far away.

Front-line leadership is where the leadership process takes on an aura of personal interaction between the leader and his followers. This is the level where the leader has personal knowledge of all his people This knowledge extends to detailed information about a subordinate's personal situation, her family needs, and other personal issues that are likely to affect her sense of personal drive and motivation. Jaques called this organizational setting a "mutual knowledge unit." The leader has firsthand knowledge about those central personal factors that could affect a subordinate's behavior in a given situation.[112]

The mutual knowledge unit (MKU) is the basic front-line management structure (see Figure 9.2). As shown, it contains the first-line manager (FLM) and his or her subordinates. The number of subordinates that a first-line manager can effectively get to know in a personal sense is limited. If everyone is doing essentially the same job (level I roles), then a first-line manager can handle up to sixty individuals.

In a practical sense, sixty people is the maximum number that a given person can get to know in-depth to be able to sensitively react to their personal needs and their families' constantly changing needs. If the workforce is operating on multiple shifts or at multiple site locations, then the front-line manger (FLM) may need a supervisor to assist him in doing his job.[113]

Figure 9.3 depicts the nature of how this supervisory role applies to the first-line level. Note that the supervisor assists the FLM in carrying out his managerial accountabilities. The supervisor is not the immediate manager and should not be seen as such. The supervisor is not a layer: she is essentially straddling two levels with the role of assisting the manager in getting his work done.

The practice of effective leadership at the front-line level requires that individual employees perform essential tasks on time and to appropriate standards, cope effectively with typical problems encountered at the front-line level, and process critical information in a timely and responsive manner. A key challenge facing the front-line leader is to not only deal with the workforce individually but to also build and sustain high-performing

---

112 Jaques, Elliott. Requisite Organization, Cason Hall Publishers: Arlington, VA, 1996. Page pair 91.

113 Jaques, Elliott and Clement, Stephen D. Executive Leadership, Cason Hall Publishers: Arlington, VA, 1991. Page 126.

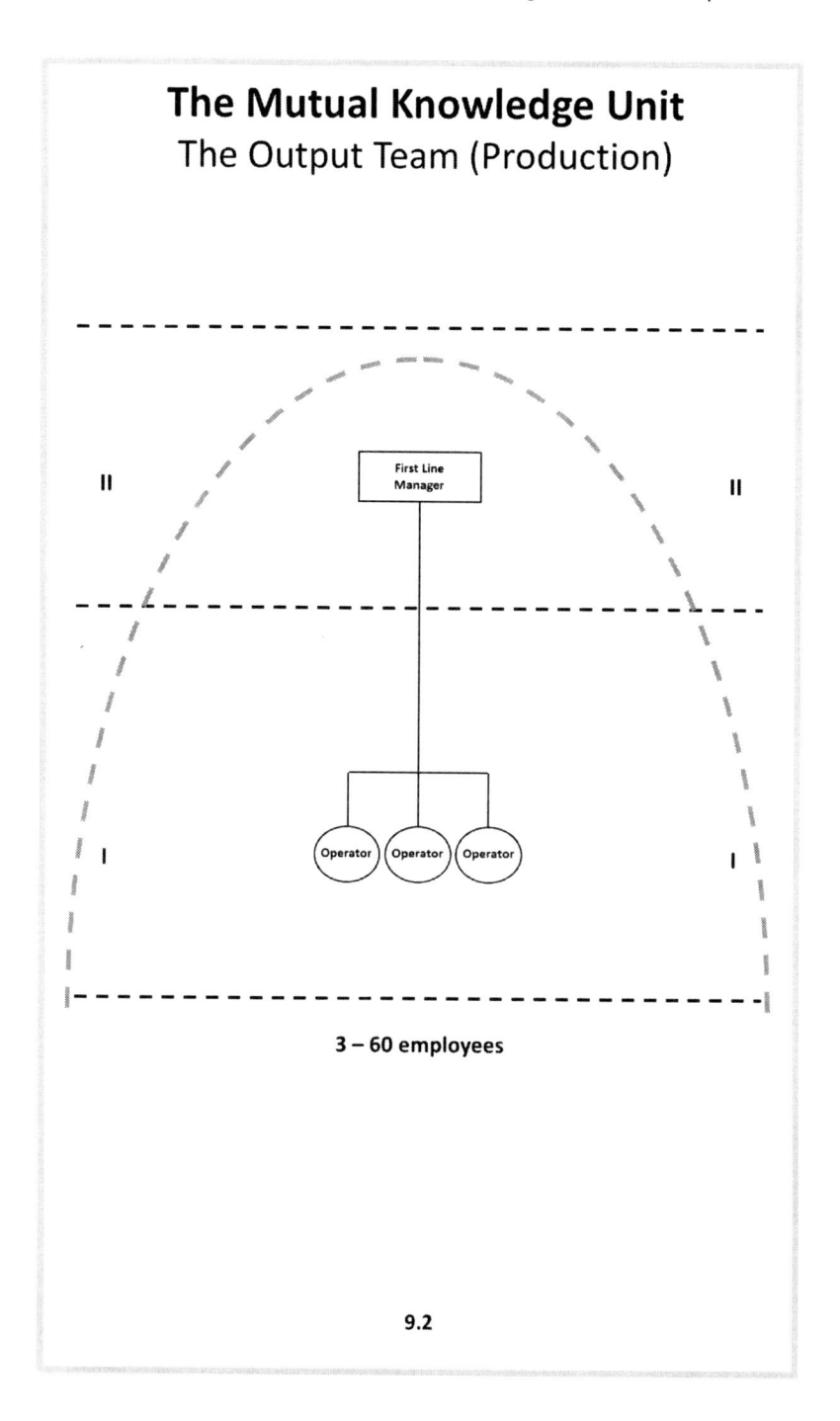

Principle #5: Provide Effective Managerial Leadership

The Mutual Knowledge Unit
The Output Team (Production)

First Line Manager

Operator Operator Operator

3 – 60 employees

9.2

Supervisor Accountability and Authority

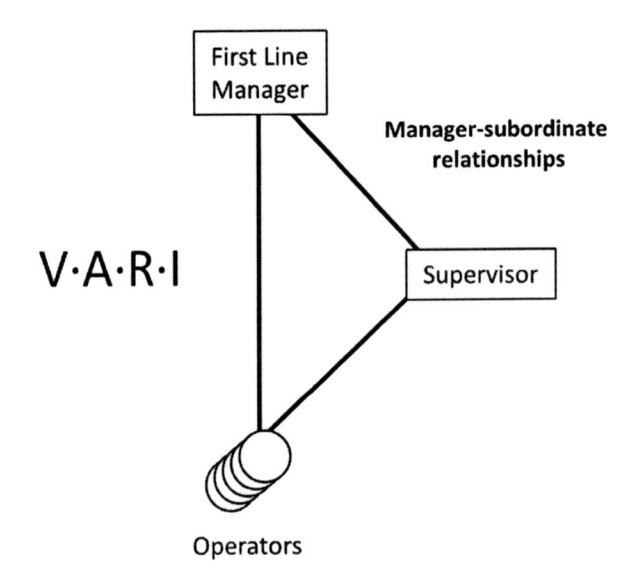

V·A·R·I

First Line Manager

Supervisor

Manager-subordinate relationships

Operators

1. Does not have accountability for the decision on Veto of selection or Initiation of removal (no V and I)

2. He/she does have accountability for work assignment (A), technical, scheduling & leadership task within the range of authority designated by the first line manager. Has the authority to reward (R) and discipline within prescribed limits.

3. Does not change the manager-subordinate relationship between FLM and his operators

9.3

Principle #5: Provide Effective Managerial Leadership

output teams. Thus, teamworking is also an essential competency of the front-line leader. Somehow he must integrate individuals into teams without destroying or suppressing individual creativity. This skill set requires the front-line leader to thoroughly understand the psychological dynamics underpinning individual and team behavior. The judicious application of a basic set of leadership practices encompassing skills such as task assignment, coaching, performance review, applying rewards and punishment, induction, and teamworking are essential to achieving and improving front-line operational effectiveness.

At level III, the basic production unit, it is impossible for the leader to personally know all of her people in the same manner that she did as the front-line manager. What is possible, however, is that they all recognize one another as belonging to the same unit. Thus, this level is referred to as a mutual recognition unit (MRU).[114] The important point here is that the leader should personally know at least half of the people assigned to her unit and at least recognize the rest as belonging to the unit. There are some practical limitations that pertain to the MRU. The maximum number of people that should be assigned to an MRU is approximately 300 (level I roles).

Figure 9.4 depicts a typical MRU organization. Note that the MRU is ideally made up of four to six output teams. Each of these teams contains approximately thirty to sixty individuals, depending upon the complexity of the work inherent in their operational function. For example, one of these teams may be an analytical section while another may be a sales management team. Note also that the MRU is the first level where specialized experts are assigned, such as a process engineer or HR specialist. These specialists are colleagues of the output team leader but report directly to the MRU director. As stated previously, there is an interesting observation that can be made about the MRU. This unit is widely perceived by many leaders as their last "fun job." According to these individuals, this attribute is chosen because this is the last level where the manager actually feels in charge of events. For example, when she gives an order there is a concomitant expectation that the order will actually be followed. Above these levels, anonymity sets in, and leaders at the higher levels report that this sense of personal accountability and accomplishment are lacking.

---

114 Ibid. Page 128.

Mutual Recognition Unit

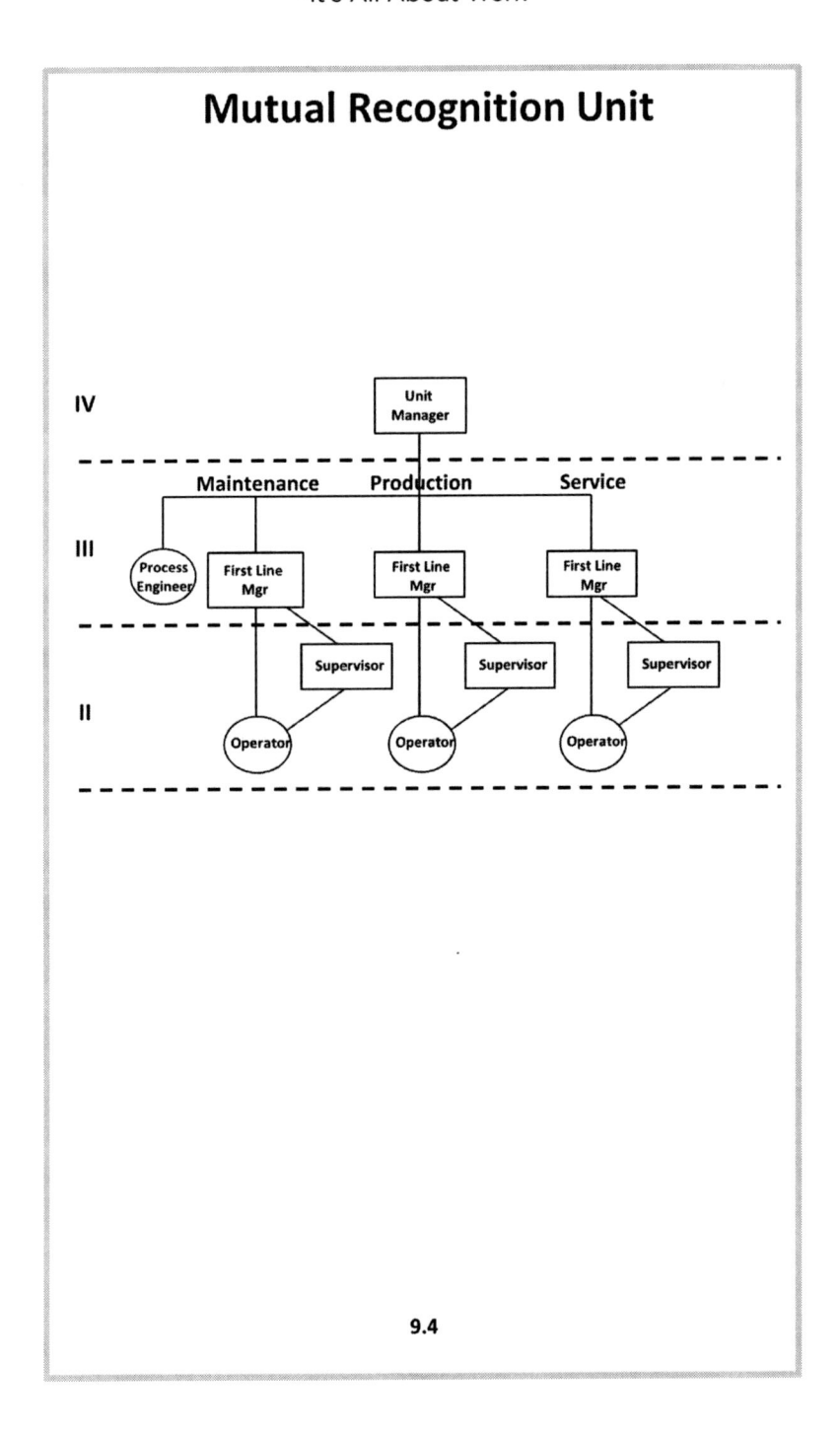

IV — Unit Manager

Maintenance   Production   Service

III — Process Engineer, First Line Mgr (Maintenance); First Line Mgr (Production); First Line Mgr (Service)

II — Supervisor, Operator (×3)

9.4

Operational Leadership:

Operational leadership begins to occur at levels IV and V. A leader at this level still retains all of the accountabilities and expectations of direct leadership for his immediate subordinates in addition to his operational leadership accountabilities. This is the level of the stand-alone operating unit (the division or brigade in the military and the business unit in industry) that contains all of the roles required for autonomous operations in the marketplace (or on the battlefield). This is also the level of many small businesses; however, many small business owners function at multiple levels. A small business owner may have a manager hat (level III) and an owner hat (level IV).

The level IV and V executives have three main concerns in running an effective operating unit. First, he must profitably meet customer and market needs. Second, the executive must ensure that supportive operating systems, processes and procedures are in place that facilitate getting work done efficiently and effectively. For example, the information system must provide the right information, in the right format, at the right time (i.e., timely system performance data). Third, the executive must provide the organizational leadership necessary to establish an operating environment that fosters individual creativity, innovation, and the commitment required to remain competitive.

Effective operational leadership is the process through which the activities of all key subordinate functional elements are directed, coordinated, and controlled in order to accomplish the assigned goals and objectives of the business unit. Key functional areas include the facilities, equipment, communication, operational procedures, and personnel essential to an executive for planning, directing, and controlling the operations of assigned subordinate business elements. These systems must be successfully integrated to support the executive's operating plan. For example, it does no good for the marketing department to develop new products or services if the company's distribution system cannot deliver them on time. Similarly, if the company is not a best in class leader in its core business functions—product design, quality, execution, and so on—then quality marketing and advertising methods are likely to be ineffective.

The executive cannot run a competitive operation alone. He must

- Rely on his staff and subordinate managers for advice and aid in planning and supervising operations

- Understand team and organization limits and capabilities

- Train his subordinate teams to execute the business plan in his absence

- Institute cross training among staff so the unit can continue to operate under difficult conditions

Because a key competency of an effective executive is to successfully integrate key business functions into a unified system, the management and leader development process must be reoriented from differentiation to synthesis and integration. True operational effectiveness is predicated on the assumption that the whole is greater than the sum of the parts.

The executive exercises operational leadership by attending to the business unit policies, rules and regulations, customs and practices, and values of the business unit climate. It is these control mechanisms that convey the most powerful messages about what is acceptable, even more so than any stated values could do. Social structure and organizational values must be consistent or people become confused and develop cynical attitudes toward the organization.

As described previously, sustaining a sound business unit organizational structure is a necessary foundation for organization leadership. For example, the procurement (buying) process is steadily increasing in internal complexity as a natural by-product of the increasing consolidation that is taking place in many industries throughout the world. As buying has become more sophisticated, so also must the sales process to keep abreast. To maintain effectiveness, the business unit must ensure that there is a proper match between the sales force and buyer in terms of their underlying capabilities. In other words, in consolidated markets, today's sales force must be capable of operating one or more organizational levels above those historically associated with the sales process. It is an accountability of the executive to ensure that the structure and underlying roles keep pace with changing industry demands.

There are two other aspects of operational leadership that come into

Principle #5: Provide Effective Managerial Leadership

play at levels IV and V in every organization. First, individuals operating at these levels need to instill and reflect a sense of enterprise thinking.

> **ENTERPRISE THINKING:** Enterprise thinking is taking into account the impact of impending decisions, directions, and plans on the entire company and the entire organization. Enterprise thinking should demonstrate knowledge of second order consequences on all other teams or organizations within the entire organization or company.

Thus, goals and objectives must be viewed from two very different perspectives: a business unit perspective (my team and organization) and an enterprise perspective (the entire company or organization). Sometimes the enterprise view must preempt local interests. Second, the operational leader needs to drive continuous improvement initiatives or projects as a routine practice and methodology for running her respective functional element (e.g., sales) or fully integrated business unit or departments.

Operational Leadership and the Manager-once-Removed:

Previously we discussed the role of the Manager-once-Removed in assessing the working capability of employees. However, the MoR has additional accountabilities that are crucial to being an effective operational leader. Once an organization's structure is correctly designed, it is then necessary to ensure that leaders at each operational level create a supportive leadership climate to reinforce a proper focus on goals and objectives. The immediate manger plays a central role in this effort at the lower organizational levels (the direct or tactical level). He does this by ensuring that goals and objectives are a routine part of the task-assignment process. At higher levels, however, this accountability falls on the shoulders of the MoR.

There are several other aspects of an MoR's role that profoundly affect the operational effectiveness of the company and the building of a climate of continuous improvement. First, the MoR must ensure the equitable allocation of resources across subordinate units.[115] This includes the scope and complexity of assigned work (tasks), financial resources,

---
115 Ibid. Page 256

and human resources and rewards. Each of these resources must be equitably applied across all of his operational units. Second, it is up to the MoR to ensure that his immediate manager is practicing effective leadership with her respective subordinates two levels lower in the organization. Third, the MoR must also assess the health of the leadership climate and culture of the team. And last, the MoR is personally accountable to facilitate three-level teamworking. This means an MoR must develop an effective working relationship with subordinates at these lower levels. Such a relationship must be handled with care so as to not usurp the immediate manager's accountabilities vis-à-vis these same subordinates.

A full-scale description of this role is beyond the scope of this book (such a description is a separate book in itself). Nonetheless, if the MoR role is clearly established, it would be possible to hand off some of the current centralized sign-off authorities to the MoR. In this way, the MoR would act as a bridge between the tactical level and the strategic level. For example, the MoR would maintain a semblance of management control over critical business decisions while simultaneously freeing up senior executives to concentrate on other tasks appropriate to their respective organizational levels. Thus, with an MoR role in place, not everything would have to go to the topmost levels for sign-off.

In summary, operational leaders wear three separate leadership hats. First, they continue to exercise face-to-face leadership of their immediate teams. Second, they function as MoRs in their respective functional areas. Finally, they implement operationally focused tasks designed to specifically improve the overall efficiency and effectiveness of their operating units, such as continuous improvement initiatives, project improvement work, and so on.

Strategic Leadership:

Strategic leadership accountability is the exercise of leadership accountability from one to many. The top tier of leadership in any company must be focused on running the enterprise as a whole. Strategic leaders, however, are still accountable to practice sound operational leadership and direct leadership. Strategic leadership appears at levels VI, VII, and VIII. At these levels, policies are formulated, vision and strategies are set, and the future direction of the enterprise is envisioned.

Principle #5: Provide Effective Managerial Leadership

The Manager – once – Removed Role

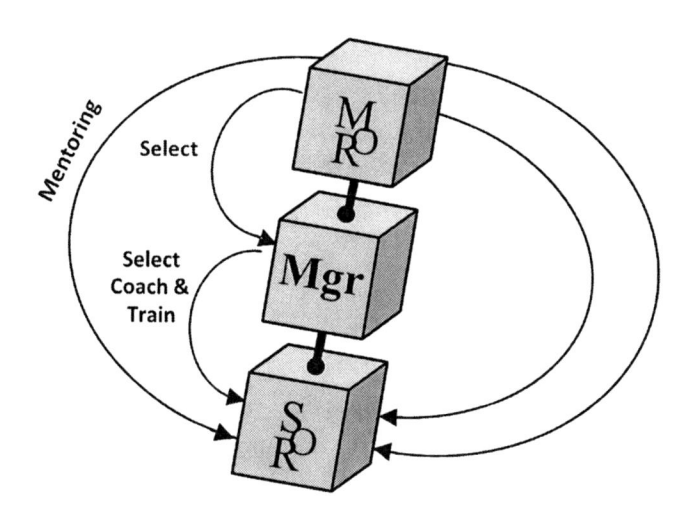

[Diagram: MoR, Mgr, SoR cubes with "Select" from MoR, "Select Coach & Train" from Mgr, and "Mentoring" loop around all]

- **Equitable allocation of resources**

- **Establish three level team working**

- **Establish SoR candidate slates**

- **Evaluate Mgr-Sub leadership relationship**

- **Assess SoR potential and plan career development**

9.5

Strategic leaders are also charged with articulating corporate values and establishing a supportive enterprise culture to ensure that the work of the organization gets carried out effectively.

The chief executive officer (CEO) must exercise leadership accountability over the whole organization. To do so she must set direction and win the collaborative support of all employees collectively, at all levels of the organization, to move in the direction set. The essence of strategic leadership is that the CEO is in a working relationship with *all subordinates*, at *all successive organizational layers*, at one and the same time[116].

Vision:

In particular, the CEO must be concerned with setting and sustaining an effective corporate vision. It is impossible to get all of the people moving in a common direction if the CEO does not have a clearly articulated conception of where he is trying to take the company. The vision statement is essential for inculcating throughout the organization the secure feeling that the CEO is on top of things and knows both the direction and future destination of the company. The executive delivers the same message to everyone at the same time, using various company- wide communication processes and establishes a common context with everyone in the same way, not relying on interpretation by intermediate managerial levels. This process is essential to achieving a shared outlook across the whole organization and for establishing a unified enterprise culture.

Vision flows logically from a company's basic mission. Strategy, in turn, reflects how the company intends to achieve the vision. Finally, structure provides the organizational context necessary to achieve the vision. The articulation of vision allows subordinate organizational elements to align their own sense of purpose and direction and is essential for building group-wide consensus.

Culture and Values:

The CEO must also be concerned with establishing a supportive corporate culture designed to facilitate the attainment of the long-term

---

116 Ibid., pages 264–275.

vision. Utilizing culture as an integrating mechanism oriented on the future requires that the CEO ensure that key cultural components be internally consistent with one another. A key cultural element is the quality and nature of the company's value system. Values can serve as a great unifying force because they bond people together as they move toward future goals and objectives, provided that both organizational values and individual values are reasonably congruent. For example, do restrictive financial control procedures (authority) conflict with the valuing of individual initiative (accountability)? Aligning corporate and personal values is no small feat because values are elusive and often difficult to articulate. It is a fundamental axiom, however, that operating values be congruent with stated values.

> **STATED VALUES:** Stated values are often seen in a company's mission or vision statement. Value statements are posted on company websites, marketing materials, and generally communicated to the public and consumer base. For example, XYZ is a green company (environmental consciousness).

> **OPERATING VALUES:** The company practices reflects operating values both internally and externally. They include the processes and procedures the company utilizes to meet its goals—the actual work that may or may not support the stated values. For example, XYZ company has hazardous material–handling procedures that are universally accepted as bad for the environment, with evidence supported by citations from the EPA for environmental infractions.

Thus, CEOs must periodically assess the degree of congruence between the various value systems operating throughout the company. CEOs must ask themselves, "Are we walking the walk and talking the talk from a values perspective? And can we profitably live up to the expectations of our public value statements?" These questions become even more critical when discussing employees. Many companies have a stated value of "respecting and valuing all employees" yet in practice do the opposite, perhaps tolerating a culture of harassment and intimidation. Figure 9.6 depicts how values can be used to positively shape employee behavior.

Social Exchange: Using Values to Shape Behavior

If an Organization Wants Employees Who Are:

- Creative and Innovative
- Committed & Enthusiastic
- Competent
- Reliable & Consistent
- Trustworthy & Honest
- Quality Oriented
- Courageous & Compassionate
- Customer Focused
- Cooperative

Then the Organization Will Have to Provide a Working Environment (Culture and Climate) That Reflects:

- Openness and Candor
- Fairness and Justice
- Freedom From Fear
- Trust
- Clear Accountability & Authority
- Reasonable Assurance of Continued Employment
- Participation in Work Assignment
- Opportunity for Advancement
- Challenging Work
- Competent Leadership

The factors above are, in essence value statements and Values are reflected in a work unit's climate (as well as in the institution's culture). Culture and climate, in turn are Operationalized through existing politics, procedures, rules and a variety of other day-to-day implementing practices.

9.6

Principle #5: Provide Effective Managerial Leadership

Talent Pool:

A key element of strategic leadership is concern over the long-term health of the enterprise as a whole. As organizations grow and mature, they must ensure that they have sufficient organizational capacity (people) capable of driving that growth. Thus, strategic leaders must ensure that there is a steady flow of talent throughout the organization sufficient to fill the roles inherent in implementing the long-term corporate vision and strategy.[117] The task of developing future leaders is thus an inherent part of the enterprise's talent pool management system. The senior leaders in the enterprise need to meet periodically to discuss the health of the current talent pool and decide on key developmental moves required to successfully grow the next generation of leaders.

As the world has gotten more complex, the demands on existing and future leaders have also gotten more complex. Leader development programs are thus integral to the long-term survival of the enterprise. However, it is no longer sufficient to simply replace today's leaders with competent successors. Tomorrow's leaders must be more competent to effectively cope with steadily increasing complexity. In other words, tomorrow's leaders must be capable of surpassing today's counterparts. In fact, as we described previously, we no longer use the term *succession planning* when discussing talent pool issues; we now prefer to talk about *surpassion planning*.

Great care must be given to the design and implementation of the company's leadership development program. While skills and knowledge are an important part of any such program, they are not the most important element. Varied job assignments coupled with varying experiences are also critical to individual development. However, leadership development does not depend on individuals rotating through all possible assignments. Rather, it requires a carefully thought out program that mixes experience with education and training.

---

[117] Ibid. Page 288.

The Three Pillars of Leadership

Direct Leadership

1. Context
   - Role Specific
   - Model - task oriented
   - Authority base
   - Role Related vs. Earned Authority

2. Specific Competencies
   - Technical Competence
   - Planning Competence

3. Supervisory (Individuals)
   - Task Assignment
   - Coach
   - Performance Assessment
   - Performance Feedback
   - Skills
   - Rewards/Disciplines
   - Induction on to team
   - Communication
   - Knowledge

4. Team Building

5. Create a supportive climate/work environment

Operational Leadership

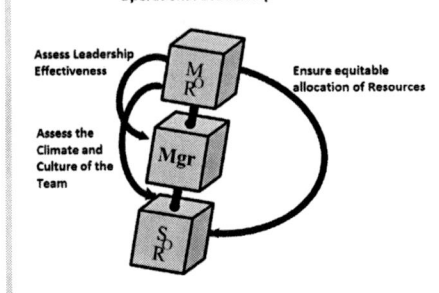

Assess Leadership Effectiveness

Ensure equitable allocation of Resources

Assess the Climate and Culture of the Team

Influencing the effective integration of Individuals and teams into the organization.
- Assessing future potential
- Health of leadership culture/climate
- Mentoring and career development
- Assessing leadership effectiveness
- Equitably allocating resources across subordinate work units
- Facilitating three level teamworking

Strategic Leadership

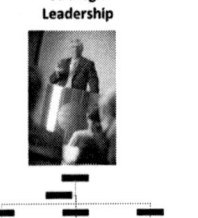

- Vision, Culture, Values
- Putting Culture/Values to work
- Organizational Design
- Structuring & Working
- Relationships
- Systems Development
- Planning, Information & HR
- Talent Pool Management
- Succession Planning

9.7

The Leadership Challenge

The challenge facing an organization's senior leaders is that they have to be competent interpersonal leaders with their immediate subordinates (and their staffs); they also have to be capable operational leaders (Manager-once-Removed leadership) and effective strategic leaders. These accountabilities constitute three completely different sets of leadership competencies. The first entails face-to-face leadership capabilities, whereas the latter two require a totally different set of competencies (see Figure 9.7). The cost of exercising effective leadership is management time. As one can surmise from the previous discussion, leadership at the higher organizational levels consumes a great amount of executive time. To cope with these increased demands on their time, senior executives must be able to delegate appropriate work and tasks to subordinates operating at lower organizational layers.

Leadership Time Demands

The impact of leadership demands on a manager's time should not be underestimated. Interacting often and effectively with subordinates and carrying out all of the accountabilities associated with the leadership role at varying organizational levels will consume a considerable amount of a manager's available time. Previously, we mentioned the concept of applying arithmetic equations, or leadership math, to the leadership process to attempt to ferret out the precise nature of these time demands. This section addresses this topic in greater detail. For example, at the tactical level, the front-line leader needs to develop a strong personal relationship with her team. That is why front-line operating units need to be properly sized so that the managerial leader has sufficient time to actually carry out this accountability. At this level, we recommended that work units be sized according to the complexity of the work being performed by team members. These front-line organizations are called *mutual knowledge units (MKU)* because of the personal nature of the interaction that must occur between the managerial leader and her subordinates. Depending upon the complexity of work, these units should never exceed sixty individuals.

At the operational level, the leader's time demands continue to grow.

Not only does she have to personally lead her own team, she also picks up Manager-once-Removed leadership accountabilities. For example, let us take a level IV executive who manages a geographic region that contains 150 small operating units; these could be stores or sales reps. One of the critical MoR tasks is that the level IV executive must assess the working capacity of the level II unit managers (or sales reps). Thus, it is essential that the MoR get to know each SoR well enough to render such a judgment. Second, the MoR is also accountable for the career development of SoRs. This task includes mentoring the SoR in such a way that he can operate to his full individual potential. To perform these two tasks, the MoR must spend sufficient time with an SoR to make this effort meaningful.

Each SoR is minimally entitled to sitting down with his respective MoR to discuss his career and how that career may be actualized in the company. This task generally requires at least one hour of an MoR's time. If the SoR is at a different location than the MoR, then travel to his location will require still more time. Thus, the level IV executive, in the above situation, will be required to spend at least 150 hours annually with her SoRs and whatever additional travel time is required. Further, in many cases the MoR will want to talk to her immediate subordinate managers about the current performance level of a given SoR. This effort will take additional time. Thus, it is not surprising that an MoR will spend approximately two hours per year with each SoR to perform a valid potential assessment and to subsequently mentor the SoR. If a level IV executive has 150 level II SoRs, this amounts to a 300-hour annual time demand, around seven to eight weeks of her available time.

If these time demands prove to be too cumbersome, then the MoR should consider restructuring her organization so that she doesn't have as many subordinates two levels down. It is absolutely unacceptable for an MoR to foist off the tasks of assessment and mentoring to a subordinate manager or to one of her staff principals (e.g., HR). This is not their work, and an SoR will not be motivated by talking about their careers with such individuals. The only real solution is for the MoR to spend adequate time preparing for and carrying out the assessment process and then following up this process with value-added mentoring. All of this will require the expenditure of substantial management time. These time demands, in turn, should be factored into the design of the organization (e.g., span of control, number and size of geographic regions, number of business units, etc.). Failure to properly consider the time demands imposed on managerial leadership roles will likely lead to some leadership work not getting done.

Chapter 10

Organizational Structure and Customer Impact

It All Starts with Customers

For some unfortunate organizations who lose sight of their customers, it can end very quickly with those same customers. Today's customers have ready access to more information about a company, product, or service than they could possibly ever use. Countless websites are devoted to ranking, analyzing, critizing, and complimenting essentially every organization imaginable. Whereas this information was originally focused on companies and their products, it has now spread to social organizations, charities, and even individuals themselves. Social media has replaced the coffee shop with almost instant gossip and disussions impacting churches, schools, and even little league teams. Large advertising agencies have teams devoted to creating viral campaigns and ads, with the intent that consumers will push the message virally through cyberspace. Churches and schools are monitoring Twitter and Facebook to see what people are saying about their organizations. A school incident can spread to parents within minutes, all while their children are actually sitting in that very school. Today, it is entirely possible for a parent to gain knowledge of an incident before the school principal does. Simply put, the amount of information your customers have about your organization is staggering, and the speed in which they receive or access it can be in measured in seconds. So what impact does this have on your organization and its structure?

Recall that mission drives vision, which, in turn, drives strategy, and strategy drives structure. The customer has an impact on all of these variables. An organization's relationship with its customer base begins in many ways: for many, it is via the Internet, and yet for others it is with a physical employee. For today's customers, their first interaction with a company is often that ogranization's website. This initial exposure should naturally give rise to these structural questions: What does my site need to look like? Do we design and manage our own site or should we outsource it? How many employees and what roles do we need to manage this customer focal point?

Yet, for other organizations, it is likely that your organization's relationship with customers occurs within the lower tier of your company. Many customers' initial physical interaction with your organization occurs with a front-line level employee (salesmen, delivery driver, retail floor associate, etc.). How many drivers do you need? How many employees are required on the retail floor? What is the work that they should be doing? Your front-line structure has an immediate impact on these customer-facing roles and, thus, the customer. And your mission, vision, and strategy drive this front-line structure, or they should. Gaining and utilizing customer information both from customer touches and market research are a crucial component of an organization's vision and strategy development. This knowledge should then be reflected in the mission and vision of the organization. Afterall, a vision that is out of touch with customers will likely drive a strategy that will also be out of touch with these same customers.

Gain an Intimate Knowledge of Your Customers:

First, companies need to clearly distinguish between *consumers and customers*. These two terms are often used interchangeably, but it is important for our language to be precise. We shall define the terms as follows:

CONSUMERS: A grouping of individuals that acquire goods or services for direct use or ownership (rather than resale).

CUSTOMER: An individual that buys goods or services.

We shall therefore refer to consumers as a category, or grouping, of individuals, whereas a customer is a specific individual.

Distinguishing between consumers and customers is important because it allows one, in turn, to differentiate out a separate and distinct business function to address each.[118] For example, the marketing function historically deals with customer groups (in our terms consumers), whereas the sales function tends to deal with an individual customer. The work to be performed in each of these functions is thus very different. Marketing is concerned with monitoring changing trends in consumer needs and identifying new product and service offerings that would be perceived by consumers as worthwhile. So a marketing organization would contain a market research function, a market analysis capability, category managers managing a specific grouping of products (e.g., dishwashers), brand managers managing separate and distinct brands (e.g., KitchenAid versus Whirlpool), an advertising group managing corporate brand advertising, a customer loyalty group focused on building and maintaining customer loyalty programs, and a marketing service activity designing and distributing various advertising tools.

While marketing information is important in the broad sense, knowledge about individual customer needs is crucial to the long-term success of a given enterprise. At the macro level, an understanding of your customers should be an integral part of the decisions your company makes about market position and strategic goals. For example, voice of the customer (VOC) is a central concept to any Lean Six Sigma initiative.[119] Figure 10.1 depicts how the voice of the customer process is used to describe customers' needs and their perception of a given company's products or service.

---

[118] Jaques, Elliott. Requisite Organization, Cason Hall Publishers: Arlington, VA, 1996. Page pair 88.

[119] Yang Kai, Voice of the Customer, McGraw Hill, 2007

Voice of the Customer

1. Identify customers and determine what you need to know

↓

2. Collect and analyze reactive system data, then fill gaps with proactive approaches

↓

3. Analyze data to generate a key list of customer needs in the customer's language

↓

4. Translate customer language into CTQs (Critical to Quality Requirements)

↓

5. Set specifications for CTQ's

10.1

There are two basic ways to gather VOC information. An organization can go out and get the information—proactive methods. Or an institution can let the data come to them—reactive methods. These two methods are described in greater detail below:

> PROACTIVE Methods: The organization takes the initiative to contact customers. Methods include surveys, questionnaires, focus groups, interviews, and point-of-sale contact. Because the organization controls the timing and content of the customer contact, proactive methods can be used for a wide range of purposes, including product and service design, process improvement, and performance monitoring.
>
> REACTIVE Methods: The information comes to the organization through a customer's initiative. Methods include customer calls (complaints, compliments, queries, requests for technical support, sales), web page hits, e-mails or cards that customers send to you, point-of-sale questionnaires, referrals, and so on. It is absolutely critical that reactive methods be carefully thought out and designed to gather, track, and use the collected information correctly because it refers directly to current product and service offerings.

Because customers are more likely to contact an organization when they have problems, the reactive data source is better at detecting product and service weaknesses than strengths. This data source may also be more biased because it represents a particular customer segment that is more likely to contact the organization rather than other segments.

The following five types of VOC information are useful in making strategic business decisions:

> 1. How well your current products and services meet (or do not meet) customer needs.
>
> 2. What customer needs exist that are not currently being provided.

3. What customers report that they would like to see in a product or service offering.

4. A competitive analysis of your customer offerings.

5. Benchmarking data regarding your customer offerings.

Customer Impact on Organizational Structure:

Once customers have been thoroughly studied, how do they factor into organizational design decisions? We have already talked about the marketing function found in most corporate entities, which is focused on consumers. But dealing with individual customers is also central to most organizations. Jay Galbraith answers the question as follows:

> It means forming long-term relationships with the most valuable customers. It means interacting with these customers across multiple points of contact and integrating the results of these contacts in a consistent company position for the customers. It means learning from the contacts to customize the company's offering for different customer segments. It means learning about new customer needs and expanding the company's offering to meet them. It means using knowledge of customers to package products and services into solutions that create value for customers.[120]

Our answer to the aforementioned question is that each level of an organization must align around its immediate customers, whether the immediate customer is an internal person or an external one. It must structure itself from the outside in.

---

[120] Jay R. Galbraith, Designing the Customer-Centric Organization, Jossey-Bass, 2005, page 2.

The specific type of structure flows from an analysis of the customer base. The number of levels in an organization will depend, in part, on the number of customers, their geographic diversification, the nuances of their needs and expectations, the portfolio of products and services an agency offers to the customers or customer segments, and how the company intends to service the customer (e.g., how they reply to inevitable customer satisfaction problems, etc.). The structure, processes, and systems for the whole organization and each of its levels will be determined, in part, by customer requirements, that is, from the outside. If the customer requires operational efficiency or short cycle times, then the structure will be flat, processes lean, and systems standardized. If customers require intimacy and hand holding, then multiple levels of the structure will be customer facing or customer close, so multiple processes must link into customers and systems will need to be customized to serve diverse customer requests.

The organization's command-and-control structure may be more or less centralized depending on the organization's customer-centric strategy: efficiency, customer intimacy, or innovation. Also, value expected by customers will factor in performance measures of the agency and positions within the organization. Some positions and roles in the organizational hierarchy will be determined in terms of customer requirements. For example, a single customer may be acting as a buyer for a large organization. In order to effectively interact with that customer to negotiate a financially viable deal, it is necessary that the customer account manager (sales rep) possess sufficient cognitive capacity to be able to effectively address key underlying financial issues. Because role incumbents at higher organizational levels generally possess higher cognitive capacity than those at lower layers, account managers need to match or surpass in cognitive capacity the buyers they have to interact with if they are to negotiate effectively with the buyer. Thus, buyers for large companies are often serviced by national account sales personnel who occupy higher-level roles than ordinary sales staff.

We observed an example of the adverse impact produced by a capacity mismatch between a buyer and a seller in Mexico after the North American Free Trade Agreement (NAFTA) was reached. Prior to opening its borders with the United States, sales personnel in most Mexican companies tended to operate at lower organizational levels (I and II) and possessed the requisite (cognitive) capacity to function effectively at these levels. They sold a lot of their products to small family-owned retailers located in markets (*mercados*) and to other small retailers. Once NAFTA went into effect, large American organizations unleashed their higher-level buyers into the fray. In many cases, these buyers operated one or two levels higher in capability than their Mexican counterparts. This mismatch heavily favored American companies. Sales negotiations, in turn, also reflected this mismatch and similarly favored American companies. It wasn't until Mexican companies began to increase the capability of their sales force that negotiations became more evenly balanced. Figure 10.2 depicts the nature of this mismatch. Note that in this case the capability of the buyer was much more sophisticated than that of the seller.

The above lesson has been learned in industry because of the adverse financial consequences that occur if capability is under resourced. In government organizations, however, the same financial consequences are often not present. Many government agencies often under resource (in terms of capability and capacity) their supplier-focused staff (procurement). (A similar discussion can be made regarding the customer-service function, although the operative variables are somewhat different.) The price of under resourcing the procurement function is perhaps best illustrated by analyzing the government-contracting process. In the current process, government contracting officers often operate at a much lower level than their equivalent civilian contracting personnel. This mismatch leads to dysfunctional contracts heavily favored toward the external contractor rather than the agency or government. (This is not the only problem uncovered in the contracting process, but it has been chosen to simply underscore the application of the aforementioned principle to a key government process.)

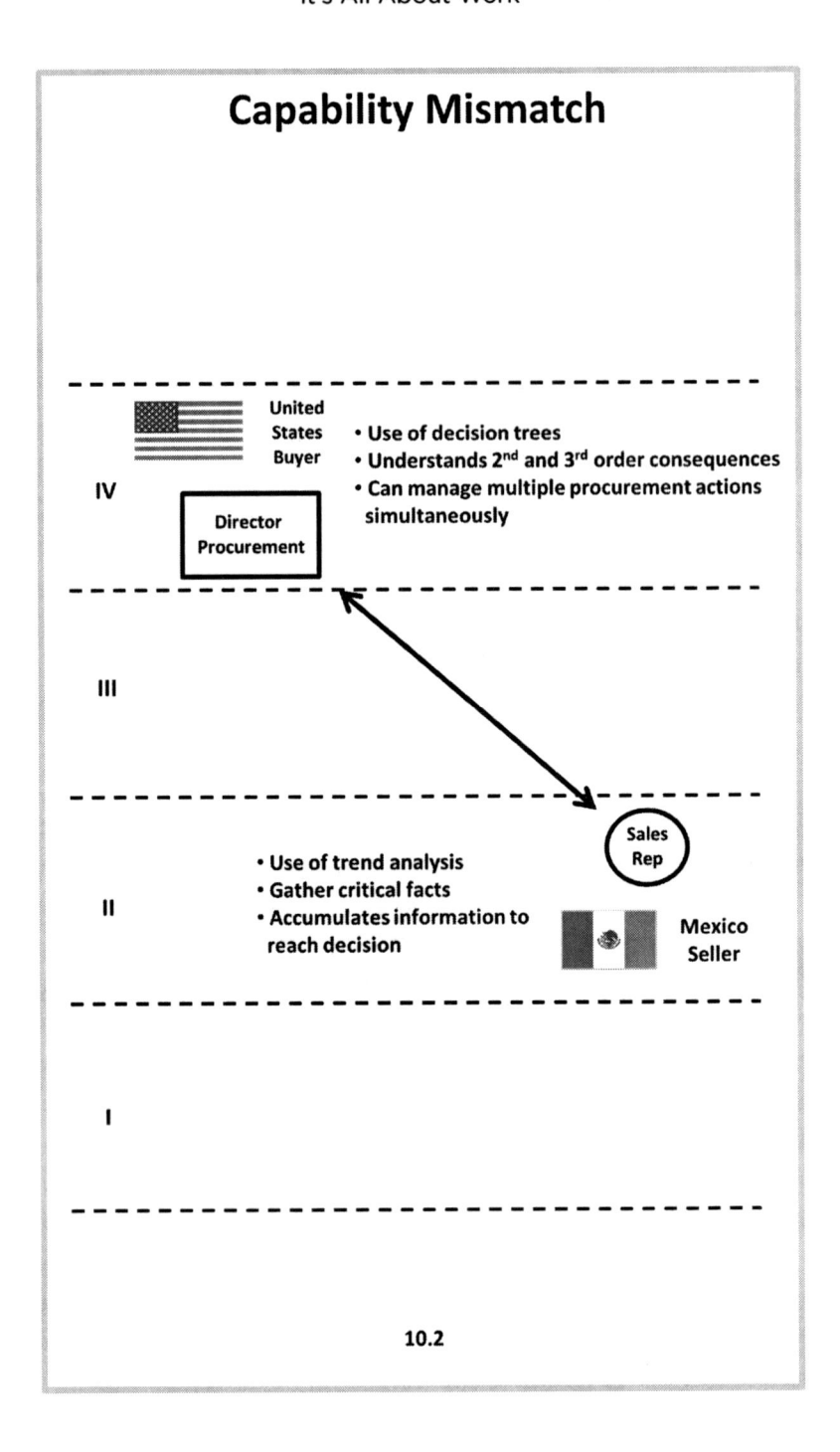

Capability Mismatch

IV — United States Buyer
- Use of decision trees
- Understands 2nd and 3rd order consequences
- Can manage multiple procurement actions simultaneously

Director Procurement

III

Sales Rep

II
- Use of trend analysis
- Gather critical facts
- Accumulates information to reach decision

Mexico Seller

I

10.2

In summation, before you can embark on applying the principles outlined in this book, your organization needs to ensure that you have properly acknowledged your customers' impact on your organization, its systems and procedures, and the organizational structure itself.

Chapter 11

Implementation Introduction, Sponsorship, and Education

As promised, this section of the book provides reader insights, lessons learned, and guidance in implementing the organizational design principles described in the previous sections. The implementation suggestions that we make are based on our years of experience in many different types of organizations. We have applied these principles personally as consultants, executives, business owners, and teachers. We have also studied and tested them in government, corporate, and academic settings as well.

Dr. Stephen D. Clement

Since the publications of *Requisite Organization and Executive Leadership,* Dr. Clement has spent the past twenty years implementing, studying, learning, and adapting the principles to numerous large organizations throughout the world (e.g., CRA/Rio Tinto, Pepsi, Whirlpool, Textron, Office Depot, and Lennox Industries, to name a few). This experience also included a variety of projects within the United States Army (more than twenty years total). Dr. Clement brings with him the experiences of working with these large organizations and weaves key lessons learned into the implementation suggestions provided in this section.

Chris Clement

Having grown up around Dr. Jaques and Dr. Clement, Chris brings forth a unique generational experience to the theories and principles. He has applied this knowledge as both a midlevel executive at a Fortune 500 company and as a small business owner. In his own small business, Chris was able to demonstrate that minor modifications and tailoring of the principles made them equally applicable in meeting the unique needs of today's smaller businesses.

It has been our experience that today's large and small organizations face similar organizational concerns, yet they have drastically different priorities pertaining to those concerns. Most of our large corporate clients (including government agencies) have spent a majority of their energy on people issues first and then only tangentially do they choose to refocus their attention on organizational structure issues. Many of them tell us they have sufficient leadership programs, personnel management, and succession-planning programs and would like us to assist them in fixing the organization: "We have good people and good leadership, but our organizational structure is a mess; it needs fixing." Over time, they have come to realize that their structure has become bloated with too many roles crowded too close together, dysfunctional working relationships clouded by excessive dotted lines, overhead driven too high by grade creep, and more recently the emergence of ineffective structures due to the removal of roles to reduce costs (as opposed to the removal of work to reduce costs). As a result, some of these clients have come to a realization that they now need help in updating their organizational structures.

While a large number of organizations seem to think they have adequately addressed the people issue, it has been our experience that many talent management and assessment programs leave much to be desired. For example, in the chapter on capability assessment, we pointed out that any valid assessment of individual potential ultimately relies, in large part, on a manager's judgment. This capability assessment is important because it forms a key element of any succession-planning system. But many of our larger clients are very uncomfortable with relying on a manager's judgment in this area; they prefer to utilize what they believe to be more fair quantitative testing, psychological profiling, and employee feedback to assess the potential of their employees. Sometimes these choices are driven by a fear of litigation, while at other times they prefer to simply rely on the latest HR leadership program.

In some cases, line managers simply do not know their SoRs well enough to render a valid assessment, so utilizing an outside assessment process resolves their problem. Unfortunately, our experience with these personality-focused assessment tools is that they have not proven to be good predictors of future individual working capability. What we have seen is that use of these tools often results in roles being filled with individuals who do not have the innate cognitive capacity to do the work of a given role (e.g., a level III person in a level IV role). This mismatch, in turn, creates severe organizational problems. Either someone is forced to step up (or down) to get this level IV work done (and, thus, is not likely to have time to do their own work adequately) or the work doesn't get done at all.

In a few cases, the company's leadership actually modifies the structure in order to get the work done. For instance, they may add another full-scale organizational layer or modify work processes to include inserting more capable overseers, thus muddying the waters in terms of accountability and authority. This modification, or work around, process is how many organizations end up with excessive dotted-line and matrix-reporting structures. If an organization fills roles incorrectly, utilizing under-capacity people for key roles, it very easy to see how that same company can end up with a dysfunctional structure. This fear of utilizing managerial judgment to assess the potential of employees is a large driver of dysfunctional organizations and their structure.

Ironically, in our work with smaller organizations, they say to us, "I don't have organizational or structural problems; I have people problems. How do I know who my up and comers are, my high potentials?" Perhaps executives in smaller organizations believe that by "fixing" the employee capability and capacity issue, the organization and its subsequent structure will right themselves. Small business executives and owners do not seem to shy away from judging people. In fact, many of them openly embrace the process, reading leadership books, articles, and so on to assist them in assessing their people. However, quite often, their judgment of their people's potential tends to be biased. This bias can be summed up as "I need him or her to be just like me; if we had three of me, we would be just fine."

By focusing on their people, small business managers sometimes neglect to look at the impact that the organization has on existing working relationships affecting those very same people. For example, a small business owner recently described to us a situation in which his CFO and COO were "fighting. "It's a real turf war between finance and the plant, and it goes all the way to the top. The CFO and COO just don't work well together." The owner tried team-building retreats and a whole host of other techniques in attempts to get the individuals to "just get along with each other" to no avail. He was happy with the performance of both individuals; however, he was now contemplating which one to terminate as he saw that as his only option left. When we began to ask questions about the work they were involved in, it became clear to us that this business owner had a role-clarity issue, specifically related to the working relationships between overlapping roles and teams. What is the finance team accountable for? What is their authority vis-à-vis plant employees? What is the COO accountable for? Can the CFO request an employee to stop work to change course or direction? What authority level does the CFO have?

Each executive and subsequent team had self-defined roles, and of course each team had arrogated as much authority to themselves as they could get away with. In this case, we concluded that the issue was poorly defined working relationships and role clarity, not a turf war or personality clashes. We said to the owner, "As the organizational (operational) leader, you are accountable to fix the working relationship issue first, before terminating one or both of these valued executives. As their direct leader, you owe them the chance to work together in an organization with clear roles, which contain clear accountability and authority descriptions before terminating them."

Most organizations face systemic challenges that require both organizational remedies as well as people remedies. Just as you can't have accountability without authority, you can't have an organization without people. In this implementation guide, we will attempt to reflect on challenges facing all types and sizes of businesses. Keep in mind, we recommend that you address the organizational challenges first and address the people issues second.

The easy part is in creating the boxes (roles) and the organizational structure. The hard part is putting the "faces to the spaces," that is, filling the roles you have created and changed with people with appropriate capability.

Executive Sponsorship and Education/Learning: Key Drivers of Successful Implementation

Recall this executive quote from Chapter 4:

My client has 80 managers and with that, 80 different opinions and beliefs on how this company should be organized, when all they really need is 1.

The last several years have had a dramatic impact on businesses worldwide. Our industry, management consulting, has also witnessed a significant amount of change as well. For many years, our client work followed a similar path. Typically, our initial contact would be with someone from the operational side of the business (sales, operations, production, CEO) who identified an issue and decided to engage us in project work to address the issue. The HR department essentially functioned as a support activity to any project work that subsequently took place. As part of this effort, we generally had an initial briefing with the CEO followed by his or her senior executive team. Our conversations started at the top and flowed down the organization. An initial briefing generally would last one to two hours and represented a general overview of our study process and underlying concepts. If the client then decided to go forward with a project, they would typically request a full-scale presentation of the principles to be used in analyzing their organizations. Such a presentation might involve an off-site meeting, which would typically last anywhere from a half day to a full day for the senior executive team. The intent of this longer session was to inform and educate the executives as to the hows and whys that would drive specific recommendations. The sponsors of a project were typically the people directly accountable for the profit and loss (P&L) of the organization being studied. Implementation, that is, the tough decisions, was also driven by these same executive sponsors.

More recently, our work has been sponsored by HR and Organizational Development departments. In addition, we have noticed that fewer and fewer clients seem to have an interest in learning about our methodology and underlying concepts of how to organize their companies. Recently, we have been tasked with providing organizational structure solutions. Nearly every business today is experiencing strong economic challenges. Time pressures to achieve economic recovery have suddenly become paramount. All of this has led to the time-compression challenges we discussed earlier. Prior to 2008, a typical conversation from a C level (Level V or higher) executive might sound like:

> *Tell me how your team arrives at your solutions? Why do you recommend what you recommend? What is your philosophy? How can you help this organization be more efficient and effective?*

Today the conversations from HR and OD executives sound a bit different:

> *Okay, so we've got organizational problems. How much will it cost to fix it and when can you be done? I have to get this approved, and we need the solution yesterday.*

Obviously, any conversation between us and a CEO is substantially different than those with the head of the HR department. The CEO clearly has the authority to schedule meetings and educational sessions with other senior executives. The HR or OD department simply does not have the same clout. They frequently have to negotiate for any time requests involving operational managers. And because they are a staff support element, line managers often ignore these time requests (or at least minimize the available time drastically). Consequently, today it is harder than ever to conduct a thorough study. But study execution is not the only challenge that has arisen. Once a study is completed, organizations then face an imposing implementation challenge.

Implementation Challenge

At the end of each project, we typically schedule a team meeting with all project personnel, similar to what the army calls an after action report. We explore the usual metrics: Did we meet the budget set by the client? Did we meet the timeline? The most important discussion surrounds the recommendations themselves. How does the company or client plan to pursue implementation of agreed-upon recommendations? Were any recommendations modified, and if so, why? How long is the implementation schedule or timeframe? Does the client have a multistage or multiyear approach to implementation?

In recent years, implementation of project recommendations has become more challenging than ever. Even minor recommendations have sometimes been fought tooth and nail by incumbent teams and individuals. It seems as if resistance to change has grown exponentially. We have developed several hypotheses regarding this issue. Perhaps because individuals in today's organizations have experienced so much rapid change, much of it negative due to the recent downturn in revenues, they have simply become fed up with organizational change. It has also occurred to us that maybe we needed higher-level sponsorship to get these changes pushed through the bureaucracy. Maybe we were not getting sufficient input (data) to adequately reinforce our recommendations. The question remains though, why is it so hard for a client to implement?

In an odd turn of events, our recommendations for right sizing (also known as downsizing) six or seven years ago met with much less resistance than recent projects. Today's resistance is present even in those situations where hiring occurs or new roles (jobs!) have been recommended. In reviewing recent projects, we found that many organizations in the recent past removed personnel due to cost constraints, but they did not correspondingly remove the work that these individuals performed. Thus, many of our recent projects ended up recommending that these eliminated roles be filled: "The work is still there and still needs to get done. You need someone to carry out those tasks (work); hence, we recommend you fill this role." Yet, even in these situations, we encounter aggressive resistance to what one would think would be an obviously embraced recommendation. The operative question is *why?*

Generally, we conduct our project work in an environment of

openness and candor, both internally and with the client. So we began to ask them. Why was implementation so difficult? Why do you think your people resisted so strongly? What could we have done differently to make implementation easier? We discovered that the resistance was not coming from those individuals most impacted by the proposed changes but from their managers and leaders. As will be described in the following section, the data that feeds our recommendations comes from all levels of the organization. As part of our analysis, we apply our principles to that data to arrive at specific recommendations. For example, a detailed analysis of work occurring at a given organization layer may result in a conclusion that individuals operating at that level were focused on the wrong work: they were performing tasks inappropriate for that level. Based on the information that we gleaned from our original interviews, we believed that we had amassed substantial supporting evidence for such a finding. Thus, we felt such a recommendation was sound and factually based.

But then during the implementation phase, we sometimes uncovered the following puzzling dichotomy: "We recommended ABC change, but you actually implemented DEF. Why? How did you reach that decision?" Sometimes the answer provided by the client was based on their efforts to achieve consensus decision making. At other times, the decision was rendered by the leader of the impacted organization: "The engineering managers didn't like that recommendation, so we compromised and did this instead." Or "The VP of sales said that wouldn't work for us. That's not how he did it at his prior corporation, so he decided we should do DEF instead."

We realized, of course, that not all of our recommendations were going to get implemented. Some were costly, some were multiyear, some involved long-term change, and some were simply too radical to do all at once and had to be broken up into steps. While many recommendations were ultimately implemented, the time and effort involved seemed to be far more than we had expected. For example, if we have a client who is still discussing and pondering recommendations made a year earlier, then we believe we have an issue.

In trying to further understand the above phenomenon, we interacted with the teams and individuals who were most vocal in their resistance. For example, in the engineering situation described above, we subsequently had a discussion with the engineering managers and the VP of engineering. How did we get here? Was the data wrong? Were the recommendations wrong? Why did it take so long?

In short, we found that much of the resistance was based on a lack of adequate information. We quickly realized that those that put up the biggest resistance did not have visibility as to the why behind our recommendations. Additionally, they had no idea about our underlying organizational principles or theories. They were never involved in any of the briefings regarding who we are, what we are doing, and the organizational principles from which we operate. The communication preceding a given study often went like this:

> *The EVP/GM and VP of HR have hired consultants to analyze the existing structure of the engineering department. The VP of engineering has spent thirty minutes with them and he or she is on board. Please accommodate them accordingly.*

The primary driver of change recommended in the aforementioned project ultimately would be the VP of engineering, yet he had little or no exposure to our principles. As a result, they would often revert back to what they knew and were comfortable with:

> *You can't decentralize engineering and have an engineer work for a program manager. A program manager is not always an engineer and thus can't manage one. They simply don't speak the language or understand engineers. All engineers must work for engineers. We're not doing that (the recommendation).*

In a follow-on discussion with the VP of engineering, we would then discuss actual work-related tasks. We focused specifically on what a program manager was accountable for and the authority they needed to carry out those accountabilities. We also focused on the engineering work that had to be performed in the program management process in order for them to accomplish their goals. This discussion was then followed by describing an ideal role of the engineer. This episode often ended with a statement such as:

> *Oh, I didn't realize that was why you recommended that the engineering role be formally assigned to the program management team. Given my new understanding of levels of work, role clarity, and accountability and authority, I can see how that might work. Let's give it a shot.*

The difference is education! After the aforementioned challenging implementation efforts, we began to modify our approach to project work. We decided to return to basics. Prior to engaging in any organizational study or project, we now require that senior-level executives of the organization being studied participate in our Essentials for Effective Organization Design workshop. We began this requirement in 2010 (we had used this upfront education approach in our army work for some time), and so far the results have been outstanding. We are now involved in less meetings with clients involving implementation issues, less of our recommendations are being modified, and the resistance to change has dropped dramatically. The clients are saving time and money and impacting their organizations more effectively.

So what does this mean for you, the reader, and your organization? Quite simply, if you believe your organization needs organizational project work, followed by possible structural changes, then you must ensure that all key stakeholders, particularly at the top of the impacted team or organization, and even other organizational associates (partners, etc.) are familiar with the principles that underpin the proposed project work. This could mean reading this book or attending one of our workshops. You might consider communicating the following message:

> *I'd like to do some organizational work in my department/ division/team. I'm going to ground my recommendations and changes in the principles outlined in this book. These changes will impact your/our organization. I'd like for you to be familiar with the principles because I will need your*

assistance in implementing any possible recommendations.

Note, we are not asking that you get buy in on the principles. You need not convince (i.e., sell) everyone in the organization that these principles are right for your team and organization. Just ask that they be familiar with the principles contained herein. When they ask:

Why did you recommend that organizational or role change?

You can respond with something similar to this:

Because if I am to hold this person accountable for X, she needs the following minimum authority to get the work done.

Or

Because this is a level III role and I believe the incumbent is a great employee, but operating at level II, I'm going to move him to another position and bring in a level III capable employee to fill that level III role.

Simply put, a key lesson learned is to educate the impacted leadership team on the organizational design principles we espouse. If you do so, you will save yourself time and money down the road.

Project Team Makeup

A key component in analyzing your organization is *who* is actually going to perform the analysis itself. While the executive sponsor is the owner of a given organizational project, that individual may or may not be involved in the analysis process. For smaller companies (less than a few hundred employees) we suggest that the owner or chief executive conduct the interviews and subsequent analysis (as described in the following chapters). We make this recommendation because the owner (or chief executive) will ultimately be responsible for any tough decisions that have to be made and the subsequent implementation of all recommendations.

For companies larger than this (or if a smaller company is complex, i.e., contains a small number of level I roles but a substantial number of level II direct output roles), a full-time project team should probably be assembled to interview managers and employees, aggregate the information obtained from them, and analyze key data elements. This team could be made up solely of external people (consultants) to conduct the study. Alternatively, it could be made up completely of internal staff members or it could be a hybrid team with both inside personnel as well as outside consultants.

A key benefit of an external team is that they bring with them an outsider viewpoint and are less likely to be swayed by existing knowledge, cultural biases, or sacred cows. Remember, the hog won't butcher itself. However, external teams can be expensive and may take additional time to get up to speed on your industry or marketplace. The second option described above is to appoint an internal team. There are no additional costs incurred (besides time and resources) and no need to gain industry knowledge. As with external teams, however, there are a few negative factors associated with this approach. For example, internal teams have a tendency to give the organization a cursory look and sometimes lack a revolutionary approach to recommendations. Internal teams also suffer from a tendency to preconceive solutions prior to gathering any actual work data. This latter factor may negate the entire purpose of doing an organization study in the first place. In addition, there are likely to be a host of leadership dynamics surrounding who should actually do the interviews and analysis if an internal team is chosen.

We have found in our consulting practice that a blended approach seems to work best. A blended approach combines the benefits of an outsider viewpoint with the insider knowledge of internal team members. The real value of a blended approach, however, is that internal company personnel will have firsthand knowledge of the underlying principles and concepts that lead to specific study recommendations. This knowledge will prove invaluable in the implementation phase.

Successful Implementation

In conclusion, successful implementation of any changes based on our principles requires two things.

1. EXECUTIVE SPONSORSHIP: The executive sponsor should be someone that is accountable for the results of the business unit or function to be analyzed and changed. While HR, finance, and other service-providing positions are certainly valuable as executive sponsors, executives in these functional areas are not accountable for actual business results. They are not accountable to make key decisions such as role realignment or role creation that impact the P&L of a given area or business function. They are, however, accountable to provide expert advice during and after the project. This advisory capacity may include initiating a review of the organization based on our principles.

2. EDUCATION IN THE PRINCIPLES: Based on our recent experiences, we feel is it crucial that as many people in the impacted organization as possible become familiar with our design principles. Senior-level personnel, particularly, should have a thorough understanding of the principles as they really need to be the drivers of change. They are the very individuals who will have to make the tough decisions required during implementation (i.e., putting the face in the space). This education can be gained by attending a seminar on the principles, thoroughly reading and analyzing this book, or possibly participating in one of our online learning modules we hope to launch in the future.

Chapter 12

Preparing to Analyze the Existing Structure

Review Mission and Vision Statements and Strategic Plan

An analysis of an organization's existing structure should begin with a review of the existing mission and vision statements. These statements should drive a company's strategic plan, which, in turn, drives subordinate functions and tasks (recall the discussion in chapter 5). If your organization does not have a clear and succinct mission or vision statement, we highly recommend you develop one. This need not be a lengthy process; a review of current articles and literature should give you enough information to write one yourself. The only advice that we would offer is to make sure that your mission statement is directly related to the work your organization actually does. Remember, it's all about work. We have seen many mission statements that do not reflect what an organization actually does. Below are the operational definitions that we use for constructing a mission and a vision statement.

MISSION: A short formal written statement of purpose. It reflects the broad objectives of the corporation.[121]

Example: NASA—Conduct manned space exploration

VISION: The CEO's overarching long-term strategic goal. Vision gives the context for the development and carrying through of strategic options. The vision can be modified as circumstances dictate but should be reviewed at least annually.[122]

Example: NASA—Put a man on the moon by the end of this decade (vision as articulated by then President John F. Kennedy)

Previously (chapter 5), we described the relationship between mission, vision, functions, and tasks. A company's mission suggests goals, objectives, and critical functions that must be performed to accomplish that mission. These functions are then reflected in an organized pattern of roles aligned in a particular way to carry out the work inherent in those functions or mission. This pattern of roles constitutes the manifest organizational structure. The manifest structure is the organization that is officially chartered by an enterprise to carry out its work. A key element of that work is planning.

Planning is the bridge between the company's current state and its desired future state. Most companies have a strategic plan. Larger companies may have a strategic planning group, whereas smaller companies may only have an informal plan known solely to the owner or CEO. A viable strategic plan should reflect those key events or activities required to achieve the company's future vision. The plan should contain vital information about markets, customers, and the overall competitive environment. The true value of the long-range plan is that it permits a company to ponder these questions:

If the plan says we are going to achieve X by 2016, then what does the organization need to look like to get there?

---

[121] Jaques, Elliott and Clement, Stephen D. Executive Leadership, Cason Hall Publishers, Arlington, VA, 1991. Page 102

[122] Ibid.

What is the work (roles) that needs to be performed to accomplish the plan?

Once again, if you don't have a strategic plan, we suggest that you develop one. Formulating a plan is a critical first step in articulating the potential organizational changes required to achieve the company's future vision.

In addition to analyzing the impact that the strategic plan may have on the existing organizational structure, it is also useful to gather and review other key information sources that could likewise affect the structure. Figure 12.1 depicts several sources central to this effort. Collectively, these sources suggest organizational changes that might be required as a company strives to achieve its future vision. At the very least, this information is likely to be central to any effort to analyze the viability of the current structure. It should be reviewed by a project team that has been specifically established to carry out an agreed-upon study.

The project team should be made up of both external and internal resources. The external resources provide subject-matter expertise useful in the analysis of the existing work system. The internal team should include operating personnel chosen from the organizational development group or specially selected personnel from the prospective study area. As will be shown, the external team can also provide essential training to the study sponsors and key operating personnel selected from each major study area.

The value of having an internal team paired with the external team is to facilitate the implementation process. By participating directly in the study process, the internal team will understand the rationale behind specific study recommendations. This understanding includes an in-depth knowledge of the principles and concepts used in the analysis phase to develop specific study recommendations.

Information Sources

| Situational Awareness 1.0 | Mission Functional Analysis 2.0 | Customer Analysis 3.0 | Stakeholder Analysis 4.0 |

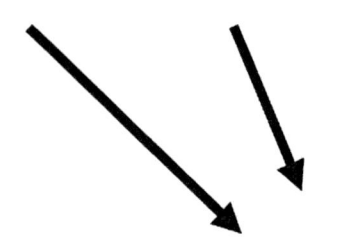

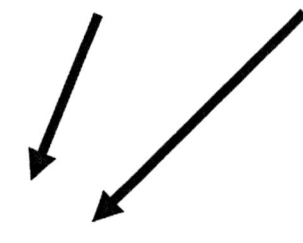

Information

12.1

Gather and Review Various Organizational Data Sources:

The data sources described in Figure 12.1 provide an individual and his team's key "homework," which is reflective of the current state of the organization. This homework ensures that one is familiar with all programs, projects, initiatives, and changes that could impact the current and future organization. For example:

> 1.0 SITUATIONAL AWARENESS: What key external factors are likely to influence enterprise operations in the immediate future? Are there any major changes that could dramatically affect current operations, such as major tax changes, changing trade barriers, emerging federal or state statutes, and the like? What is happening in the competitive environment? Can one expect increasing or decreasing price pressures or more or less foreign competition? Does the company have any copyright or patent-protected material that is at risk? Monitoring situational awareness should be an on-going task, challenging every executive no matter where they may be located in the existing organizational structure.
>
> 2.0 MISSION/FUNCTIONAL ANALYSIS: Is the company experiencing mission "creep," such as new missions being added by stakeholders (shareholders, governing bodies, etc.), without a concomitant increase in resources? Is the company moving away from or toward a shared-service activity? Are existing functions being consolidated or expanded in response to cost constraints or growth initiatives?
>
> KEY PROJECTS OR INITIATIVES—Key projects or initiatives that aim to change the existing organization or the future organization should be reviewed. This might include such projects as Lean Six Sigma, business process improvement, sales training, new products or markets, customer service initiatives or technological advances or system rollouts).

COMPENSATION SYSTEM AND KEY PERFORMANCE INDICES—What does the compensation system currently reward (in terms of behaviors)? What key performance indices reflect role-output levels, (sales growth, margin, expense-to-revenue percentages, etc.)?

ROLE DESCRIPTIONS, JOB POSTINGS AND CURRENT EMPTY ROLES—Are there roles that are currently sitting open? How long have they been vacant? Are you currently hiring for roles? Should you put in place a hiring freeze or a no-transfer policy until after an organizational review has been completed?

3.0 **CUSTOMER/CONSUMER ANALYSIS:** Any insights, reports, or projects surrounding customer data should be reviewed. Customers and consumers have a significant impact on every organization. If you have commissioned detailed studies or internal teams to provide insights into customer trends or patterns, you need to review the output from such projects thoroughly.

How do you analyze potential customer segments, decide on which customers to pursue, communicate with those customers, develop and retain customers, design loyalty programs to keep them, find ways to reactivate them, and so on?

Are there any changes occurring in the procurement section of key customer accounts? Are procurement activities being further centralized? What impact do changing procurement patterns have on the company's existing sales force? Are your sales reps matched in capability to their respective buying organizations?

4.0 **STAKEHOLDER ANALYSIS:** What are the desires and needs of your key stakeholders, shareholders, investors, and state and federal overseers? What are the concerns of the board and CEO? Does the workforce have any strong feelings about the current culture or leadership climate?

In gathering and reviewing the above information, a study team increases their awareness of the challenges, changes, and state of the organization. This awareness can ease the transition to implementation and prevent an organizational review from being misguided. You and your project team will want to avoid any surprises similar to this:

Why are we talking about reorganizing that business? The marketing and finance team just did a project analyzing that business area. The marketing guys say the marketplace is shrinking and moving to product and services that we don't currently offer ... and the finance team stated that we are losing money in that business anyway. They both recommended that we look at pulling the plug on that business.

There are several outputs to be garnered from analyzing the aforementioned information. First and foremost, it permits an organizational project team to identify key organizational issues that may need to be analyzed in greater depth. Second, knowledge of these issues then permits the project team to construct a study plan and a supporting interview guide. Third, the development of a comprehensive study plan identifies topical areas to be analyzed in greater detail and specific individuals to be interviewed in the process. (Both of these topics are described in greater detail in the next section of this chapter). Fourth, awareness of significant changes occurring in the surrounding business environment also suggests potential concomitant personnel changes that might be required. Finally, all of this permits the project team to construct the manifest and extant organizational structures. Knowledge of these two structures is useful in that it suggests the depth of change required to construct a requisite organization.

Construct the Manifest Organizational Structure:

Once you have reviewed the mission or vision, strategic plan, and other key information relative to any organizational design project, it is then useful to gather existing organization charts from various sources in the organization. In large organizations, you may find different organization charts for the same activity or team. The organization charts produced by the HR department likely represent the pattern of roles as described by the formal personnel system, such as those reflective of the performance management system or the compensation system. The organization charts you receive from the various operating units likely represent their description of how they believe work actually gets done in their respective functional areas. Differences between these two sets of charts often reflect practical differences between who actually works for whom versus who may report to whom. For example, sometimes line management modifies the reporting scheme to get a specific role compensated at a desirable level. These varying organizational charts (if any) need to be reconciled into a single organizational representation. This representation is referred to as the *manifest organization*.[123] The value of the manifest organization is that it allows one to focus in greater depth on specific functional areas and individuals worthy of further study.

Many organizations use various software tools to create their organizational charts. Over the years, we have received numerous chart formats. Figures 12.2 and 12.3 are representative samples of some of the more unique charts we have seen. Figure 12.2 features the CEO at the bottom with subordinates above him; this format most likely stems from the recent popularity of "servant leadership." Figure 12.3 aims to show everyone as "collegial" or a "networked" organization. Most organizations, however, have their charts flowing from the top down as evidenced in Figure 12.4. You might call this your traditional format.

We only demonstrate these formats because we have a very specific way in which we draw and format our organization charts. First, a box indicates a manager with at least one direct subordinate. Second, a circle demonstrates a nonmanagerial role. Such a role could be located at any level of the organization and could relate to countless different functions or types of roles. This role is not a manager and thus does not have the same accountabilities and authorities of a manager.

---

[123] Jaques, Elliott. Requisite Organization, Cason Hall Publishers, Arlington, VA. Page pair 11

Preparing to Analyze the Existing Structure

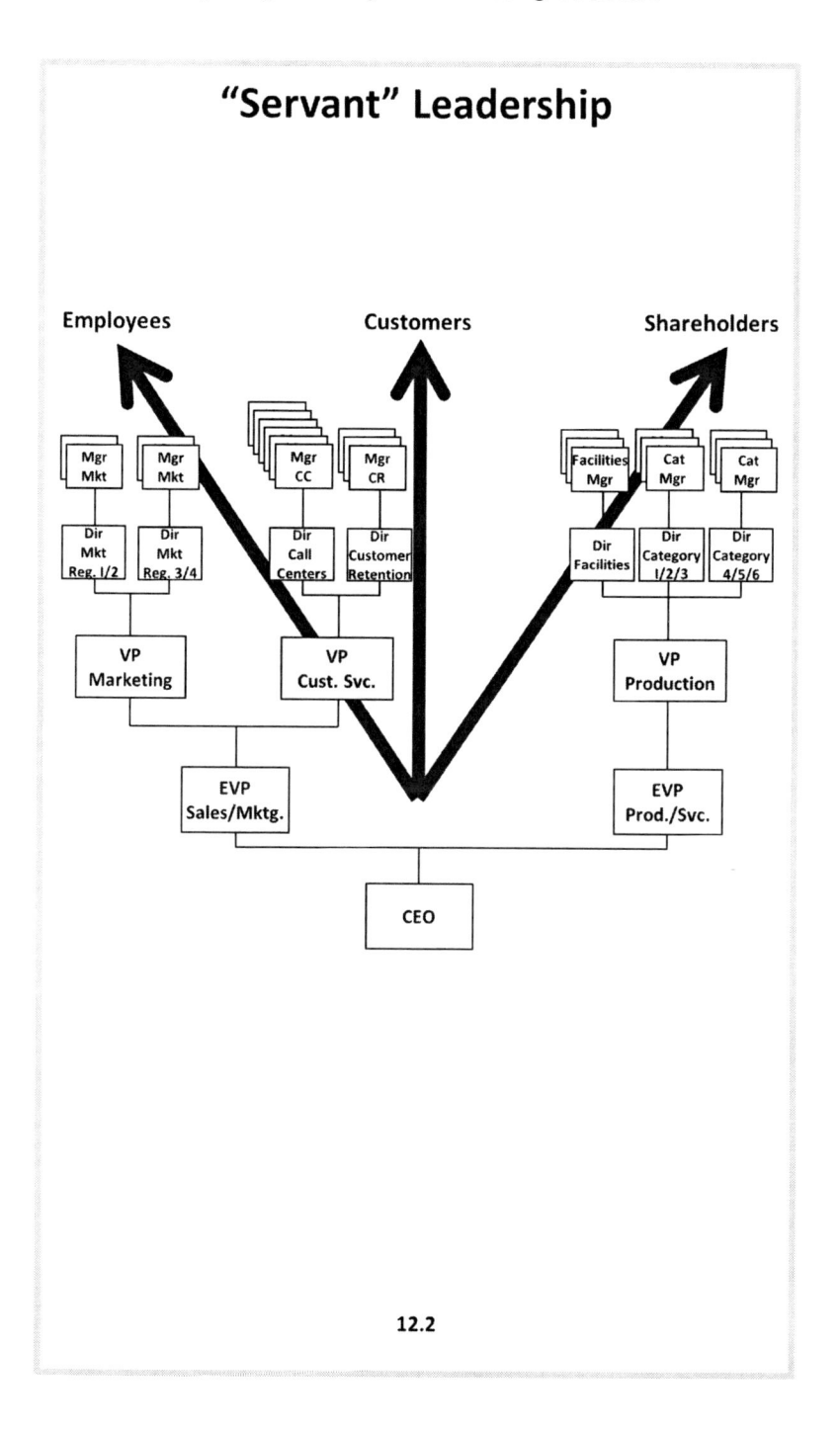

"Servant" Leadership

Employees — Customers — Shareholders

- Mgr Mkt | Mgr Mkt | Mgr CC | Mgr CR | Facilities Mgr | Cat Mgr | Cat Mgr
- Dir Mkt Reg. 1/2 | Dir Mkt Reg. 3/4 | Dir Call Centers | Dir Customer Retention | Dir Facilities | Dir Category 1/2/3 | Dir Category 4/5/6
- VP Marketing | VP Cust. Svc. | VP Production
- EVP Sales/Mktg. | EVP Prod./Svc.
- CEO

12.2

221

The "Networked" Leader

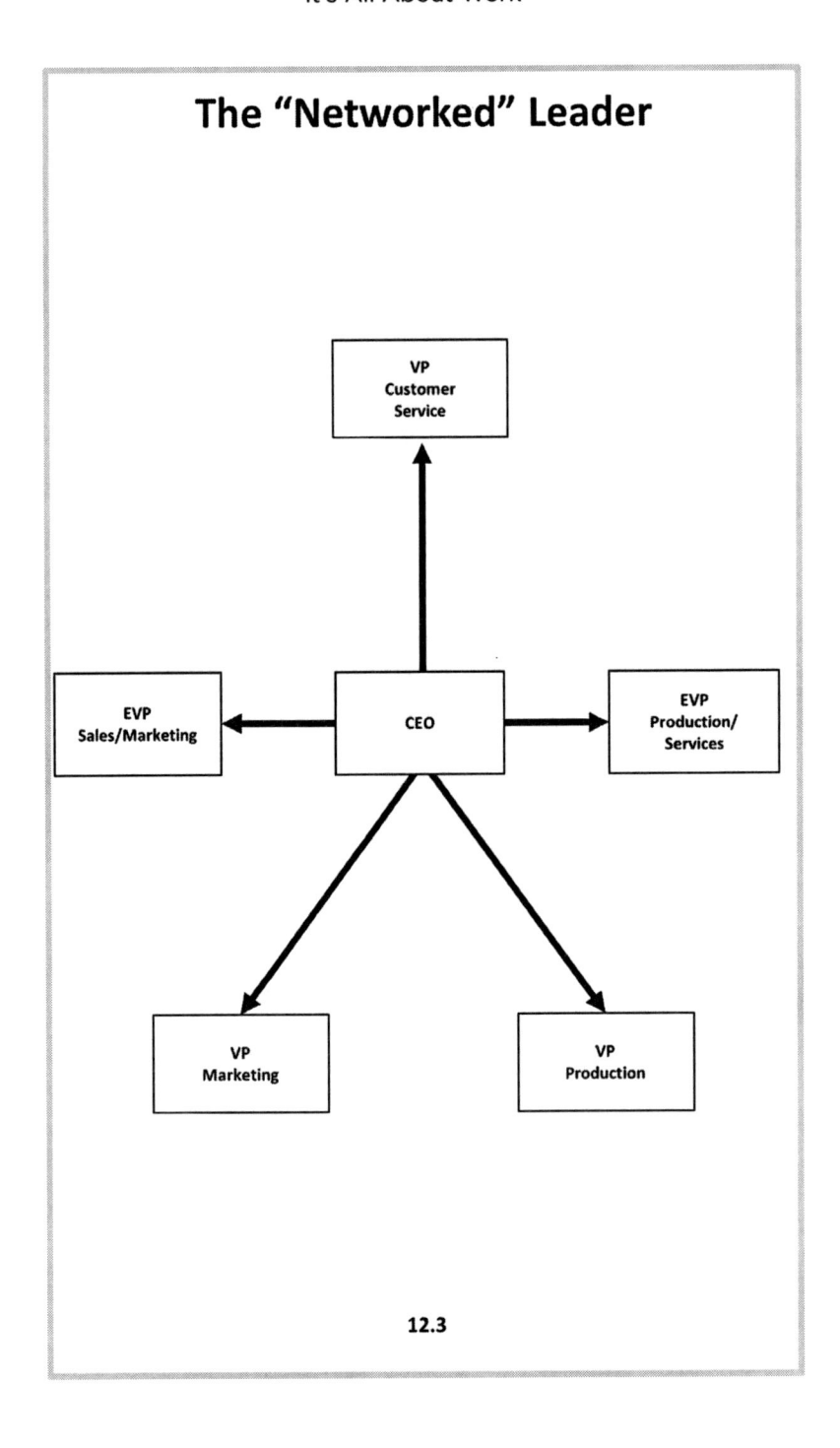

```
                    ┌──────────┐
                    │    VP    │
                    │ Customer │
                    │ Service  │
                    └──────────┘
                         ▲
                         │
┌──────────────┐    ┌─────────┐    ┌──────────────┐
│     EVP      │◄───│   CEO   │───►│     EVP      │
│Sales/Marketing│    │         │    │ Production/  │
│              │    │         │    │  Services    │
└──────────────┘    └─────────┘    └──────────────┘
                     ╱       ╲
                    ╱         ╲
                   ▼           ▼
            ┌──────────┐   ┌──────────┐
            │    VP    │   │    VP    │
            │Marketing │   │Production│
            └──────────┘   └──────────┘
```

12.3

Preparing to Analyze the Existing Structure

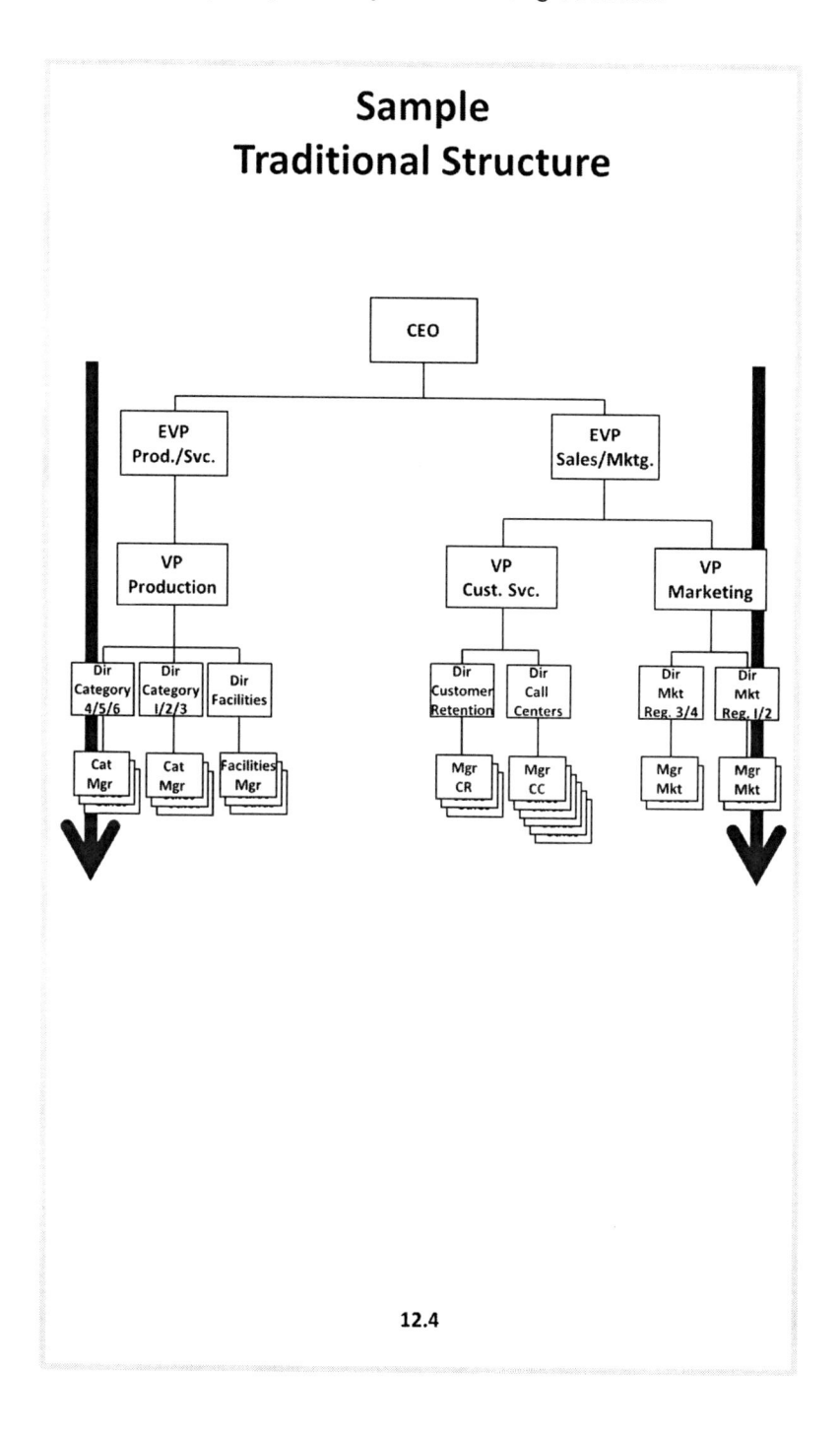

Sample Traditional Structure

```
                          CEO
              ┌────────────┴────────────┐
          EVP                         EVP
       Prod./Svc.                  Sales/Mktg.
            │                ┌────────┴────────┐
           VP               VP                 VP
       Production       Cust. Svc.          Marketing
      ┌─────┼─────┐      ┌─────┐             ┌─────┐
     Dir    Dir   Dir   Dir    Dir          Dir    Dir
  Category Category Facilities Customer Call  Mkt    Mkt
   4/5/6   1/2/3          Retention Centers Reg. 3/4 Reg. 1/2
     │      │      │       │        │        │       │
    Cat    Cat  Facilities Mgr      Mgr     Mgr     Mgr
    Mgr    Mgr    Mgr      CR       CC      Mkt     Mkt
```

12.4

We next take whatever organizational charts we receive and reformat them based on our tentative assessment of levels of work. The key is to visualize the differentiation of work at each consecutive level. Because we do not know at this early stage in a given study what level of work individuals are actually performing, we typically level the chart based on the titles of existing roles or the compensation level related to a given role. Figures 12.5 and 12.6 show how we apply this initial leveling process to a given organization chart. Note the presence of multiple titles. At this point, it is logical to ask, are these roles really in different levels or do they just reflect different pay scales?

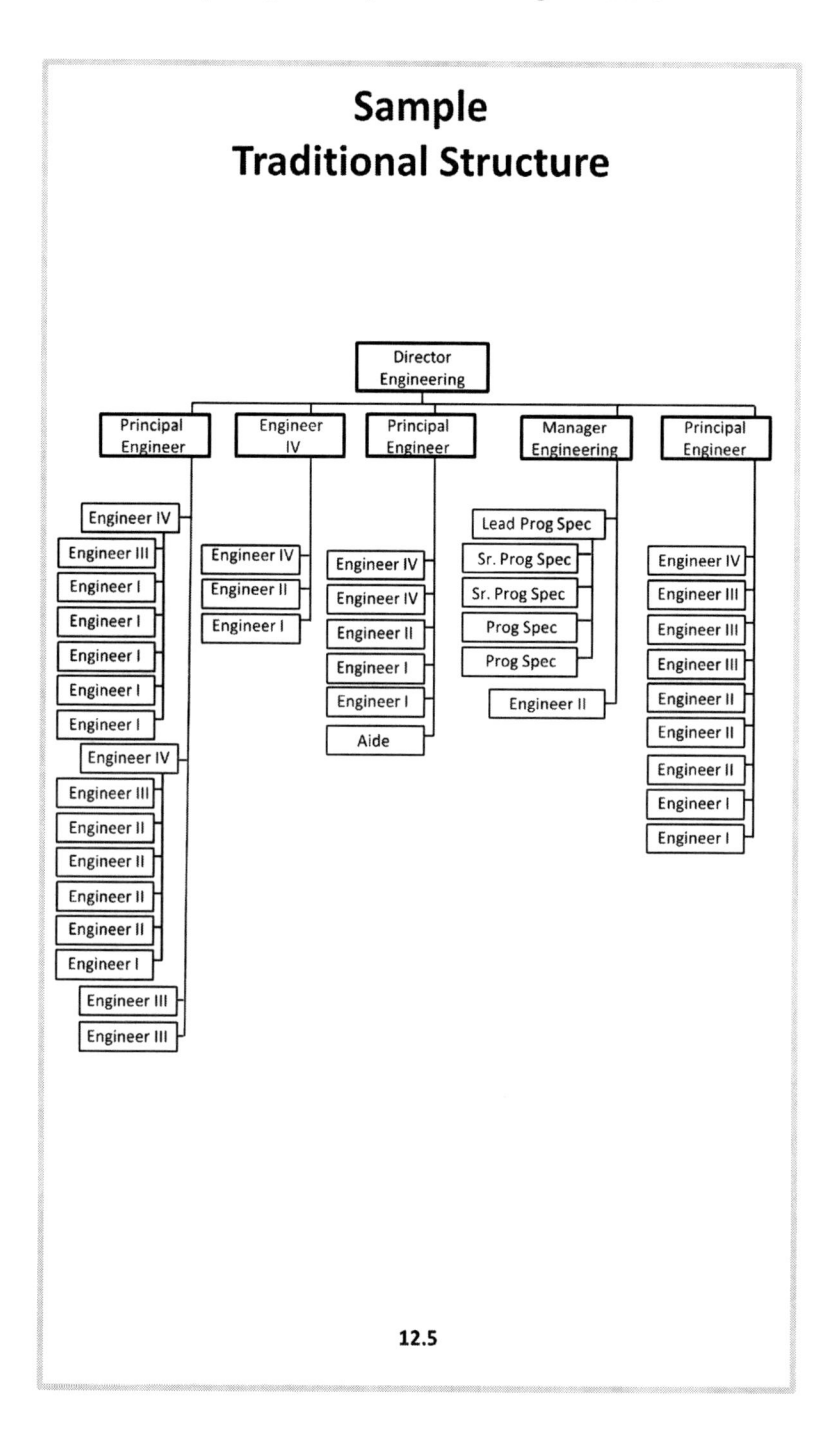

Sample Traditional Structure

```
                         Director
                        Engineering
    ┌──────────┬──────────┼──────────┬──────────┐
Principal   Engineer   Principal   Manager   Principal
Engineer      IV       Engineer   Engineering Engineer
```

Principal Engineer:
- Engineer IV
  - Engineer III
  - Engineer I
  - Engineer I
  - Engineer I
  - Engineer I
  - Engineer I
- Engineer IV
  - Engineer III
  - Engineer II
  - Engineer II
  - Engineer II
  - Engineer II
  - Engineer I
- Engineer III
- Engineer III

Engineer IV:
- Engineer IV
- Engineer II
- Engineer I

Principal Engineer:
- Engineer IV
- Engineer IV
- Engineer II
- Engineer I
- Engineer I
- Aide

Manager Engineering:
- Lead Prog Spec
- Sr. Prog Spec
- Sr. Prog Spec
- Prog Spec
- Prog Spec
- Engineer II

Principal Engineer:
- Engineer IV
- Engineer III
- Engineer III
- Engineer III
- Engineer II
- Engineer II
- Engineer II
- Engineer I
- Engineer I

12.5

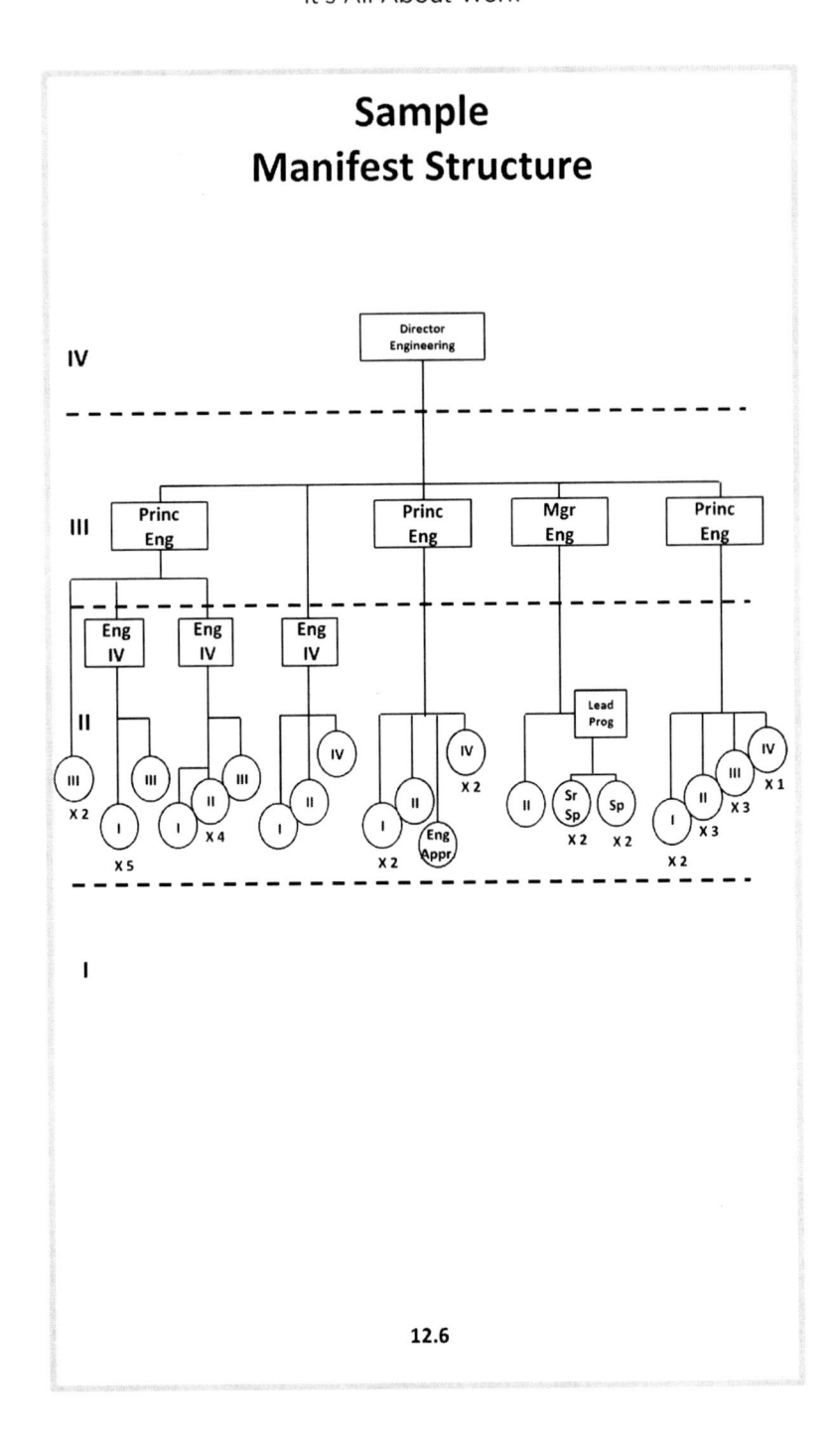

Sample Manifest Structure

IV

III

II

I

12.6

Sample Company and Structure

Figure 12.7 depicts a typical manifest structure after we have put all the roles into a "guestimated" level. We will use this sample company organization chart in the following discussion. We realize that your organization is probably more complicated than this, but in the interest of brevity and learning we have decided to use a very simple sample.

Note that figure 12.7 depicts a level IV organization made up of four discreet operating functions and a separate branch role. Each role is supposedly functioning at level III: a sales function, production function, service (delivery) function, and support functions (office manager). In essence, this organization constitutes a stand-alone level IV business unit. In this case, there is a corporate office that provides additional services to the local team as well. The value of going through this process is that it suggests possible areas requiring further exploration. For example, in the above situation, is the office manager really functioning at level III or, more likely, at level II, thereby filling the gap between the office manager and the office workforce? A similar question relates to the production manager and her supervisors. The value of this tentative manifest organization chart is in identifying potential interviewees.

Identifying Key Data Points (Potential Interviewees):

As described above, the utility of this effort is that it often provides useful insights as to who specifically should be involved (interviewed or surveyed) in any subsequent project work. Constructing a manifest organization chart in this manner is difficult because the information analyzed in the process is not always relevant. For example, titles are often misleading and compensation data is sometimes skewed by experience or the job market. Thus, any attempt to assess the level of complexity of roles without the benefit of time-span data or other detailed work assessments requires one to utilize several different techniques to put roles into a given organizational layer. In other words, how do you assign a level to a role you have not analyzed or studied in any depth? Below are some techniques that can help in this initial leveling process.

It's All About Work

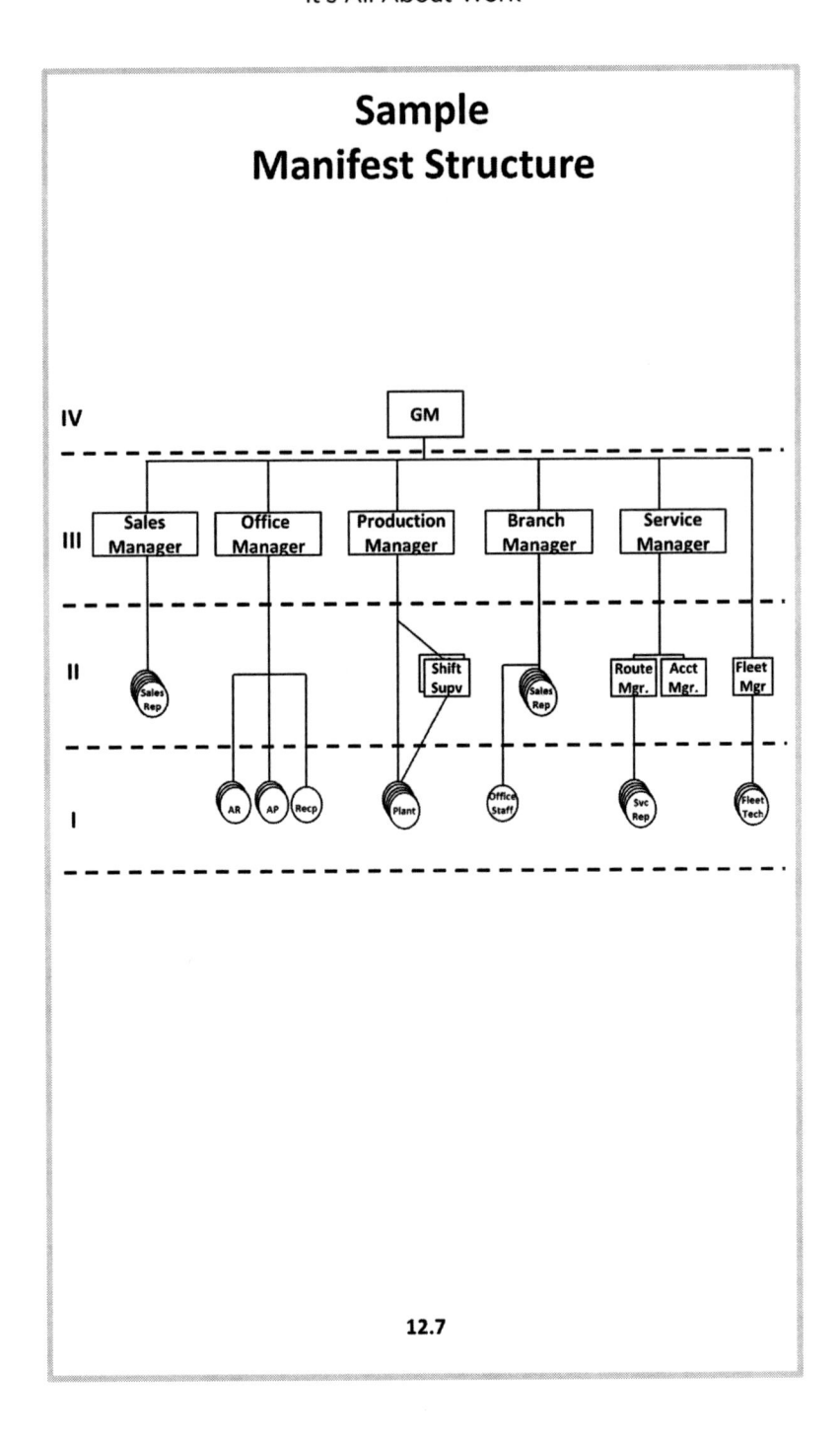

Sample Manifest Structure

Stratum	
IV	GM
III	Sales Manager — Office Manager — Production Manager — Branch Manager — Service Manager
II	Sales Rep; Shift Supv; Sales Rep; Route Mgr, Acct Mgr; Fleet Mgr
I	AR, AP, Recp; Plant; Office Staff; Svc Rep; Fleet Tech

12.7

228

First, you can examine existing reporting relationships (who works for whom) and fit the corresponding pattern of roles into the level you think they are currently working at. Do not be surprised if you see multiple roles within one level or far too many layers within a given level. For example, you might find seven levels of management in what you believe is a level IV operation. During this initial leveling process, you may very well have more titles than levels. Ask yourself, is that additional manager really another level or simply a title (or pay scale) above the subordinate manager? Other things to look for are managers with only one subordinate. What does that manager do to add value to just one subordinate? Also note any independent contributor roles (no subordinates) or specialty roles (engineers, quality control). In addition, when looking at a tentative manifest organization chart, you might ask yourself the following question:

What other teams and organizations perform work or provide input for this team/role to get their work done?

Second, the project team can build on experiences gained during previous studies where similar roles were analyzed in greater depth. Finally, the project team can analyze existing job evaluation data, such as Hay system data, to estimate the level of complexity of a given role. Errors made in attempting to assess the level of complexity of existing roles are not critical at this stage because they can easily be corrected during the analysis phase of the project when real work-related data is gathered. The real value of this initial assessment is simply to provide additional insights into selecting possible areas and roles of interest.

Review Role Data:

Next, review the role descriptions of all roles, if you have them. Many organizations have what we would call a "job posting" rather than what we would define as a true role description. Does the role description clearly articulate what the role is accountable for? Can you measure the output of that accountability? Is the authority to accomplish the work of the role clearly defined? Does it indicate who the role incumbent interacts with to get work done? Conducting a review of role descriptions also suggests specific areas where one might need to gather additional information.

Locate Role Anomalies:

Construction of the manifest chart allows you to identify potential organizational anomalies or areas of interest. For example, these anomalies may be areas of interest that you will want to explore further. Such areas might include the following:

- Managers with only one direct report
- Managers with a large number of reports
- Managers with no subordinates
- Specialty advisors and technical roles and their accountabilities and authorities
- The number of titles and layers
- The dotted line or matrix reporting structures

Next, lay out all the organizational charts and select people at all levels in the organization. Make sure you identify individuals from all functions, both good performers and bad, for inclusion in the data-gathering phase of the project. Identify roles that seem to be misunderstood by others, roles that work with a large number of others to get their work done (inputs/outputs), and roles that seem to have a questionable accountability and authority base. These are the individuals who will assist you in discovering how the organization really works and how its structure is currently functioning. In smaller organizations, it is often possible to include all personnel in a given work area. In larger organizations, you should gather work data from 10–20 percent of the personnel. If you are unsure of what work a particular role performs, add that role to the list.

In our sample company (Figure 12.7), here is who we would want to talk to:

- All level III managers and the level IV GM
- A random selection of two individuals chosen from each of the following roles at levels I and II:
  - Sales representative
  - Office staff
  - Production employee
  - Shift supervisor
  - Route manager
  - Account manager
  - Fleet manager
  - Branch sales rep and branch office staff

Target Organizational Anomalies:

An analysis of stakeholder concerns coupled with a review of the manifest organization suggests likely areas of interest that may need to be probed in further depth. For example, if stakeholders identify slow decision making due to excessive process-control steps, the project team will want to develop some questions around existing process steps. Further, the project team will also want to talk to some individuals involved in the current process. While reviewing the data and stakeholder information, take note of so-called anomalies. Generate specific questions to explore these anomalies. For example you might say, "Let's talk about process here at Sample Company. How do existing processes impact decision making for your role? How about for other roles?

What Is the Work?

To construct the extant organization (the organization that reflects how work actually gets done), it is necessary to analyze the work that is actually being performed by various role incumbents.[124] Thus, every project begins with a series of questions about the work that is actually done. For example, it is always useful to ask an individual, "What are the five or six critical tasks that you are being asked to perform? Who works for you? What are the five or six tasks that you are holding them accountable to perform? Which of these tasks will have the longest time span, that is, take the longest time to complete?"

Gathering actual work-related data to construct the extant organization is described in greater detail in the next chapter.

---

124 Jaques, Elliott and Clement, Stephen D. Executive Leadership, Cason Hall Publishers, Arlington, VA, 1991. Page 102

Chapter 13

Constructing the Extant Organization

The organization and the people who work there know what needs to be done. Generally, they will do whatever it takes to achieve their work goals or objectives. This is popularly known as implementing work-arounds.

The extant organization represents how work actually gets done in an organization. The value of the extant organization is that it provides a picture of how people in the organization intuitively believe that things must be organized to get work done.[125] Additionally, it provides an idea of the magnitude of change required to move from the current situation to one actually required by the nature of the work, attendant mission, and functions assigned to the activity. You can construct the extant organization from data collected from employees about the work that they actually do. As described above, this data provides insights into any work-arounds that are followed to accomplish a given mission or task. It is extremely probable that there will be marked contrasts in what people say they do (extant) versus what others think they do (their manager, role

---

[125] Jaques, Elliott. Requisite Organization, Cason Hall Publishers, Arlington, VA, 1996. Page pair 11

descriptions, and other teams).

To gather the aforementioned data, it is necessary to talk to a variety of people in the organization. Previously, we discussed identifying a random sampling of individuals from all levels and functions. We prefer to collect this work data in the form of one-on-one interviews lasting up to two hours. You can expect longer interviews for individuals occupying roles higher up in the organization. Lower-level interviews, for example at level I, may be less than an hour. The interviewer should be the project manager or someone on the project team. While these interviews can be rather time-consuming, we find that the process allows us to collect extremely useful qualitative data about actual work. In the past, however, we have utilized other data-gathering methods when we saw fit to do so. For example, you can gather data from a larger and broader audience by hosting focus groups or by sending surveys across the entire organization. In our experience, however, these methods are purely supplemental to a quality one-on-one interview. We firmly believe that the quality of one-on-one interviews cannot be matched by the quantity of data provided by surveys or focus groups.

Construct a Structured Interview Guide

Before talking to your people, you must first construct a structured interview guide. As described previously, the interview guide should focus on the work that is done. By talking to the people who actual perform that work, you are able to gather insights into the direction the organization may need to move in to increase overall operating effectiveness.

Typical Questions:

Here is a brief sampling of generic questions we ask in the interview process:

- What are the five or six critical tasks that you are accountable for in your current role?
- Who do you work for? Who works for you?

- Who provides inputs to get your work done?

- Which of the tasks that you are currently working on will take you the longest time in the future to complete?

- What five or six tasks have you assigned to your subordinate?

- Which of these tasks will take you the longest time to complete?

- What are some factors that inhibit your ability to get your work done?

- Who do you have to interact with to produce your outputs?

- Is there any work that you are doing that is non-value adding that could be eliminated?

The actual questions in the interview guide should be tailored to the specific project area one is studying. For example, if the study is focused on the Information Technology (IT) functional area, then there should be questions relating to architectural standards, data bases, service agreements, etc. Similarly, if the focus is on manufacturing operations, then questions regarding process improvement and quality need to be added. Over the years, we have developed a rather lengthy interview guide, with far too many questions and variations to include in this book. Suffice it to say, however, that the gathering of factual work related data is a critical step in any organizational design project endeavor.

Reflection:

Once all work-related data is gathered and the interview process completed, it is necessary to set aside a significant amount of thinking time for the project team to sort through all of the recently gathered information. The thinking time should allow the project team to not only reflect on the amassed data but to thoroughly discuss possible remedies for emerging issues. The reflection process should produce a comprehensive picture of the current work system. One way to do this is to begin with a single individual role and analyze the actual work this person does:

- What does this person do? What is she accountable for?
- Do the manager and others see this role encompassing the same work and accountabilities?
- What level is the role currently? What level should it be?
- What level is the individual performing at?
- If the level of the role is not consistent with the level of the individual, then why is that? (This requires judgment.)
- What or whom does she need input from to get her work done?
- What authority does she have to get her work done?
- What authorities do others (not the immediate manager) have over her work and tasks?
- Are there any major projects underway that could affect her work?
- Are projects pursued as stand-alone initiatives or as additional duty for the team members?

This analysis should be performed on each and every selected role in the studied organization. As you go through this process, a picture emerges of an organization that most likely operates quite differently from that originally reviewed. At this point, it is useful to plot every role on a new organization chart reflecting the actual level of the work that is currently being performed by the role incumbent. Figures 13.1 and 13.2 allow you to compare the manifest organization of a sample company and the extant structure (recall the manifest organization was the structure formally depicted on the company's organization charts, whereas the extant structure represents how work is actually getting done).

Figure 13.2 portrays the output of our data-gathering exercise and the subsequent plotting of roles reflecting their current work level. This plotting generally uncovers typical organizational problems, such as missing roles, incumbents working at too low a level, and role crowding. The most common issue we see in today's environment is that the work is being performed at too low a level. For example, in the situation described previously, the work of a level III role incumbent actually consists of level II tasks. In a situation such as this, you must then look to see who is doing the level III work. Is it the level IV manager or project team—or perhaps the work is not getting done at all?

At this point, it is useful to explore why this work is being performed at too low a level. For example, one should not immediately assume that such an outcome occurs because the role incumbent does not have sufficient capacity to work at the right level. In this phase of a particular study, we analyze the work, not the individual. In analyzing the work, we make an assumption that most people aspire to work to their full potential. (We will deal with a capacity shortfall in a later chapter.) Many organizations, however, simply do not allow individuals to operate to their full capacity for a number of reasons.

Review the levels of work discussion in chapter 5 and look for organizational issues that might result in work being "pushed down" a level. Does the role contain the minimum authorities necessary to accomplish this task? What authority do incumbents have in receiving service (input) from others? Do they have other people in the organization who have authority over them that might conflict with their work flow, such as multiple people assigning them tasks or giving them direction or orders? Are they inundated with lower-level tasks (meetings, paperwork, etc.)? Has the organization limited their discretion or data to make decisions? Has the organization compressed its time horizon to meet short-term goals? The issues we spoke of earlier are just the beginning of a whole host of reasons a role might be pushed down a level.

You should have amassed enough data at this point to begin a compilation of outdated tasks, tasks that no longer seem to provide value to the organization. You can then set aside these tasks for further exploration at a later date. Do not assume that when people say that a task does not add value that this contention is in fact true. Do some due diligence before eliminating a particular task. There was a reason for every task at some point in the past; make sure that original rationale is no longer valid or needed.

Once you have performed the aforementioned type of organizational analysis, the project team will begin to uncover existing organizational problems such as too many layers, unclear roles and accountability or authority, poor working relationships, and so on. These are the very problems that need to be addressed and resolved if the organization is to increase its overall operating effectiveness. How to do this is discussed in the next chapter.

Interviewee Observations and Opinions:

During the interview process, most personnel will likely share their comments, observations, and opinions regarding the current state of the organization. These are very similar to the customer comments many companies receive on customer surveys. This information reflects how existing personnel judge how the workforce deals with current problem areas and describes any specific work-arounds that they have implemented to deal with these problems. Issues identified here typically generate additional areas that may need to be explored further. Some observations may be completely unrelated to structure, accountability, or capacity and yet still warrant further exploration. For example, if several interviewee's express an opinion that their manager deals with people through intimidation and fear, you need to look at this issue in further detail as it may lead to serious morale issues.

Sample Manifest Structure

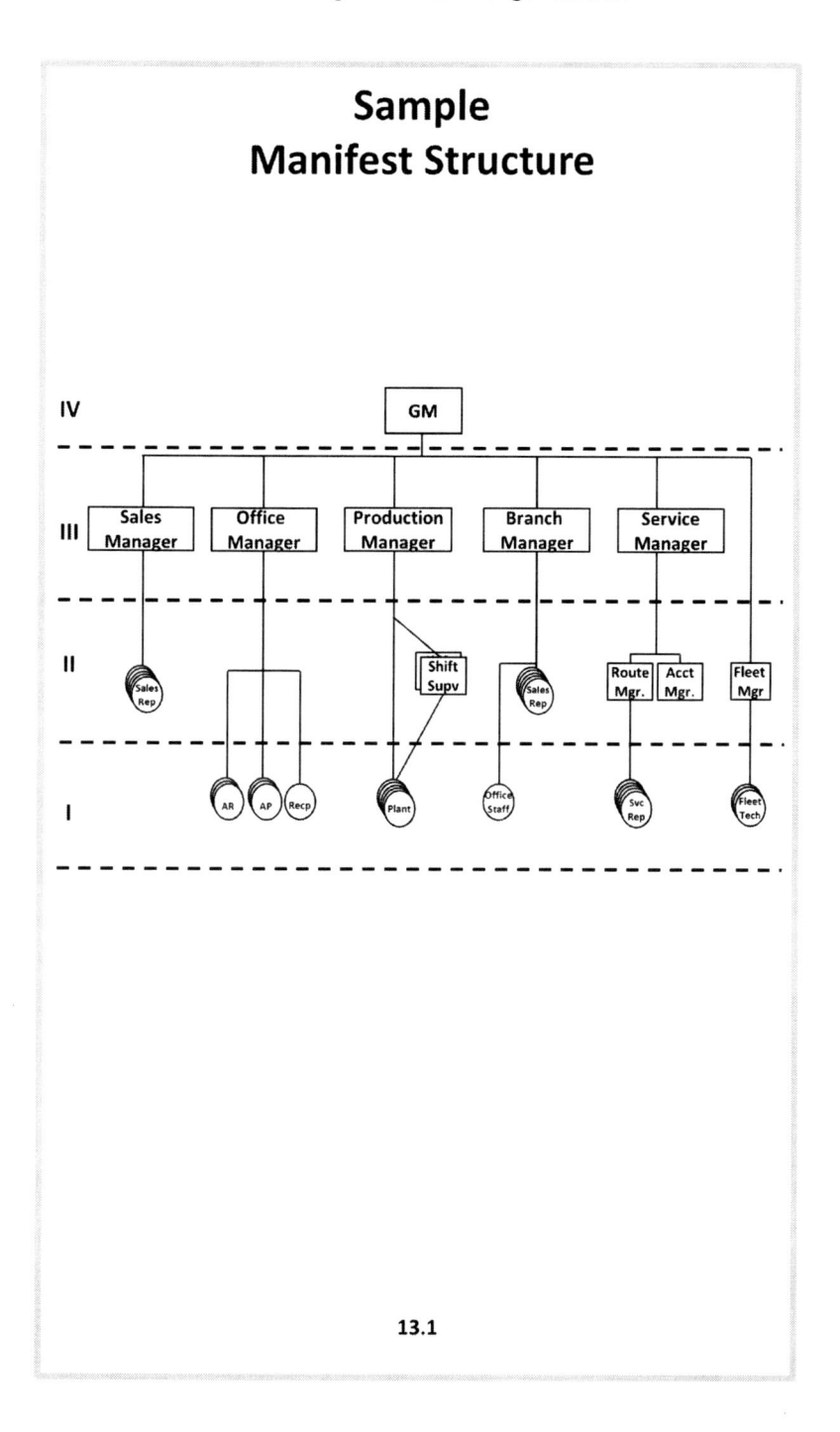

IV — GM

III — Sales Manager | Office Manager | Production Manager | Branch Manager | Service Manager

II — Sales Rep | Shift Supv | Sales Rep | Route Mgr. | Acct Mgr. | Fleet Mgr

I — AR | AP | Recp | Plant | Office Staff | Svc Rep | Fleet Tech

13.1

Sample Extant Structure

IV — GM

III — Production Manager, Service Manager

— Sales Manager, Branch Manager

II — Office Manager, Shift Supv, Sales Rep, Acct Mgr., Fleet Mgr, Sales Rep

— Route Mgr.

I — AR, AP, Recp, Plant, Office Staff, Svc Rep, Fleet Tech

13.2

COMMENTS: These are statements made by personnel related to specific questions raised by an interviewer.

OBSERVATIONS: These are observations of the current state of things. These observations can be from the project team or the interviewees. They are not just observations about structure; they may be observations about anything that was discovered during the process.

OPINIONS: These are additional responses from anyone involved in the project.

Organizational Analysis:

Once key work-related data is gathered, it is then possible to construct the extant organization. (Recall the extant organization reflects how work actually gets done). Time-span data gathered during the interview process details the level of work relative to a given subordinate. Therefore, use of the time-span instrument is a good technique to employ in determining the actual level of work of a given role. Time-span data requires you to interview all of the managers in a given work organization. However, it is not always possible to get time-span data for all individuals. Therefore, it is sometimes necessary to utilize other information sources to assess the level of work of a given role. For example, compensation data can provide insight into level of work. Similarly, leadership relationships can also provide useful input data, such as whether the individual is accountable for leading a small group of people (30–60 individuals—level II) or a number of stand-alone subordinate activities—level III.

Even titles and reporting relationships can sometimes provide useful input to the assessment of the level of work. For example, suppose an individual works in a large government agency, say the Department of the Army. He might be a political appointee (an Assistant Secretary of the Army) reporting to the Secretary of the Army. The Secretary of the Army (SA) position is well-known as a full-scale level VII equivalent position (The SA "runs" the army and works alongside the Chief of Staff of the Army—a four-star General. Four-star Generals occupy level VII positions, especially the Chief of Staff role). Thus, the Assistant Secretary of the Army position essentially constitutes a high-level VI role (a three-star general equivalent) or a low level VII role. Most assistant secretary positions in the current army structure also have three-star generals assigned as deputies. Time-span data obtained from the SA may show that a given assistant secretary is actually functioning at level IV or V. Nonetheless, the role calls for a level VI or VII individual.

Perhaps the most useful ancillary analytical technique (other than time-span) is to compare the work someone does in a given position with those tasks that a majority of other people normally perform in that type of work at that level. Over the past two decades, we have amassed a substantial database of critical tasks by level and function that we use in making normative comparisons. For example, individual X, who occupies a financial-analysis role, reports that she spends the majority of her time working on the following specific tasks:

1. Identifying financial trends in the pricing/promotion area
2. Aggregating financial performance data for quarterly business reviews
3. Analyzing the potential impact of proposed pricing changes
4. Developing a financial summary of recent promotional program initiatives

These tasks are normally associated with people working at level II in a typical financial organization. It turns out that the individual in the above example is actually occupying a level III role based on her title, compensation, reporting scheme, manager's expectation, and so on. Note the absence of level III type tasks in the above list, such as generating financial options and risk analysis. Thus, you can conclude that individual X is operating at too low a level. If such a pattern persists across multiple roles in the remainder of the financial organization, you might conclude that the whole organization is being pulled down a level. Figure 13.3 graphically portrays such a situation.

Role Being Pulled to the Next Lower Level

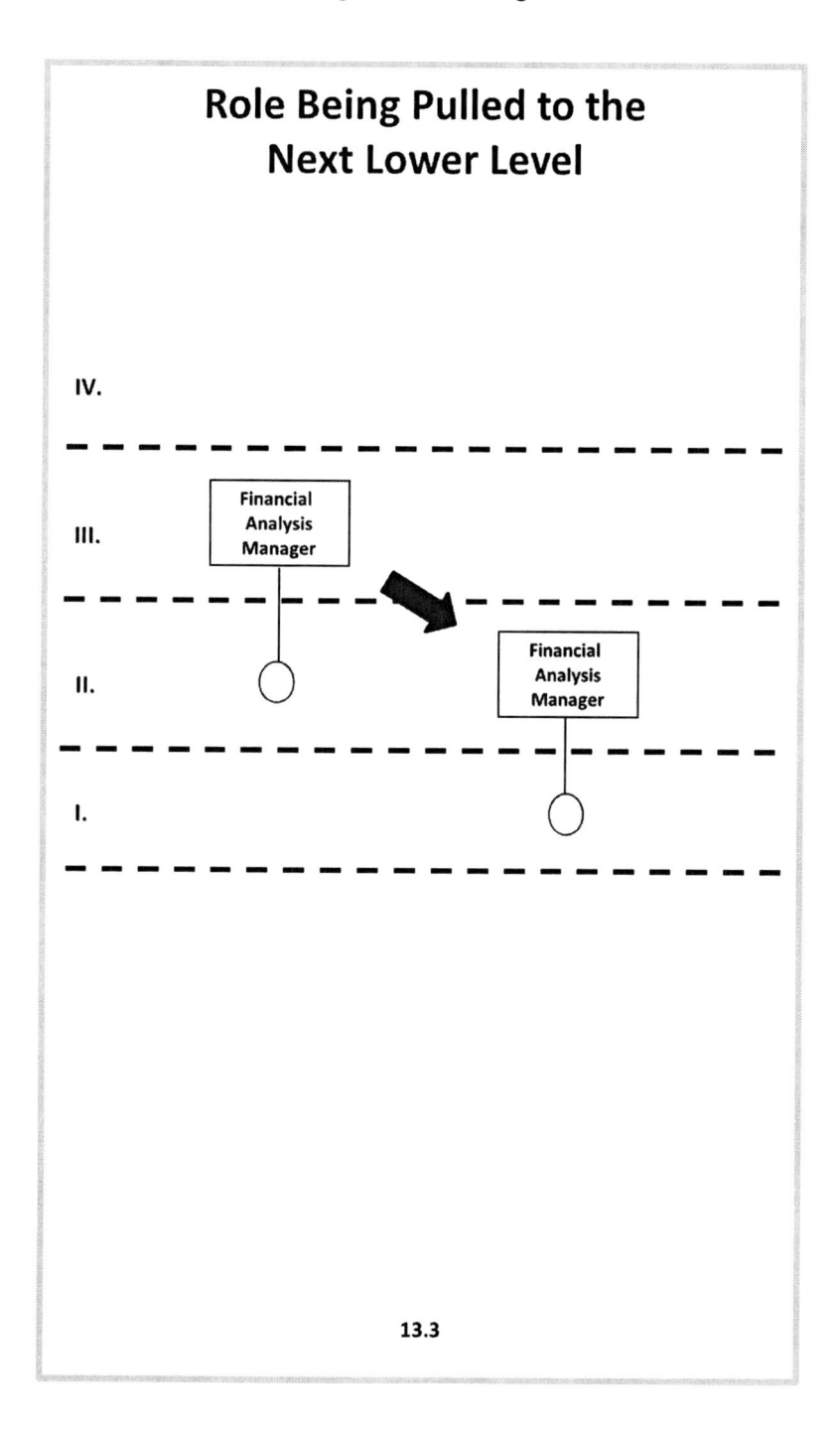

IV.

- - - - - - - - - - - - - - - -

III.   Financial
        Analysis
        Manager

- - - - - - - - - - - - - - - -

                    Financial
II.   Analysis
        ○   Manager

- - - - - - - - - - - - - - - -

I.
                    ○

- - - - - - - - - - - - - - - -

13.3

Knowledge of the extant organization is useful in that it suggests steps or actions to be taken for the organization to move toward a requisite structure. For example, in the situation described above, if the whole finance organization is being pulled down a level, it is important to figure out how to get the finance people focused on the right work for their level. This is where some organizational detective work comes in. The challenge is to find out what underlying issues may be causing people to work at too low a level. Here are some possible examples:

1. The organizational climate is such that the whole organization is being dragged down (forced to work at a lower level) due to:

    - Financial concerns

    - Competitive/time pressures

    - Leadership issues

    - History/culture

    - Narrow policies, procedures, and discretion

2. Subordinates are not competent to do their own work, thus pulling down the manger to do the lower-level work

3. The manager is not capable of working at his or her assigned level, thus pushing down the subordinate to do lower-level work

Alternatively, the detective may also ask the following questions: Who is doing the missing work? Has the organization fabricated a workaround system or process to get this work done? Is there a missing role in the current structure? Figures 13.4 and 13.5 portray the impact of a missing and combined role.

Let's revisit our sample extant structure. (Figure 13.6) Actual work data gathered during the interview process found that the sales manager was de facto performing level II work. The sales manager was essentially a sales closer with the bulk of his time and tasks spent in front of potential customers, negotiating and closing accounts. Similarly, the office and branch managers were also found to be operating at too low a level. Office staff located in the branch readily identified that they had two bosses, the local branch manager and the office manager at the main location. The service reps were confused as to who had the authority to assign them tasks and prioritize their tasks, the account manager who was accountable for the customer relationships or the route manager who was accountable to manage an efficient delivery system. The fleet manager stated that he had two bosses as well, but it was clear to this individual "who was the top dog."

The value of these findings is that it permits the researcher to ask the following fundamental questions: If the sales manager is operating at level II, who is doing the operational sales work (e.g., level III business analyses, exploring the second order consequences of proposed pricing changes, managing multiple promotional programs taking place simultaneously, etc.)? Similarly in branch operations, who is developing and adapting sales and service initiatives to the local market needs? If the sales manager or the branch manager is not doing this work, is the GM doing it? Does this detract from his or her other work? And most importantly, why are they working at too low a level? Further, why is it not clear to branch staff who they report to?

By focusing on these types of questions you will able to develop future solutions and recommendations. These recommendations form the outline to be used in designing a requisite structure.

The Impact of Combined or Missing Roles

V. Tasks

IV. Tasks / Combined Roles
- If two independent roles are combined, especially across organizational levels, the combined work load is likely to exceed the capabilities of a single person

III. Tasks
- Generally, when the workload in a given role is too much for a single person, the short-term task requirements tend to drive out the longer range work

II. Tasks

I.

13.4

The Impact of Combined or Missing Roles

V. [Tasks]

IV. [Missing Role]
- When there is a missing role, either the subordinate has to step up to perform the higher level work, the next higher level manager is pulled down to perform that work, or some (or all) of the work doesn't get performed at all.

III. [Tasks]
- Generally, the higher level manager is pulled down to perform some of the more critical tasks because the lower level individual does not possess sufficient capacity to do the work while the remainder of the work is usually ignored.

II. [Tasks]

I.

13.5

Sample
Extant Structure

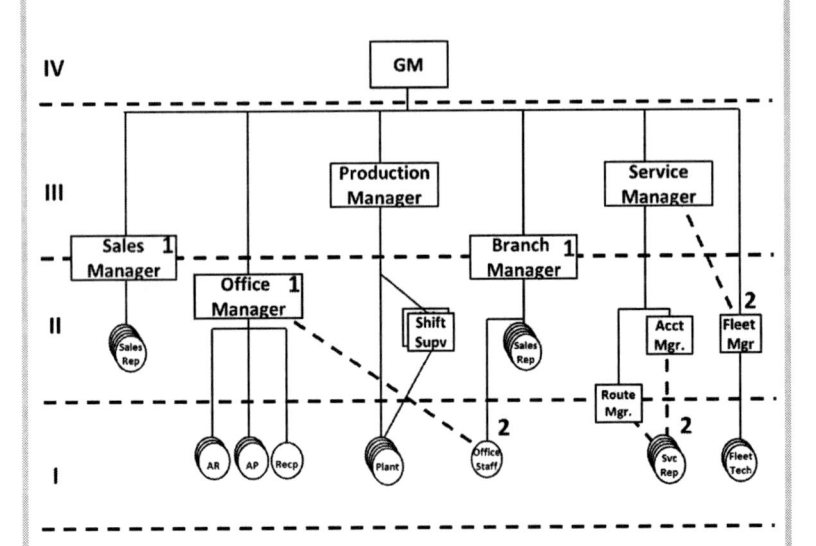

IV — GM

III — Production Manager, Service Manager

Sales Manager 1, Branch Manager 1

II — Office Manager 1, Shift Supv, Sales Rep, Acct Mgr., Fleet Mgr 2, Sales Rep

Route Mgr.

I — AR, AP, Recp, Plant, Office Staff 2, Svc Rep 2, Fleet Tech

1: Role is operating at lower level

2: Role essentially (extant) reports to multiple managers

13.6

Determining Levels of Work in Your Organization:

Every organization, or business unit, has two easily discernible layers, a boss and a worker. If the front-line worker is a level I individual, then who does that person report to? And who does her manager report to? These questions are asked until you reach the boss. This permits you to quite easily calculate how many levels of reporting exist. You can do this same exercise in the opposite direction. If you believe the boss is a level IV individual, then start going down the chain of command to see how many layers emerge.

Determining the level of complexity of the business unit can start at the top or the bottom. Refer back to the levels of work discussion in chapter 5 when analyzing your front-line worker. It is very possible that a business begins with a level II or even a level III front-line employee. If you begin your organizational analysis at level II and have four additional reporting levels above that front-line employee, then based on your reporting relationships, you have a level VI business unit. Ask yourself, are we sure that this is really a level VI business? If not, what level is the business or what level should it be? Substantial project work over the past two decades suggests that level V business units operate more effectively (i.e., they are more nimble and adaptive) than level VI BUs.

If you believe that the business unit is a level V operation, then it is possible that you have too many layers. Recall that each layer should add value to the next lower layer. Is each person or role in this chain truly adding value? Perhaps one of them is a "straw boss" or a supervisor (see earlier definition in Figure 9.3 and its limited authority).

Working Relationships:

In today's highly competitive business environment, it is not always possible to organize in an optimum fashion (i.e., maximum effectiveness). Sometimes it is necessary to centralize office support functions or roles to reduce costs. We call these centralizing initiatives *shared services*. *The output of these roles* (payroll or HR, for example) is provided to all others in the organization regardless of location, function, or business unit. The presence of shared services, however, adds complexity to an organization's leadership system. Rather than directly owning a given support activity, a business unit in a shared service environment has to receive services from this activity. This now involves the BU in complex working relationship issues. In some cases, a BU service receiver may feel that they are not getting adequate service. Generally, however, service receivers in such situations have no choice. The shared service activity is monopolistic in nature. The service receiver is forced to "buy" services internally. The operative question to broach in such a situation is, "Would you buy this service from organization A if you had a choice?" If the answer to that question is no, then the project team needs to uncover possible problems pertaining to the service activity. Is the quality bad? Are the services not provided on time?

The essence of any shared service activity is that it entails a service-providing or service-getting relationship. For such a relationship to be effective, the accountabilities and authorities underpinning the relationship need to be clear. One of the observations that we have made over the years is that the larger the company the more likely a shared service activity can lose sight of its customer. Without proper performance controls and metrics, it is very easy for a shared service activity to focus inwardly on its own performance metrics and not the customer's. This tendency is especially true in large government bureaucracies. Because they are monopolistic in nature, they never go out of business (or get outsourced). To avoid shared services from becoming irrelevant, it is incumbent upon senior management to tie their performance to the service receiver.

A service-providing relationship is simply one of a number of dotted-line relationships that can exist within a company. Support staff often report daily to an operational manager but simultaneously maintain a formal relationship with their functional manager. This dual reporting relationship can easily place the individual in an untenable position vis-à-vis either manager. Failure to be clear about an underlying authority base, whether in reference to a shared service activity or to a single individual, can seriously undermine operational effectiveness. Some organizations have gone so far as to establish a formal matrix structure where everyone reports to multiple managers. The main problem with such structures is that it becomes nearly impossible to fix accountability to a single individual. Not surprisingly, this lack of accountability can quickly lead to serious performance problems. The presence of any of the aforementioned problems provides a useful backdrop for resolving such issues in the subsequent design and fielding of a requisite organizational structure. That is the subject of the next chapter.

Chapter 14

Creating a Proposed Requisite Organization

Background:

At this point, an effective organizational study should have amassed a significant amount of information related to the existing work system. A detailed analysis of that information probably uncovered a number of organizational findings documenting the existence of specific organizational structure problems, such as missing roles, too many layers, or role crowding. Some of these findings are likely to be reflected in the extant structure, while other issues emerge as trends contained in the qualitative interview data. Once specific problem areas are identified, it is then necessary to analyze the underlying nature of these problems and to recommend the necessary changes required to resolve them. The outcome of this exercise should be the design of a requisite organizational structure. Recall that a requisite structure is one required by the nature of the work (hence, use of the term "requisite"). The construction of a requisite organizational structure requires the systematic application of a number of fundamental organizational design principles.

A Requisite Organization:

A requisite organizational structure contains the proper number of organizational layers such that each layer is engaged in work that is fundamentally different (in terms of adding unique value) than the work taking place at other layers, either higher or lower. The actual number of layers required is dictated by analyzing an organization's mission and the critical functions required to accomplish that mission. There exist some basic ground rules for determining how many layers are correct for a given organizational entity. First, if this is a large business-oriented enterprise, then you should expect to see no more than seven organizational layers from the CEO to the front-line worker. These are mainly Fortune 100 or 500 organizations employing tens of thousands of people, depending upon the type of industry. (Obviously, the pharmaceutical industry will have fewer workers than the mining industry or the retail industry.) In the government sector, "large" generally refers to major government departments such as the U.S. Department of Defense, the Department of Veterans Affairs, and the like.

Second, the number of organizational layers is also affected by the underlying complexity of the work actually being performed at successive organizational layers. For example, in a high-technology environment, the direct output produced by front-line associates may be occurring at level II or level III, such as a Ph.D. physicist in a laboratory setting. Thus, you need to exercise some judgment in determining the proper number of layers required in a given organization. If the primary output occurs at level II, no more than six layers are required.

Third, if the organization being studied employs business units to get its work done, then you can apply some rules of thumb that apply to typical business units. For example, BUs tend to operate more effectively if they can be organized into five discrete organizational layers from the bottom to the top. Further, every BU contains two easily discernible positions, a BU president or managing director and a front-line worker. Thus, there should be no more than three management layers between the two anchor points. There are some circumstances, however, when a business is just too complex to manage with five layers. In this case, a sixth layer may well be needed, but this should be the exception, not the rule. Additionally, there are size and volume limits that seem to relate to the proper number of layers in a stand-alone BU. If the size exceeds the $1 billion dollar threshold, you might think of ways to break it up into smaller units.

Fourth, smaller organizations can have anywhere from two to five total layers. Obviously, a mom-and-pop restaurant or small dry cleaner consists of two layers. Larger franchise operations such as a small drug store or a large chain restaurant might require three layers (e.g., a Macaroni Grill restaurant). Larger drug stores with a pharmacy or a larger grocery store are likely to be level IV entities as are most car dealerships. Lastly, some small business groups might consist of a number of level IV entities all working for a single level V owner or manager.

The mission, functions, and tasks required to be performed dictate the number of layers. To be useful, each layer must encompass value-adding work appropriate to that layer. Too many layers results in multiple people working on the same tasks, while too few layers results in missing roles or work being done inadequately or some work not getting done at all. Thus, the proper number of layers sets the correct context for getting work done.

Next, in a requisite organization, each role must be clearly defined in terms of its underlying accountability and authority base. Even with the proper number of layers, if roles aren't clearly defined, people could still end up working on the wrong tasks. Visit our website (www.organizational.com) for some examples of poorly defined roles versus good ones.

In designing a requisite structure, you should analyze the extant organization and then compare it to a requisite one. For example, in the previous chapter, we portrayed an extant organization where several roles were found to be functioning one full organizational level below where they ought to be. Given this finding, the challenge then is to describe the work that is not being done by the existing role incumbents. The recommendations that follow should address how best to close the gap between what is and what ought to be. It may be that a role incumbent is working at too low a level because that is all that has been expected of him by his current manager. It could also be that the current manager does not have the authority and discretion appropriate to her level and consequently is pulling down the whole organization a full level. Lastly, it might be a situation where dire economic pressures are forcing everyone to work on short-term tasks simply to survive.

Creating a Proposed Requisite Organization

Ascertaining which cause is more plausible in the above situations requires you to also analyze the qualitative comments made by various sources during the interview process. For example, an analysis of the manager's work as described by him or her personally, or as described by the next higher-level manager (e.g., the time-span data), could shed some light on this finding. Alternatively, discussions with the BU president could provide overarching general business information regarding the financial health of the current business.

Figure 14.1 depicts how the aforementioned analysis could be applied to the sample organization in order to arrive at a set of specific recommendations.

Recommendations for Our Sample Company:

1. The office personnel located in the branch will report directly to the office manager at the main office. They are in a service-providing role to the branch manager and branch staff. (Principles #2 and #3)

2. The fleet manager will report directly to the service manager. The service manager is accountable for route delivery and thus should have direct managerial authority over fleet personnel. (Principle #2)

3. Perform an in-depth analysis of the work/tasks of the roles that are working below a requisite level. The objective is to move the role to the appropriate level by either removing lower-level tasks, developing the individual incumbent, or replacing the incumbent if it is deemed he does not have the capacity to work at the level the role should be. (Principles #1 and #4)

4. Recognize that the office manager role is straddled between levels II and III (remember in this example they receive additional office support work from corporate headquarters) and adjust HR systems to reflect this situation if need be. (Principle #1)

Sample Requisite Structure

14.1

5. The route representative (sales/service/delivery) will now report directly to the account manager who is subsequently held accountable for each customer account along that route. The route manager will function as a supervisory level role to assist in this endeavor. (Principles #1 and #2).

What follows is a review and analysis of the data gathered during the interview process. This analysis is done from a perspective of how best to address existing issues. The analysis process begins by selecting a role that was interviewed and then analyzing the work of this role by applying the following design principles:

Organize around Levels of Work—Principle #1

- What does this role do? (Tasks)

- Of all these tasks assigned by the immediate manager, which one will take the longest time to complete? (Time-span)

- What is the level of complexity of the bulk of their tasks?

- How much of their time are they spending on lower-level tasks (e.g.; administrative work, which is Level I or II)?

- Are there issues/parameters that prevent them from working on higher-level tasks (e.g., limited discretion or authority)?

Establish Clear Accountability and Authority—Principle #2

- Who does this role work for (direct manager)? Are there any other quasi managers they report to?

- Are the *accountabilities* of the role clear to them? Clear to others?

- Are the *authorities* of the role clear to them? Clear to others?

- Who can assign tasks to this role?

- Who measures/monitors individual performance?
- What is the output of the role?

Establish Clear Working Relationships—Principle #3

- Who (individuals, roles, or teams) provides this role with inputs they need to get their work done?
- Who do they interact with to get their work done?
- Can they request services from others to assist them in getting their work done?
- Who can assign specific tasks? Who can request that they perform other tasks?
- How does the individual prioritize his or her task list?

These are a sampling of the questions we ask ourselves during the analytical phase of project meetings. From an analysis of interview response data emerges a picture of the organization that is likely to be fairly different from how you or others anticipated that the organization actually worked. Hopefully the emergent picture is not totally dysfunctional. The challenge you now face might sound like this:

> *Okay, so we know we have some roles working at the wrong level, some roles/people who are unsure of what they are accountable for, and, to top it all off, everyone essentially believes they need more authority to be successful. Now what do we do?*

Levels of Work—Reaching Specific Recommendations:

Start with principle #1: is this organization or role working at the appropriate level? If not who is doing this work? Try to discover the possible reasons why the correct level of work is not getting done. What can be done about these issues? For example, if a level III role spends a lot of time doing level I admin work, can this work be off-loaded to administrative staff or can some of this work be eliminated altogether? Are there any additional admin staff needed? In many cost-cutting exercises, companies often eliminate administrative staff but fail to concomitantly eliminate administrative work. Consequently, higher-level managers tend to get pulled down to do the administrative work.

Recommendations should be aimed at removing work that is not appropriate for a given role. It is also important that discretion be correct for the level of work expected of the individual. The overall general theme to be applied here is the systematic removal of barriers that might prevent a person from working on the correct level tasks. At this point, we are attempting to get the *role working at the proper level, not the individual (that will come later).*

After you go through this exercise with a few roles you will start to see how many true layers you have in the organization. The obvious question to be answered is, do we have too many or too few layers? As described previously, however, do not be surprised if you discover missing layers. For example, in a level V business unit, the CEO/president is appropriately working on level V tasks. Unfortunately, his or her immediate subordinates (VPs) all seem to be working on tasks that are level III in nature. Their subordinates (directors), in turn, may be working on level II tasks. If the entire organization, minus the CEO, are working at level III and below, then who is doing the level IV work? What can be done to fix this?

Each organization and its attendant reporting system are going to be different. No two organizations are the same nor will they likely face the same issues. Your recommendations may be similar to some of the following:

- Add roles to perform missing work

- Remove roles from the organization to get the proper number of layers

- Implement process-improvement projects to streamline work and processes to allow roles to work at the proper level

- Get people to focus on the proper type of work for the role they occupy

Establish Clear Accountability and Authority—Specific Recommendations:

It is highly likely that you will have recommendations surrounding the number of organizational layers that exist within your company. These and other recommendations will likely have a significant impact on existing roles and possible new roles. Review chapter 6 at this time. The output of this stage of the project is to produce written role descriptions that clearly state what *every role* is accountable for and the commensurate authority that goes along with that accountability. Start with a task list. List all major tasks for a given role; these form the basic accountabilities of the role. Creating a list of accountabilities is somewhat simple. The difficult part, which is often forgotten, is identifying the proper authority to complement this accountability list. Each accountability should have a specific output, and each task should be able to be defined in terms of a what-by-when. Avoid the self-defined role. Do not allow people to make assumptions about what they are accountable for and what authority they have or need.

As the project chief, you are accountable (with input from others) to define each role. It is the accountability of the role incumbent's manager, however, to accept or approve a proposed role description. This finding should not be surprising for it is ultimately the manager who is held accountable for role performance. In summary, project personnel are accountable to build role definitions, but the immediate manager is accountable for approving them. Next, it is essential to ensure that each task contains the proper authority. Finally, it is important to ensure that both the accountability and authority are appropriate for the level of a given role.

Establish Clear Working Relationships—
Specific Recommendations:

In addition to laying out accountabilities and authorities by task, the role description should spell out the who and what (in terms of input) this role needs to interact with to get their work done. For example, if role A (marketing director) needs analytic financial reporting from a support team and vendor expense data from the accounting staff to perform their marketing work (marketing plan), then this should be spelled out in the role description. This identification of key working partners lays the groundwork for defining proper working relationships.

Depending on the level of complexity and size of your company, you may need to do this between two roles in a general sense or between two roles in terms of specific tasks.

Examples:
An IT support person is accountable as a service provider to the marketing director.

If we look at another role relationship it may be more dynamic than this.

- HR director and marketing director functioning at the same organizational level. The HR director has advisory authority as it pertains to the marketing director's accountability for vetoing someone to the marketing director's team.

- The HR Director may have monitoring authority with the marketing director to ensure the marketing director is in compliance with the company's sexual harassment policies.

Working relationships are dynamic in nature; thus the idea of examining individual interactions by task can be daunting at times. However, it is vitally important to have a candid conversation about the proper accountability and authority relationship between roles. It is not necessary, however, to always try to define this relationship for every single task.

Summary:

Over time, roles, tasks, and work change, thus necessitating that you periodically update organizational levels, roles, and working relationships. While we cannot prescribe for you how often you may need to do this, we can suggest that you look at the rate of change within your organization. The faster things change externally and internally and thus affect your organization, the more frequently you may need to revisit these principles. In essence, by following the steps outlined above, you are implementing principles 1, 2, and 3. Once you have completed these steps, you have essentially created the *spaces. Now comes the hard part, the faces.*

Chapter 15

Implementing Your New Structure

Once you have conducted an organizational study and identified changes required to improve your structure and its related work system, it is then incumbent upon the company's senior leadership to actively oversee the implementation of any agreed-upon study recommendations. Recommendations generally vary from specific structural changes to process and system changes. In many cases, changes relative to all three categories are required. Many recommendations require making tough decisions about the potential capability of current role incumbents to perform the work of newly established roles or positions that have been substantially redesigned. This challenge of putting a "face into the space" is perhaps one of the most difficult tasks facing a company's leadership. It is intensely personal in nature but absolutely critical to the long-term success of the enterprise. Putting people into roles for which they are not qualified does neither them nor the company a favor, no matter how hard the decision.

Regardless of what recommendations are finally agreed upon, the senior leaders need to continue to play an active role in a given study initiative. First, they need to continue their active sponsorship throughout the implementation phase. They cannot simply appoint a transition team and hand off project implementation to that team. They must continue to be seen as involved in the overall process. Second, they need to ensure that any implementation plan follows a proper sequence. For example, it has been our experience that structural changes should be implemented before process changes. In our army project work, we found that the introduction of structural changes sets a more fertile ground for the subsequent application of Lean Six Sigma process work. (In one major command, organizational structure changes led to five times as many Lean Six Sigma projects than occurred in other similar commands that chose not to follow this sequence.) Third, the senior leadership should inform the workforce of all agreed-upon changes and the underlying rationale for these changes. Communicate, communicate, communicate! Communication is critical to any successful implementation plan.

Also central to any successful implementation plan is a concomitant change-management plan. The purpose behind the change-management plan is to involve the workforce in the change process. By so doing, the organization can reduce the normal friction and resistance to change that routinely accompanies a change initiative. One of the fundamental reasons why we utilize an in-depth interview process is because such a process involves large numbers of individuals in the study effort. In addition to providing valuable study content, the participation of these individuals in the process goes a long way toward involving them personally in study outcomes. In nearly all studies conducted to date, interviewees responded that they were excited to be part of the overall change-management process and that they sincerely appreciated an opportunity to participate in the effort.

Implementing Study Recommendations

Nearly all Organizational Development (OD) projects uncover findings that address one or more of the six steps depicted in Figure 15.1. For example, some findings may relate to the existing work culture in the organization, such as whether the current culture is supportive of desired work outcomes or undermines individual efforts. Remember, culture is never neutral.

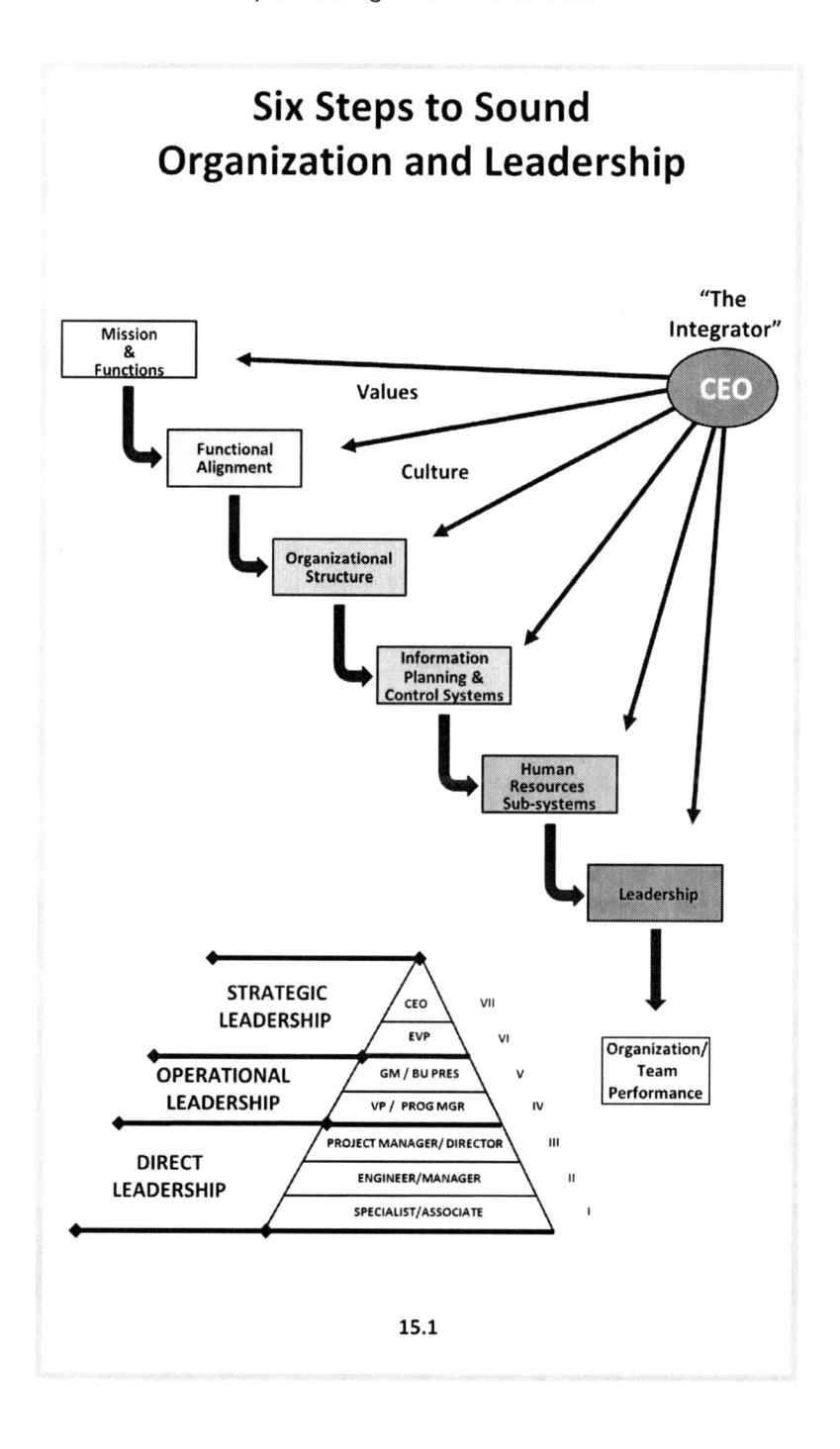

Implementing Your New Structure

Six Steps to Sound Organization and Leadership

"The Integrator"

- CEO
- Mission & Functions
- Functional Alignment
- Values
- Culture
- Organizational Structure
- Information Planning & Control Systems
- Human Resources Sub-systems
- Leadership
- Organization/Team Performance

STRATEGIC LEADERSHIP
- CEO — VII
- EVP — VI

OPERATIONAL LEADERSHIP
- GM / BU PRES — V
- VP / PROG MGR — IV

DIRECT LEADERSHIP
- PROJECT MANAGER/ DIRECTOR — III
- ENGINEER/MANAGER — II
- SPECIALIST/ASSOCIATE — I

15.1

Other findings relate to the nature of the work actually being performed in a given functional area (the extant organization). As was described in the previous chapter, the extant organization is useful in that it provides insights into the depth of required changes and a possible pathway necessary to get to a requisite structure. The magnitude of change required is likely to be in direct proportion to the gap between the extant organization and a requisite one. If that gap is large—for example, the extant organization reflects a number of roles crowded together into a single layer with missing work occurring at higher layers—then the changes required to implement a requisite structure will be large. If the gap is small, then it may be possible to introduce incremental improvements that tend to be less disruptive than large-scale change.

Not all study recommendations involve simple structural changes. For example, if the organization contains a large number of complex working relationships, such as excessive dotted-line relationships or a large number of individuals reporting to multiple managers, then the changes required to clarify the requisite nature of these relationships is likely to be substantial. Most dotted-line relationships are characterized by a lack of clarity as to who can tell whom to do what and with what authority. Clarifying complex working relationships requires that one first get clear on the exact nature of specific accountabilities and authorities for all existing roles. In complex situations, this often entails tailoring a specific authority base for each major role accountability. This is a fairly ambitious undertaking and, as such, is often avoided in most implementation plans. Of course, the cost of not clarifying such relationships is considerable friction and dysfunctional conflict.

Some studies might encompass the application of major system changes. These system changes can involve work processes that, in turn, typically involve the application of continuous improvement tools such as Lean Six Sigma or total quality management. Other change may involve the further tailoring of existing key management systems to more effectively support desired work outcomes. For example, the performance-management system should clearly recognize and document substandard performance as it might pertain to selected individuals. Without such documentation, it is difficult (if not impossible) to take subsequent disciplinary action. Similarly, if the planning system forces everyone to focus solely on short-term results, it should not be surprising to find managers at all levels working on the wrong tasks, and they are likely to be pulled down one or more levels.

Faces and Spaces

In most study efforts, the aforementioned changes represent the easy steps in any change-management effort. As described, previously (and discussed in-depth in chapter 9), the hard part comes when one deals with the human dimension. Once a proper structure and supporting systems and processes are in place, it is then up to the senior leadership team to address related people issues. One of the most significant challenges facing a company's leadership team is to ensure that the right people are placed in the right roles. This requires senior leaders to make candid judgments about individual working capabilities.

Recall that improving operational effectiveness requires both the right structure and the right people assigned to key roles in that structure. By "right people," we mean individuals who possess the requisite capability and capacity to do the work assigned to a given role. Assessing an individual's capacity to handle more complexity, including their potential to work at a different organizational layer, is more an art than a science. The assessment relies on an individual manager's judgment about another individual's working capacity. Recall the discussion in chapter 8 where it was shown that managerial judgment, especially in a properly structured organization and rendered by the next higher-level manager (the MoR), was better than existing testing instruments. Further, what makes judgment even more reliable is when subordinates are part of a comprehensive talent-management system. Such a system compares and then calibrates judgments across multiple functional areas. This comparison and subsequent calibration allows senior management to compensate for hard versus easy judgments.

Individual Working Capacity

Working Capacity (f) =

Information / Problem Solving Capacity

   X   Values

       X   Skills/Knowledge

          X   Wisdom

             X   Temperament

15.2

Recall, that *capacity* is only one component that makes up an individual's working capability (see Figure 15.2). Revisit the definitions of both of these terms in chapter 8. One of the difficulties encountered during an assessment process is the tendency for an assessor to overly focus on skills, knowledge, and experience. This tendency is hard to overcome because most of us tend to view job requirements in terms of their underlying skill, knowledge, and experience base rather than innate cognitive capacity. Unfortunately, focusing on skill, knowledge, and experience often causes us to overlook a subordinate who has loads of potential but is young, new to the job or company, inexperienced, or not trained in a given functional area. Hence, we are prone to underutilize our human capital unless we work extra hard to overcome these natural assessment biases. Having the right people assess, using a valid baseline normative work-related database, and calibrating assessments in regular talent pool management meetings are ways to overcome the aforementioned assessment biases.

Role Calibration:

Role calibration means determining where in the organizational structure a given role should be positioned based on an assessment of the complexity of work assigned to the role, that is, which organizational layer and which band within the given layer. In a properly structured organization, each layer can be broken down into three distinct bands: low, medium, and high. Executives in most organizations are readily able to discern differences in roles corresponding to these three distinct bands.

Properly calibrating roles facilitates the prioritization process because it identifies possible role overlap, non-value adding crowding, and roles whose underlying work-related complexity no longer supports the emerging corporate strategy. In an era where requirements outpace allocations, the use of agreed-upon decision rules is likely to be perceived by all affected parties as both fair and impartial. The calibration process can also prove instrumental in determining training and development needs, job distribution patterns, and appropriate compensation levels for roles.

The real challenge in calibrating and prioritizing roles across a large organization made up of many diverse functions and numerous subordinate organizations is how to determine whether role A is more or less equal to role B in terms of level of complexity. The only effective way to make such a comparison is to apply a consistent set of organizational design principles to all roles. Once this is done, an executive role located in layer IV in one department is no more or less important than another executive role also located in the same layer in another department. Both are of equal importance: they are both layer IV roles. If a shortage of executive talent has to be dealt with, then the top-most executives in the enterprise need to apply their own judgment and decide where best to absorb the risk generated by not filling a given role.

Role calibration begins with this question:
What level is this role?
The output of such a query could be:
This is a level IV role.
The response, in turn, can lead to these types of follow-on questions:

- Does the incumbent have level IV (or greater) capacity?

- Who do we have with level IV capacity to fill this role?

- If the individual (incumbent or otherwise) does have the capacity, do they have the capability? (Values, skills/knowledge, wisdom, and temperament plus capacity)

Assessing Capability and Capacity—Specific Recommendations:

At this time, you should have a relatively solid implementation plan aimed at achieving a requisite structure based on our first three principles. A key component of this is a clear understanding of the level at which each role should operate. This is your space. You now need to fill these spaces with people, faces. Develop a plan of action, if you haven't already, aimed at assessing the potential of every individual in the organization. Remember that this assessment is to be performed by the managers and MoRs, not by the OD project team or HR specialist. In fact, the project team might very well consider beginning this process simultaneously with the organizational study to speed up the implementation of any organizational changes. In other words, the aim is to have all the faces assessed in terms of capacity and capability at around the same time the spaces are agreed upon. Review the potential assessment guidelines in chapter 8 for assistance.

Utilize the assessment data to fill all the new or modified roles with individuals who demonstrate, at a minimum, the current capability or possible future capability and capacity to operate at the level of the role. These assessments form the foundation of an overall talent pool management system. Ensuring that the organization has a constant flow of talent is one of the most important strategic leadership tasks facing the senior leadership team in any institution. Without sufficient talent to fill unexpected vacancies or newly evolving roles, a company will simply not be able to keep up with the pace of change inherent in the external environment. Change has become the new constant. Thus, change management is also a new constant. As will be shown in the next chapter, managing both revolutionary change as well as evolutionary change is an inherent responsibility of a company's senior leadership. The very survival of the company is at risk if this work does not get done.

Leadership—Specific Recommendations

Once a requisite organizational structure has been put in place and the roles in that structure filled by competent people to do the work inherent in those roles, it is then incumbent upon those individuals who occupy roles carrying leadership accountability to exercise effective leadership to the fullest extent possible. Recall the specific leadership work described in chapter 9. For an organization to be effective over the long haul, leaders at every organizational level have to competently carry out leadership tasks appropriate to their level. One of those key leadership tasks is the ability to create a culture that fosters both evolutionary change as well as revolutionary change.

Chapter 16

Other Lessons Learned

Governance

Complex organizations continuously evolve their organizational structure, management control systems, and governance as they adapt to constantly changing economic, political, and competitive pressures. That evolution may reflect new missions or strategies assigned to the organization or it may be reflective of changing strategies to meet new challenges. The net effect is that change is constant. Evolutionary changes accumulate and often drive the need for revolutionary changes in organizational structure, management control systems, and governance systems. Further, we believe that leadership, organization structure, and governance are the driving forces behind any organization as it strives to achieve its mission and goals.

Governance, in its simplest form, ensures that everyone in an organization understands the *mission of the organization,* their role in carrying out the mission, and the accountabilities and authorities associated with their role. If, through a clearly communicated and documented governance system, individuals understand mission, roles, accountabilities, and authorities, they will add value to the organization in accomplishing its overall goals. Consequently, one of the critical success factors underpinning an organization's ability to accomplish its mission is an effective governance system.

An effective governance system requires clearly defined and documented accountabilities and authorities for all roles in an organization's structure. As described previously, in the absence of clarity and documentation, especially in the underlying authority base that defines the web of working relationships extant in any organization, employees establish their own rules about who does what and who can tell whom to do what. In these organizations, management control becomes blurred, and the effectiveness and efficiency of the organization wanes. By contrast, the outcome from a clearly defined and documented governance system is more likely to be a practical and effective management control system and a well-structured, effective, and efficient organization. Failing to meet its mission is the cost of a nonexistent or weak governance system.

Without a Formal Governance System

Best business practices (from business literature and academic research) tell us that organizations who fail to clearly define and document a governance system are likely to suffer the following problems:

- Its people are not aligned with the organization's mission (an effectiveness issue).
- People fail to perform the work for which their role was created (e.g., people at corporate headquarters running operating units).
- Accountabilities for and the output expected from work are not defined and measured.
- Authority that accompanies an accountability is not carefully and uniformly documented (e.g., allowing one organization (or team) to define oversight as *supervision, another as prescription, and yet another as monitoring*).
- Working relationships essential for getting work done across functional boundaries are left to individuals to define for themselves or for organizations to turn to the latest management fad for resolution (e.g., social networking where everyone interacts with everyone else).
- There are issues of taking on or duplicating other people's work, overlapping work, or friction points on whose work it is (an

efficiency issue) and what authority one individual has for telling another what to do (an effectiveness issue).

Our development of an effective governance system encompasses the following key steps:

1. Implementing an education phase (workshops, executive briefings, and white papers) to teach principles of a well-structured organization and normatively what is value-adding work at various levels in that structure.
2. Categorizing the level of work of key roles throughout the organization and comparing that categorization to a normative system of work that research has found appropriate for typical roles operating at various organizational layers.
3. Clearly defining a system of what organizations and people in their roles should be accountable for, especially at the strategic levels of work in corporate headquarters.
4. Formulating and fielding a carefully defined lexicon of authorities to accompany individual roles and accountabilities, especially as they relate to other people in the headquarters or in subordinate organizations.
5. Constructing a working document describing key functions, roles contained within specific organizational structure, key cross functional working relationships, and desired performance metrics.
6. Using the document itself, supported by appropriate organizational and analytical tools to define overlapping work, missing work (voids), and communities of practice—again, normatively defining what should and should not be done, who should do the work, what is their underlying accountability and authority.

Evolutionary Change versus Revolutionary Change:

Previously, it was mentioned that organizations often face a two-pronged challenge: they need to become both more efficient as well as more effective. Sometimes these two goals are mutually exclusive. Efficiency gains are generally sought through continuous improvement efforts (evolutionary change), whereas effectiveness is pursued through increased innovation (revolutionary change). Most large-scale transformational efforts pursue both strategies simultaneously. For example, our work with the U.S. Army was to help them embark on a two-pronged approach to business transformation. One strategy focused on introducing revolutionary change to both *warfighting and warfighting support organizations.* The second approach focused on developing and fielding an evolutionary-oriented continuous improvement capability.

On the warfighting side, the Chief of Staff led the charge in successfully restructuring warfighting organizations into smaller, more responsive, yet more lethal units. This was a massive multiyear undertaking moving the army from a division centric force (a level V organization) to a brigade-centric organization (level IV units). While transforming warfighting units was a difficult endeavor to undertake, this effort took place in a culture of "adapt or die." Sustaining a culture of adaption and innovation has long been a necessity and a source of pride for the warfighter. The presence of this culture facilitated the widespread acceptance of major organizational change among soldiers in warfighting units, for their very lives were often at stake.

On the support side of the army, however, transformation proved to be far more difficult. In the absence of the warfighters' culture of innovation and the lack of an accepted internal burning platform, the generating force (the non-warfighting support army) was reluctant to embrace true transformational change. Instead, non-warfighting organizations were far more comfortable embracing continuous improvement efforts, that is, evolutionary change (Lean Six Sigma projects, ISO 9000, etc.).

Continuous improvement is evolutionary in nature because it involves taking something we already do and figuring out ways to do it better, cheaper, and faster. It is about driving down costs, improving productivity, and reducing waste. Innovation, on the other hand, is the process of looking for ways to do something fundamentally different. True innovators challenge all assumptions. They take nothing for granted. They are not afraid to ask, why not? Innovation is thus revolutionary. The civilian employees of the army embraced evolutionary change, whereas their military counterparts were much more comfortable with revolutionary change. Our experience in this enterprise-wide transformational project allowed us to codify the following key lessons learned. That is the subject of the next section of this chapter.

> *Organizations are created to achieve order. They have policies, procedures, and formal or powerfully informal (unspoken) rules. The job for which the organization exists could not possibly get done without these rules, procedures, and policies. ... Creativity and innovation disturb order. Hence, organization tends to be inhospitable to creativity and innovation, though without creativity and innovation it would eventually perish.* [126]
> —*Theodore Levitt*

Avoiding the Continuous Improvement Trap

As described previously, to remain competitive and cost-effective, organizations must continuously improve their operational efficiency and effectiveness. Thus, the concept of Continuous Improvement is on the forefront of nearly every manager's work agenda. Most contemporary managers spend a considerable amount of their time seeking ways to achieve incremental improvements that can produce steady increases in overall productivity levels. In the long-term, however, continuous improvement alone is not enough. Such improvements will only take you so far. If you are focusing primarily on doing the same things better year after year, you don't think about the big threats that lie further down the road.

Simply stated, the continuous improvement (CI) trap is unduly focused on improving rather than innovating.[127] Academic research has found a trade-off between the two in business organizations. Organizations that only continuously improve become lulled into thinking that they are changing with the times (the environment, the

---

126 Levitt, Theodore, "Creativity Is Not Enough," Harvard Business Review, 2002.
127 Clement, Stephen and Harvey, Roger. Improving Organizational Effectiveness in Government Agencies. White Paper. Organizational Design Inc. 2009

marketplace, the demands of their customer), when in fact, they are on the verge of irrelevance and nonexistence. Business history is full of examples: Polaroid and Kodak, U.S. Steel, J.I Case, and General Motors, to mention only a few. CI can squash innovation in any organization.

Continuous improvement (CI) seeks ways of doing what we're already doing better—cheaper, faster, or of higher quality. CI typically focuses on processes, with its tools today being Lean Six Sigma (LSS), total quality management (TQM), and the like. CI falls under the broader category of *change,* but is a more evolutionary change than revolutionary change. It is less threatening to people than revolutionary change or less threatening than radically changing the way an organization does things, including manage. Because CI in an office or administrative setting (as opposed to a manufacturing setting) is incremental, less threatening, and typically focused on saving dollars rather than replacing people, buy-in is easier. The antibodies don't rise up to kill CI initiatives as they might with innovation.

The CI trap occurs when what is needed is revolutionary change, meaning doing what we're doing in radically new ways or possibly not doing it at all. What is needed is innovation. For example, on the warfighting side of the army, the Army Chiefs of Staff could have applied CI methods to all elements of doctrine, organization, training, leadership, materiel, personnel, and facilities (DOTLMPF), but this strategy would have had the army improving on how it fought the nation's last conflict. Doctrine had to be radically rewritten to address insurgency warfare; divisions transformed to brigades; training centers made into villages; warfighters taught to be diplomats; improvised explosive device (IED) detection researched, developed, and deployed; and equipment dramatically reconfigured.

Since 9/11, the operating army did not limit itself to CI; rather, it engaged in radically changing the way it operated—essentially it engaged in innovation. There was, of course, resistance to some of these changes, but the cost of resistance or moving too slowly with innovation was soldiers' lives. The risk of not changing was too high, so innovation and radical change happened.

The Lean Six Sigma initiatives in the non-warfighting force were basically CI initiatives; therefore, they experienced little resistance.

They were most successful in the depots and arsenals of Army Materiel Command (AMC), where the workload was high and the elimination of non-value-adding tasks permitted these organizations to more effectively cope with higher throughput. The up-tempo of war meant that there was always more demand waiting to be met. As a result, people did not lose their jobs. Thus, the workforce (and the union) was less intimidated by the proposed changes.

The organizational development and design (ODD) initiatives (our project work), on the other hand, were more radical and frequently innovative (at least in Headquarters, Department of the Army—HQDA). The radical restructuring of organizations is generally disruptive and challenges the status quo. In those organizations, people were expected to embrace significant change, and many found this difficult to accept.

As a result of the aforementioned efforts at introducing both evolutionary change as well as revolutionary initiatives, the following corollary lessons learned were discovered.

LESSON 1: Innovation initiatives require following the rules of change management much more closely than CI initiatives. Innovation in large organizations, especially government organizations, is much more threatening and generates more resistance than CI projects. Innovation projects need continuing senior leadership sponsorship and monitoring; they must be started early and continuously pushed along in light of shorter senior leadership tenure in many organizations such as the U.S. Army (usually four years but often shorter). They should be recognized as culture changes, which mean long-term time horizons and laying permanent foundations for change beyond one administration or leadership team.

LESSON 2: Clear communication to senior leaders and others impacted by innovation projects (e.g., a new governance system) that the initiative is in fact innovative and not continuous improvement is important. Develop a communication plan to continually inform the workforce so as to minimize their anxiety and defensiveness.

LESSON 3: A large, complex organizational unit such as the U.S. Army, with both civilian and military roles, needs a much more comprehensive governance system than a forty-page document with each agency's interpretation of their duties as stated (or not stated) in federal law (Title 10). Large business organizations have a single chain of command while the army has both a civilian chain of command (the secretariat) and a military chain of command (the army staff). And the secretariat has other direct lines of authority over its staff; it also has lines of authority (e.g., oversight, monitoring, advisory, coordinating, and collaborating) over the army staff. All of these lines are complicated, all are complex, and all require more than a simple listing of functions.

LESSON 4: Innovation requires not only the development of new doctrine but also new training to support that doctrine. Much of the effort associated with introducing a new governance system involved developing and promulgating new doctrine and new army operating procedures.

Chapter 17

Bringing It All Together

This book has taken a different approach to the subject of leadership and business performance improvement. Rather than focus on the individual and the skills and knowledge or competencies required to exercise effective leadership, we chose instead to concentrate on the necessary preconditions that enable the process. We firmly believe that a strong foundation is central to empowering leaders to get results. If the foundation is strong and built on time-tested principles, then leadership will naturally occur. If the foundation is weak and structurally deficient, then leadership will only emerge as an afterthought and likely to be practiced by a select few who naturally would do so regardless of the prevailing dysfunctional conditions. Our experience to date in over fifty years of consulting, research, and practice is that leadership is a personal capability that resides in all of us. Whether that capability is allowed to flourish to its full potential is dependent in large part upon the organizational foundation within which it occurs.

The process of getting work done begins by recognizing that nearly all work gets performed by individuals who occupy roles in some sort of organizational structure. It is the structure that sets the context for all subsequent behavior. If the structure is built around architecturally sound organizational design principles, then an effective work system will emerge. And, as described above, if the structure is weak, then the emergent work system will also be weak. But organizational structure and its attendant work system have never generated much excitement or interest in the business or academic communities. In fact, the opposite response occurs more often than not. Structure has often been widely viewed as a necessary evil or even as an impediment to getting work done. Pejorative terms such as *bureaucracy and hierarchy* have been routinely tossed around to describe the impact of structure on employee behavior. In the past, the clarion call was to somehow construct an organization devoid of structure altogether. Terms like matrix management, networked organization, or servant leadership organizations, emerged as preferable options.

This book attempted to refute this antistructure bias. On the contrary, a main thesis was offered that it is structure itself that actually empowers leaders and enables them to get results. In support of this thesis, we draw upon our extensive experience where historically structure and its basic foundational underpinnings have always been a key part of the leader development system. It was suggested that the military had intuitively discovered and applied a comprehensive set of basic organizational design principles that proved to be critical to their existing leader development process. These principles were shown to have stood the test of time and had been validated on numerous battlefields throughout history.

In summary, a main theme of this book has been that everyone is capable of exercising effective leadership so long as they value the leadership role and are supported in their endeavor by a work system and structure that embodies the following set of fundamental design principles. These principles include such basic concepts as:

a. Organizing around levels of work, where each level engages in fundamentally different types of work, with the proper number of organizational layers

b. Establishing a culture of clear accountability and authority for getting that work done

c. Defining clear working relationships, especially those that go across functional boundaries

d. Filling roles with people who have the innate cognitive capacity to do the work inherent in the role

e. Providing effective leadership at successive organizational layers to support getting the work done

Extensive reference was made throughout the book on how these principles had become institutionalized in the military work system and how that process had set a fertile stage for the ongoing development of effective leaders.

Accountability and Authority

Empowering leaders to get results requires that leaders at every level clearly know what specific results they are accountable for producing. Further, it is equally important to ensure that these same individuals have been given the requisite authority to carry out those accountabilities. Clearly defining accountabilities and authorities was thus seen as a crucial first step in establishing a culture of achieving results. It was also shown, however, that some authority is role-vested in nature while other aspects must actually be earned by the authority figures themselves. Role-vested authority is authority that resides in the role, position power. But role-vested authority by itself was shown to only achieve minimal compliance on the part of most subordinates. To get people to operate to their full individual potential, enthusiastically and creatively, required the managerial leader to utilize personally earned authority. The process of winning personally earned authority was shown, in turn, to be related to an individual's character and competence. Thus, character counts. That is why the U.S. Army adapted the concept of Be-Know-Do some thirty-five years ago. "Be" was related to character, "Know" referred to subject matter expertise (technical competence), and "Do" related to specific tasks required of individuals operating at a given organizational layer.

Closely aligned to the aforementioned accountability and authority concept is the notion of also getting clarity around the nature of work at successive organizational layers. Having people throughout the organization focus on the correct work for their level is absolutely central to the long-term success of any enterprise. It was reported that one of the most common organizational pathologies found in contemporary organizations was the tendency for people to work on tasks that were simply not appropriate for their respective organizational layer. This tendency often resulted in people working at too low a level or on tasks that they had previously mastered but were now assigned to one of their subordinates for execution. A common result of this gravitational tendency to focus on lower-level work was the emergence of missing work at higher organizational layers. For example, if a level IV VP is actually doing level III work, then who in the organization is doing the more complex level IV work, such as the simultaneous management of multiple functional areas (parallel processing) and their subsequent integration into a total system? Similarly, at higher organizational layers, if the senior executive is unduly focused on day-to-day operational work, then who is doing the strategy development work?

A key organizational factor that reportedly contributed to the emergence of missing work was the tendency for the present to drive out the future. In far too many of our organizational projects, we found managers at middle to higher organizational layers working on lower-level tasks. There were many rational explanations provided to justify this phenomenon such as "This was a crisis situation" or "The subordinate was simply overwhelmed." At the end of the day, however, the practice undermined the development of an effective work system.

Thus, a critical challenge facing every senior executive in any enterprise is how to ensure that his or her people are working on the right tasks at each and every organizational layer. Most executives readily understand the necessity for broad distinctions in their work systems. For example, front-line workers concentrate on producing and distributing products and services to a customer base, midlevel managers carry out functional tasks, and senior executives develop strategies and secure critical resources. But is this broad breakdown of work sufficient to ensure that an organization contain just the right number of organizational layers with people at each layer focused exclusively on work appropriate to that layer? The answer to that question has all too often been no.

Over time, non-value-adding work naturally creeps into any organization setting. Additional reports are demanded to deal with emergency situations. More and more business reviews and meetings get put on the agenda as companies struggle with difficult economic issues. All of a sudden, there is no time left for the manager to do his or her own work. In response to this development, additional management layers get established, and organizational layering occurs. Eventually, most organizations get stultified and bureaucratic in nature because of too many layers or people at each layer working on the wrong tasks. The company gradually gets bogged down by excessive reporting requirements with decision making slowed down by excessive checking. Competitors then rush in to fill the void because they are quicker to respond to fast-changing market conditions. Finally, the cry for more effective leadership emerges as employees at all levels get concerned about the very survival of the firm as a whole.

In response to the aforementioned organizational "health" problems, we described how to establish a work system around a set of time-tested organizational principles. One of those principles suggested that most large enterprises should be able to get their work done and accomplish their missions with no more than seven organizational layers from the front-line worker to the CEO. In such a system, workers at each level focus on tasks appropriate to their respective layer. This principle was called organizing around levels of work. The development of a thorough understanding of levels of work was designed to permit the leader at a given organizational layer to compare existing tasks being done by his or her subordinates with normative tasks that one would typically expect individuals to be working on at that level. This comparison allows the manager to more effectively align his or her expectations regarding likely results and to subsequently take corrective action to bring existing tasks more in line with desired tasks for a given role incumbent. A key enterprise output of the aforementioned comparative analysis is to put in place a work system that ensures that workers at successive organizational layers are focused on value-adding tasks appropriate to their respective layer.

Getting people clear about their respective accountabilities is a key step in building a sound organizational structure. But not all work in an organization is done by individuals operating alone. In many cases, individuals have to work with other colleagues on cross functional management teams. At other times, a specific role incumbent has to work across normal functional boundaries with individuals operating at lower organizational layers. In order for people to work efficiently outside of their chain of command, the accountability and authority base that defines these relationships must be crystal clear. An entire chapter was devoted to clarifying the nature of cross functional working relationships. Failure to achieve clarity on these key relationships was shown to lead to dysfunctional conflict. This conflict, if left untreated, can ultimately suck the creative energy out of an organization. If one of these relationships involves a headquarters staff member ensuring that subordinates are adhering to existing policy guidelines, then that staff member must be able to monitor the behavior of others. The term *monitor* must be clearly defined and agreed to by all parties involved in order to avoid the aforementioned dysfunctional conflict. A limited number of working relationship terms were subsequently described in great detail. This definitional process was intended to minimize the potential for conflict between organizational members who might have different agendas.

It is our contention that getting the structure right is the easy part in any organizational design effort. Dealing with the human dimension is considered far more difficult. This challenge is commonly referred to as "putting the face into the space." Ensuring that individuals at all levels in an organization possess sufficient working capacity to perform the tasks required of them at a given level was shown to be absolutely critical to the long-term success of any enterprise. Failure to be competent to do so undermines all other attempts at practicing effective leadership. Judging a given subordinate's capacity to do work at the next higher level was considered fundamental to any successful talent management system. Accountability for actually making these judgments was elevated from the immediate manager to the next higher level manager—the Manager-once-Removed (MoR). To assist the MoR in rendering a valid judgment, we described normative work requirements operative at successive organizational layers. These work requirements were thought to serve as solid baseline criteria to assist in the judgment process.

In summary, this book has been about establishing the necessary foundational principles to set the stage for the subsequent practice of effective leadership. These foundational principles are not new; they have been around for many years. What is new, however, is the recognition that their absence will clearly undermine existing leader development initiatives. Thus, the path to empowering leaders to get results begins by first establishing the necessary foundational conditions. This is the real challenge facing today's senior executives.

Acknowledgments

Readers of Dr. Stephen Clement's earlier book *Executive Leadership* (coauthored with Dr. Elliott Jaques) will know of the debt that the authors have to Dr. Jaques. The opportunity to closely collaborate with him for over a twenty-year period was instrumental in fashioning many of the ideas we have presented. This early introduction to these concepts was particularly useful for Chris Clement in his roles as a midlevel executive and later a small business owner. Perhaps equally important, however, were the ongoing discussions and interactions with Sir Roderick Carnegie and General Maxwell Thurman, which led to the tailoring and further refinement of the aforementioned ideas and concepts.

Particular appreciation is rendered to Sir Roderick Carnegie for his collaboration and sage advice over the past twenty-five years. Sir Roderick brought to the table a unique perspective of making sure that the principles described herein were always crystal clear to operating personnel. We also benefited immensely from Sir Roderick's background as a former CEO of a large international company.

It will also be clear to those familiar with the U.S. Army that our work has been influenced by our experience with the army's training and leader development process. That experience was realized by Dr. Stephen Clement over many years of active duty and many additional years as a special consultant to several army secretaries.

In addition, valued support has come over the years from Neil Austrian, CEO of Office Depot; Fred Strader, EVP Textron; the Honorable Francis Harvey, former Secretary of the Army; Tom Kelly of

Acknowledgments

Lockheed Martin Corporation; and Leigh Clifford, former CEO of Rio Tinto and current chairman of Qantas Airlines.

Michael Allen and his consulting team worked alongside us on notable projects at Pepsi and G&K Services. It was through this partnership with Michael Allen that we learned the true impact of strategic planning on organizational structure and design. Michael Allen was the originator of the surpassion planning concept.

Maurice Dutrisac and Jim Mishler have been valuable sources of ideas and stimulation throughout the years.

Chris Clement would like to acknowledge and thank his former employees as he experimented with and modified Dr. Jaques's and Dr. Clement's theories to his own small business.

A special thanks to the Office Depot Executive team, who were instrumental in providing pragmatic insights that assisted us in ensuring that the principles are practical in today's challenging economic times.

A special thanks to countless executives, generals, officers, and clients worldwide who were unwitting test subjects for our theories and hypotheses over the years.

The illustrations and charts were created by Carleton Clement of Organizational Design, Inc.

Bibliography

Argyris, Chris, and Donald A. Schon. *Organizational Learning: A Theory of Action Perspective.* Redding, MA: Addison Wesley, 1978.

Chandler, Jr., Alfred. Strategy and Structure: *Chapters in the History of the American Enterprise.* Cambridge, MA: MIT Press, 1963.

Clement, Stephen D., and D. B. Ayres. *A Matrix of Organizational Leadership Dimension.* Leadership Monograph Series, no. 8. Ft. Harrison, IN: US Army Administration Center, 1976.

Clement, Stephen D., and Roger Harvey. *Improving Operating Effectiveness in Governance Agencies,* White Paper. Organizational Design, Inc., 2009

Galbraith, Jay. *Designing Organizations: An Executive Guide to Strategy, Structure, and Process.* San Francisco: Josey-Bass, 2002.

Harvey, Jerry. *How Come Every Time I Get Stabbed in the Back My Fingerprints Are on the Knife?* Josey Bass Publishers, San Francisco, 1999.

Jaques, Elliott. *"In Praise of Hierarchy." Harvard Business Review, 1990.*

Jaques, Elliott. *Requisite Organization.* Arlington, VA: Cason Hall Publishers, 1996.

Jaques, Elliott. *General Theory of Bureaucracy.* London: Heineman Educational Books, 1976.

Jaques, Elliott. *Time-Span Handbook.* London: Heineman Educational, 1971.

Jaques, Elliott, and Stephen D. Clement. *Executive Leadership.*

Arlington, VA: Cason Hall Publishers, 1991.

Jaques, Elliott, and Kathryn Cason. *Human Capability*. Falls Church, VA: Cason Hall Publishers, 1994.

Levitt, Theodore. "Creativity Is Not Enough." *Harvard Business Review*, 2002.

Raynor, Michael E. *The Strategy Paradox*. New York: Doubleday, 2007.

Royce, Joseph R. "Toward the Advancement of Theoretical Psychology." *Psychological Reports, 1957*. Reprinted in James Grier Miller, Living Systems, McGraw Hill, 1978.

Stodgill, Ralph. *Handbook of Leadership*. New York: Free Press, 1974.

Yang, Kai, *Voice of the Customer*, New York: McGraw Hill, 2008.

Other References

Headquarters, Department of the Army, Secretary of the Army, Briefing Charts, 2007.

Numerous references and biographical information for Max Weber may be found by following the link: http://en.wikipedia.org/wiki/Max_Weber. The link for Fredrick Taylor is http://en.wikipedia.org/wiki/Frederick_Winslow_Taylor.

Empirical research and publications may be found on the Global Organizational Design Society (GO) website: https://globalro.org/en/home.html. The GO website also contains a comprehensive bibliography on Dr. Jaques's work authored by Ken Craddock.

Glossary

Chapter 1

MILITARY STRUCTURE - The historical salience of military structure and supporting concepts
- The presence of 7 echelons of command since Roman Legion days
- Clear accountability for command roles especially in combat situations
- Clearly defined working relationships across organizational boundaries
- Significant time spent on assessing and developing leadership capabilities
- Leaders must lead from the "front" and must possess the character and competence to do so

Chapter 3

DR. ELLIOTT JAQUES - A Canadian born social scientist (MD Johns Hopkins, Ph.D. Harvard) who spent his entire life studying modern organizations and how people behaved and worked in those organizations. He was a prolific writer and author of over twenty books. His work on the nature of managerial hierarchies' substantially expanded our knowledge regarding the role of the vertical dimension in organizational theory. He is especially well known for introducing the concept of time as a significant measure of the complexity of work. In our opinion, the seminal value of Dr. Jaques contribution is that he presented the world with the beginning of a General Theory of Organizational Science.

REQUISITE ORGANIZATION THEORY - an all encompassing systems theory focused on designing, staffing, and managing work in organizations. Developed by Dr. Elliott Jaques. Dr. Jaques' empirical-based theory is normative in the sense that it <u>prescribes</u> organizational structure parameters (dimensions); human cognitive capabilities, compensation and rewards; accountabilities and authorities; and managerial attributes "required" to bring the most satisfaction to people in organizations and, at the same time, maximize the value produced by those organizations. His years of research lead him to identify basic "requirements" for organizational design in large organizations, that is, what is "requisite" to meet the aspirations and goals of individuals in organizations and of the organizations themselves. "Requisite" to Dr. Jaques was "required by nature" -- in this case, required for an organized workplace; hence, the name Requisite Organization Theory.

DR. JERRY HARVEY - Author of the book "The Abilene Paradox". Dr. Harvey's reflections on the importance of Dr. Jaques work are featured in his book, "How Come every time I get stabbed in the back my fingerprints are on the knife?..and other Mediations on Management".

SIR RODERICK CARNEGIE - CEO, CRA Limited (Australia), former McKinsey Consultant – sponsored Dr. Jaques field research project at CRA in the 1980's.

STRATIFIED SYSTEMS THEORY - Dr. Jaques early formulation of principles of organizational management and hierarchy. SST evolved from his early work at CRA and with the U.S. Army. It was the precursor to the development of Requisite Organization Theory.

Chapter 4

Customers - impact some components of every role, therefore customers drive organizational structure and all of its dimensions.

Principle Based Theory – all individuals have theories on how business's should be organized. Educating the workforce in our organizational principles is a suggested method to change their individual theories to a research based (and field tested) theory based on sound principles.

Chapter 5

Mission - A short formal written statement of purpose
- Pepsi - The world's premier consumer products company focused on convenient foods and beverages (Pepsi.com)
- The U.S. Army - Win the nation's wars

Function - A grouping of related tasks, supporting a basic organizational function/need or an externally imposed directive or generalized activity
- The training function includes conducting a front-end job task analysis; identifying critical tasks; designing training programs to master task performance; setting training standards; evaluating training performance

Task - An assignment to produce specified output (including quantity and quality) within a targeted completion time, with allocated resources and within specified limits
- The marketing function includes gathering and analyzing marketing data; evaluating consumer behavior and identifying new products/service needs, and developing new methods / procedures for communicating company solutions sets to meet such needs.

Key Variables by Level
- Task Complexity
- Information Complexity / Processing Characteristics
- Resources

- Planning and Decision Making
- Problem Solving Requirements
- Leadership Requirements
- Working Relationships
- Time Horizon (Time Span)
- Staff Role Requirements

TACTICAL WORK - work occurring at levels I-III of the organization.

OPERATIONAL WORK - work occurring at levels IV and V of the organization.

STRATEGIC WORK - work occurring at levels VI, VII and VII of the organization.

COMPLEXITY - The number of variables; the clarity or uncertainty of those variables, the rate of change and the interdependence of the variables.

STRATEGIC UNCERTAINTY - Developing and investing in strategic options to mitigate against the possible adverse effects of an uncertain future.

TIME-SPAN - A key tenet of Requisite Organization Theory is use of the time-span measurement of the complexity of work. According to Dr. Jaques, the time-span measure reflects the furthest forward in time that an individual is focused in terms of his or her current role. The higher an individual sits in an organizational hierarchy, the further forward in time he or she should be focused.

TIME COMPRESSION - In certain situations, characterized by rapid change, high degrees of uncertainty, and the need for continuous adaptation, managers at all levels become focused on much shorter time horizons. This pressure has resulted in managers "furthest forward " or longest task being much shorter than Dr. Jaques original Time Span theory.

DELEGATED DIRECT OUTPUT (DDO) - Tasks delegated by a senior manager to individuals occupying roles at lower organizational layers who produce the outputs at those layers and distribute them directly to customers.

ASSISTED DIRECT OUTPUT (ADO) - Work produced by subordinates to assist their "boss" in doing his/her work. The work flows up to the "bosses" layer.

Chapter 6

ACCOUNTABILITIES - those aspects of a role that dictate the things that the occupant is required to do by virtue of being in the role.

AUTHORITIES - those aspects of a role that enable the person in the role to act legitimately in order to carry out the accountabilities with which he or she has been charged.

> **ROLE VESTED AUTHORITY** - Authority associated with occupants occupying a given role. It allows an incumbent to require others to follow orders or instructions. Used by itself it will only produce minimally satisfactory results.
>
> **PERSONALLY EARNED AUTHORITY** - Authority gained by an individual by virtue of the strength of his/her character, competence, or the personal qualities of the authority figure themselves. Used together with role vested authority, it will release the full creativity and innovation of subordinates.

TASK - an assignment to produce a given output or achieve a given goal (a what-by-when) with allocated resources and methods within prescribed limits (See Figure 6.1 for more information).

GENERAL RESPONSIBILITY - an instruction which applies indefinitely (unless amended) and specifies conditions, which, when they arise, require a person to take appropriate action within prescribed limits.

Minimum Managerial Accountabilities - In the context of organizational design and the workplace, a manager is a person in a role (a managerial role) which inherently carries the following minimum accountabilities:

1. Their own work
2. The output of others (subordinates)
3. Building and sustaining a team
4. Leadership – leading subordinates individually and as a team so they are capable of producing the outputs required by the organization

Minimum Managerial Authorities
- **Veto** the assignment of an unacceptable individual to his or her team. If the manager is to be accountable for the output of a team, then he/she must have some say as to who is on that team.
- **Assign** tasks to subordinates consistent with the organizational level within which the roles are operative.
- **Recommend** rewards and punishments consistent with an individual's performance.
- **Initiate** removal of an individual from his or her team, after due process, whom the manager judges to be unable to do the work of the role.

Chapter 7

Working Relationships - Working relationships describe how people work together in any organizational setting. These working relationships contain the volatile ingredients of interacting accountabilities and authorities. Working relationships are both internal to the organization and external (customers, suppliers etc.).

Diagonal and Horizontal Relationships - The second major category of working relationship involves interactions between individuals across normal functional boundaries or across different organizational layers. These comprise diagonal and horizontal relationships as opposed to vertical ones.

Due Diligence Actions - Reasonable accountability required by an authority figure as a normal part of exercising their working relationships with another individual.

Information Rights - Data or information pertaining to a given working relationship that is within the purview of the authority figure to request.

Responses - Generally expected actions to be taken by an accountability/authority figure in a given working relationships.

Prescribing - A prescribing relationship is the strongest of any potential diagonal relationship between two individuals. It nearly rivals the normal relationship between a manager and his/her subordinates because a "prescriber" has the authority to order an individual to take specific actions.

Oversight - To ensure that the quality of programs and/or processes are operating within specified limits; these limits may be set by company policies, legal statutes or accepted cultural practices. Examples include financial procedures or limits; product tolerances; quality standards; or operational procedures.

Monitor - Some roles in an organization's headquarters hold an individual specifically accountable for tracking the efficacy of programs or tracking the work of other individuals or organizations because they provide inputs to his or her own work or represent central steps in an overarching planning system. In these cases, the individual is granted the authority to monitor the work of those other organizations (or individuals). The monitor cannot be held accountable for the success or failure of the monitored operation. However, he/she may be held accountable for not keeping their superiors aware of the state of the monitored operation or for being ignorant of the state of that operation. A monitor is accountable for identifying potential problems and discussing possible solutions to those problems with the monitored individual (or organization).

Glossary

ADVISE - There are many incumbents in an organization who require expert advice in order to accomplish their assigned work. A specialist expert who has been given advisory authority by the organization will need to take the initiative in identifying individuals in the company who could benefit from his or her expert advice. The expert is then accountable for approaching a potential advisee and presenting information that may be of use to them. This means that the expert cannot sit back and wait for the advisee to solicit needed input.

COLLABORATE - Individual's who work at the same level in an organization, usually for the same manager but not always, are generally held accountable to work together harmoniously. These individuals are expected to collaborate with one another. Colleagues generally should have a good idea of what needs to be done in a given situation because they should mutually understand the overarching context of the work expected of them. Collaboration is the most basic of working relationships. If colleagues simply can never seem to get along, then their manager is well within his or her rights to consider replacing one or both of them.

COORDINATE - An individual is designated as accountable for assembling the proper mix of skills and representatives to achieve cross-functional coordination. The "coordinator" should propose how tasks should be approached; keep the group informed as to on-going progress and help overcome problems and /or obstacles encountered in the effort.

SERVICE PROVIDER - The service provider must know what services he or she is accountable to give and to whom. In addition, they must be aware of the resources and time available to complete assigned services and tasks.

SERVICE RECEIVER - The service getter must know what services he or she is authorized to receive and from whom. If the service getter is unhappy with the quality and/or responsiveness of the services he or she receives, he or she is accountable for notifying their manager of perceived service shortfalls.

Chapter 8

CURRENT WORKING CAPABILITY (CWC) - the maximum level of work related complexity a person could currently handle given an opportunity to do so and within the confines of reasonably favorable working conditions. These conditions include an assumption that the work is of inherent value to the person, and takes into consideration full awareness that the individual has not had a previous opportunity to acquire the necessary skills or knowledge to perform this specific type of work.

FUTURE POTENTIAL WORKING CAPABILITY (FPWC) - is the maximum level at which a person will be capable of working, say in, 1, 3, or more years in the future.

COGNITIVE CAPACITY - is the maximum amount of task complexity, information processing and problem solving skill that a given individual can handle and/or apply at any given point in his or her development.

VALUES - those things an individual wants to do or to give priority to doing.

SKILL - the routine application of facts and procedures that have been learned through practice, for example; producing a financial analysis report; designing a weekly production schedule; working with spread sheets; solving simultaneous equations, machining a bearing, drilling a blast hole or riding a bicycle; Once acquired, skills generally remain in one's inventory, some are relatively resistant to decay, e.g., riding a bicycle; while others require periodic updating, e.g., solving mathematical equations.

KNOWLEDGE - objective facts, including procedures which can be stated in words, formulae, models, or other symbols that one can learn, in the sense of being able to pass examinations or tests about them. Knowledge is useful in that it can be applied to specific situations to resolve problems, make decisions, etc. Examples include: knowledge of market factors; competitive intelligence; impact of incentive awards, etc.

Wisdom - soundness of judgment about the nature of people and the world around us

Temperament (T and −T) - tendencies in a person to behave in given ways, traits or characteristics, gives the emotional color to personal interactions. Personality and style.

> **Performance Review (Immediate Manager)**
> - An ongoing process, formalized at least annually.
> - Focuses on outcomes and judgments about how well an individual worked to achieve those outcomes.
> - Accountability rests with the manager.
>
> **Potential Review (MoR)**
> - Sometimes a less frequent event.
> - Focuses on approaches to tasks and capacity to handle more complex work.
> - Accountability rests with the Manager-Once-Removed.

Task Complexity - A what by when. An assignment to produce a what by when; that is to say, a specified output (including quality and quantity) within a targeted completion time, within allocated resources and methods, and within prescribed limits (policies, rules, procedures). The output is the target or goal.

Information Complexity - Aggregating of data to solve problems and make decisions.

Resource Complexity - The allocation and use of resources, tools, dollars and time to accomplish a goal.

Planning and Decision Making Complexity - The making of a choice using discretion and judgment. The design of a pathway (plan) to take you from your current position to your future vision.

Problem Solving Complexity - The ability of an individual to handle complexity in solving problems.

LEADERSHIP COMPLEXITY - Leading a group of subordinate(s) or subordinate units; leading a staff section.

WORKING RELATIONSHIP COMPLEXITY - Working relationships describe how people work together in any organizational setting. These working relationships contain the volatile ingredients of interacting accountabilities and authorities. Working relationships are both internal to the organization and external (customers, suppliers etc.).

TIME HORIZON / TIME SPAN - Level of work as measured by those tasks in the role with the longest maximum target completion times.

MENTORING - the process by which one individual (a Manager-Once-Removed) helps another individual (a Subordinate-Once-Removed) to (1) understand their work related potential and how that potential could be maximized within the organization and (2) to help those individuals (SoRs) grow in wisdom, the use of good judgment, skills/knowledge and temperament.

TALENT POOL - Career development and mentoring together feed a company's talent pool management system.

TALENT POOL MANAGEMENT - the design and implementation of a management system which identifies, assesses and develops a sufficient pool of people capable of filling key managerial positions.

SURPASSION PLANNING - a succession planning system whose primary goal is to fill future open positions with individuals who have <u>greater capability and capacity</u> than current incumbents.

Chapter 9

LEADERSHIP - is that process in which one person sets the purpose or direction for one or more other persons, and gets them to move along together with him or her and with each other in that direction while exercising their full individual competence, innovation and commitment.

DIRECT LEADERSHIP - a relationship between the leader and his direct subordinates one or two levels below him. Involves face to face contact and personal knowledge about subordinates and their personal life situations (family etc.)

OPERATIONAL LEADERSHIP - The leadership focus shifts to key operating systems, processes and procedures. Effectively executing key business functions and subsequently integrating them into a smoothly functions total system.

MANAGER – ONCE – REMOVED (MoR) – The next higher level manager for a given subordinate. The MoR must be two full organizational levels above the subordinate for the incumbent to effectively discharge the full set of accountabilities associated with the role

STRATEGIC LEADERSHIP - Exercising key accountabilities (e.g., visioning culture, values and talent pool management) to the entire organization at once and at the same time.

ENTERPRISE THINKING - taking into account the impact of impending decisions, directions and plans on the entire company and the entire organization. Enterprise thinking should demonstrate knowledge of "second order consequences" on all other teams/organizations within the entire organization/company.

STATED VALUES - those values that are often seen in a company's mission/vision statement, value statements are posted on company websites, marketing material and generally communicated to the public and consumer base. Example: XYZ is a green company (environmental consciousness).

OPERATING VALUES - the values the company actually practices internally and externally, including processes and procedures the company utilizes to meet its goals, the actual "work" that may or may not support the stated values. Example: XYZ company has hazardous material handling procedures that are universally accepted as bad for the environment, with evidence supported by citations from the EPA for environmental infractions.

LEADERSHIP TIME EQUATION - Assessing actual time demands imposed on a leader in a given situation utilizing such data to affect organizational design decisions.

Chapter 10

CONSUMERS - A grouping of individual's that acquire goods or services for direct use or ownership (rather than resale).

CUSTOMER - An individual that buys goods or services.

VOICE OF THE CUSTOMER - A detailed process for gathering key information about customer needs.

>**PROACTIVE METHODS** - the organization takes the initiative to contact customers. Methods include surveys, questionnaires, focus groups, interviews, point-of-sale contact etc. Because the organization controls the timing and content of the customer contact, proactive methods can be used for a wide range of purposes including product/service design, process improvement, performance monitoring, etc.

>**REACTIVE METHODS** - the information comes to the organization through a customer's initiative. Methods include customer calls, (complaints, compliments, queries, requests for technical support, sales), web page hits, emails or cards that customers send to you, point-of-sale questionnaires, referrals and so on. It is absolutely critical that reactive methods be carefully thought out and designed to gather, track and use the collected information correctly because it refers directly to current product/service offerings.

Chapter 11

EXECUTIVE SPONSORSHIP - Getting senior executives sponsorship for a project preferably from an individual who is accountable for the result of that specific area (e.g., function of business unit).

EDUCATION IN THE PRINCIPLES - Providing a thorough understanding of the organizations design principles used in the study process to all senior executives and managers in a given area prior to commencing a given project.

Chapter 12

MISSION - A short formal written statement of purpose. - reflects the broad objectives of the corporation.
　　Example: NASA – Conduct manned space exploration

VISION - the CEO's overarching long term strategic goal. Vision gives the context for the development and carrying through of strategic options. The vision can be modified as circumstances dictate but should be reviewed at least annually.
　　Example: NASA – Put a man on the moon by the end of this decade (Vision as articulated by then President John F. Kennedy)

SITUATIONAL AWARENESS - What key external factors are likely to influence enterprise operations in the immediate future.

MISSION FUNCTIONAL ANALYSIS - How have the mission and related functions changed over the years? Has "mission creep" set in, e.g., new missions/functions added without new resources? What functions have been eliminated?

CUSTOMER/CONSUMER ANALYSIS - Key data or information regarding existing or changing customer needs/expectations including response patterns, etc.

STAKEHOLDER ANALYSIS - Desires and needs of key stakeholders, e.g., shareholders, investors, employees, State and Federal, overseas, etc.

MANIFEST ORGANIZATION - The organizational structure officially represented in the existing company or institution's organization charts.

Chapter 13

COMMENTS - These are statements made by personnel related to specific questions raised by an interviewer.

OBSERVATIONS - these are observations of the current state of things. These observations can be from the project team or the interviewees. They are not just observations about structure they may be observations about anything that was discovered during the process.

OPINIONS - additional responses from anyone involved in the project.

EXTANT ORGANIZATION - The organizational structure that represents how work actually gets done in the enterprise (it includes specific "work arounds" and shortcuts).

LEVEL OF WORK - The weight of responsibility of a role due to the inherent complexity of work assigned to that role.

Chapter 14

REQUISITE STRUCTURE - The organizational structure required by the inherent nature of work being performed by the organization.

Chapter 15

CHANGE MANAGEMENT PLAN - A carefully thought out plan to implement specific study recommendations to resolve existing organizational problems. An effective plan must involve continued high level sponsorship as well as substantial employee involvement.

Chapter 16

GOVERNANCE - in its simplest form, ensures that everyone in an organization understands the *mission* of the organization, their *role* in carrying-out the mission, and the *accountabilities* and *authorities* associated with their role.

EVOLUTIONARY CHANGE - Taking something we already do and figuring out ways to do it better, cheaper and faster. It is about driving down costs, improving productivity and reducing waste. It's tools are process improvement focused, e.g., Lean Six Sigma, Total Quality Management, etc.

REVOLUTIONARY CHANGE (INNOVATION) - Looking for ways to do something fundamentally different, challenging all assumptions, taking nothing for granted, not being afraid to ask "why not".